PUB2PUB

Ben Coombs

www.veloce.co.uk

First published in July 2019 by Veloce Publishing Limited, Veloce House, Parkway Farm Business Park, Middle Farm Way, Poundbury, Dorchester DT1 3AR, England.
Tel +44 (0)1305 260068 / Fax 01305 250479 / e-mail info@veloce.co.uk / web www.veloce.co.uk or www.velocebooks.com.
ISBN: 978-1-787113-60-2; UPC: 6-36847-01360-8.

Ben Coombs

VELOCE PUBLISHING
THE PUBLISHER OF FINE AUTOMOTIVE BOOKS

ACKNOWLEDGEMENTS

I WOULD LIKE to thank all those who helped make the Pub2Pub Expedition a reality. While the list is long, particular mention must firstly go to those who travelled with me for parts of the trip – Ed Johns, Nick Hughff, Pat Hillier, Claire Scully, Anthony Neville, Olivia Gentile, Kimberley Croft and Alvaro Pinzon.

Then there are the people and organisations who helped make the journey possible. In this respect, I'd like to say a hearty thank you to Richard Sails and the TVR Car Club, Richard Smith of Dartmoor Brewery, Dom Trickett of Powers Performance, and Peter Wheeler for making such strong cars, as well as Drivetribe, Racing Green TVR, GAZ shocks, Classicline Insurance, IMS Panama, ACT Performance Engineering, Mountain Hardwear, Columbia, TVR Parts, and last but not least, TVR Engineering themselves.

There are also hundreds of people whom we met on the road and who brightened up our days with their kindness and hospitality. It's impossible to mention everyone by name, but special mention has to go to a few who went well beyond the call of duty to help us. These include Helge Skjelford, Barry Nicholson and Melissa Chacon for their help at the Costa Rican border, Alex Williamson for his help with the Dodge purchase, and Dylan Dale for his help with the Dodge repairs. I'd also like to thank Jessica Hardy and Veloce Publishing for their help in preparing this book for publication.

Last but not least, I have to thank my parents, both for their support and for the loan they gave the expedition when the budget was looking marginal in South America.

CONTENTS

THE ROUTE

EUROPE

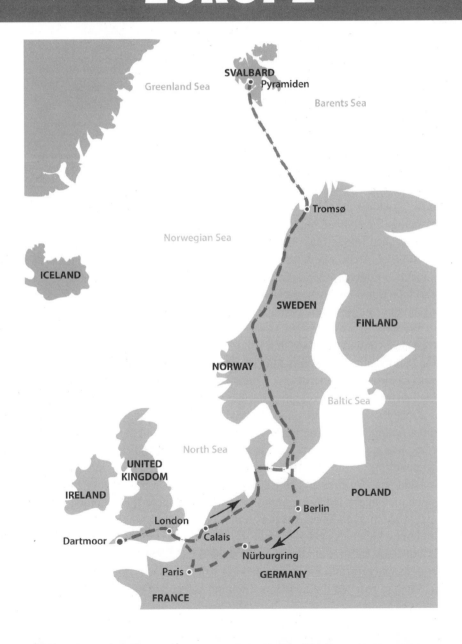

01. THE FJORD

10th July 2017
78°35'N, 16°28'E. Isfjorden, Svalbard.

A DEEP TRANSLUCENCE flooded the fjord, painting its depths with an inky blackness. Our boat pushed on, rippling the surface almost apologetically. The water seemed to possess a lethargic thickness, as if the lifeless permafrost all around had somehow leached the energy from it, rendering it thick like oil or syrup.

We were travelling along a fjord about a mile wide, the shores of which soared upwards, their conglomerate cliffs baring entry to Svalbard's interior. In various places, glaciers tumbled down from the land mass into the water. Icebergs calved dramatically from their faces. Seabirds wheeled and turned in the chill air, but the signs of humans were few and melancholy. A shipwrecked wooden hull lay abandoned on a stony beach, bleached white by the High Arctic sun. A wooden hut slowly succumbed to the elements, its sanctuary from storm and polar bear no longer needed. And all the time the sun beat down intensely, providing a warmth beyond the air temperature, which hovered just above zero.

We were in a world where man's presence had always been fleeting and exploitive, drawn to a place that wouldn't sustain him, to risk everything for the rich rewards. The waters through which we were sailing were once thick with whales, a clarion call which drew in the first European visitors. But as the water ran red and numbers declined, the islands were abandoned again.

Once the whales were gone, the next source of potential wealth left a more lasting presence on the landscape. As we rounded the headland, it came into view: a concrete pier stretched into the chill black waters, its angular bulk jarring against this empty world. On the pier was the detritus of a failed port. Winches and conveyors rusted silently in the salty air. Cranes stood motionless, lighting gantries towering high above them. Behind the quay was an abandoned power station, while accommodation blocks, offices, and mine buildings stretched away from us into the tundra. Beyond this rash of buildings, rails ran up the pyramid-shaped mountain behind the settlement and disappeared into the mine workings, where coal was once extracted.

We had reached the abandoned mining settlement of Pyramiden.

* * *

A FORMER JEWEL in the crown of the Soviet Union, Pyramiden is an unlikely settlement where 1200 people once lived and worked, less than 800 miles from the North Pole. In its heyday, it was a living expression of the Soviet Union's ability to prevail over adversity, and the town did more than simply prevail. It provided its residents with an existence above and beyond that available to many of their comrades further south.

Pyramiden was a place of extremes. It boasted the world's most northerly swimming pool, its most northerly grand piano, the most northerly gymnasium, and looking out across this outpost of civilisation was the most northerly bust of Lenin. And while we're on the subject of records, there's one more that Pyramiden can lay claim to — the world's most northerly bar.

Yes, we weren't just there for the sunny weather and the slim chance of bumping into a polar bear, we'd travelled all the way to this outpost of civilisation to kick off Pub2Pub with a pint.

IN MANY WAYS, Pyramiden's history mirrors that of the Soviet Union, for the collapse of one brought about the end of the other. Following the disintegration of the Union, it became clear that the mine had never turned a profit, and in 1998 it was shut down. From a buzzing home to 1200 people, Pyramiden has now slumped to only four permanent residents, a number that swells to around 15 each summer. Obviously, these people have to live somewhere — 'somewhere' being the old town hotel, the only building in the settlement that is still functional. And with this now being a Russian settlement, the hotel has a functioning bar, which provided the starting point for our journey from the northernmost bar on the planet, to the southernmost.

Our boat slid alongside the pier and we were met on the old dock pontoon by a few of the residents, who were sporting a fine selection of guns and pyrotechnics to scare away any passing polar bears. With them acting as our guides and protectors, we proceeded to explore the town.

When the mine closed its doors in 1998, the town was mothballed. The accommodation blocks, the cultural centre, the mine workings — everything except the hotel was deserted. Exploring these relics of the Soviet ideal was a step back in time. Reels of cine film lay abandoned on the floor of the former cinema. Cyrillic newspapers still rested on desks, their headlines coming to us from the last millennium. Sheet music was still present on a piano, equipment lay sprawled on the floor of the gymnasium, and mosaics of polar bears still jewelled the stairway into the canteen. Meanwhile, the bust of Lenin continued to stare across the bay, to where the glacier swept down to meet the sea.

We spent several hours exploring the ghost town before dropping into the hotel and heading to the bar for a beer. But it wasn't just any beer: it was the Pub2Pub Expedition's green light, a symbolic drink that signalled the start of my 20,000-mile journey to its southernmost equivalent on the far side of the world. As I watched the Russian bartender pour the most important beer of my life, beneath a painting glorifying the CCCP, I could barely comprehend what lay in store for me over the coming months.

I took a sip of the cold beer, and as I did, all I knew was that the journey of a lifetime was ahead of me. Though, truth be told, I felt like I'd already overcome one of the biggest challenges by just making it to the start line; it had been an incredibly close-run thing, and the Pub2Pub Expedition very nearly hadn't happened at all.

02. THE WEDDING

10th December 2016
50°44'N, 3°22'W. Rockbeare Manor, Devon, England.

I WAS ON the verge of tears as I sat motionless at the end of the bed, feeling like a rabbit trapped in the beam of a car's headlights. Fate seemed to offer me only a looming inevitability. I stared at the square foot of beige carpet between my feet, trying to lose myself by focussing on the repeating patterns of its weave, or the patches of dust settled on it. My mind couldn't do anything else, and everything outside that square foot of floor seemed strangely blurred. While I was vaguely aware of what was around me, I couldn't see it. The exposed roof beams above me, the other beds in the attic room of the old manor house my friends had rented for us – it was all invisible to me. Laughter echoed up from below. Laughter that cut through me, immobilised me. There was no way I could go downstairs and join in my friends' revelry. I was so crushed by depression that I couldn't face their smiles or the conversations I'd surely be forced to have. All I could do was sit motionless, my mind completely shut down, staring at the floor in front of me, and gradually becoming more and more angry at myself.

I looked at my watch. One hour to go.

One hour until Laura would walk down the aisle and be married. The greatest day of her life, shared with all her closest friends and family.

But I knew I couldn't be part of it.

Laura and I had known each other for a decade. Years before, we'd teamed up to drive a Porsche across Africa. We'd dated for three years and remained close ever since. But I felt terrible. Terrible because by virtue of my absence, it would seem like I was taking some of the attention away from the marriage and diverting it to me. Terrible because people would assume I was distraught that Laura was marrying someone else, after all we'd been through, though that wasn't the case. I felt like I was letting her down, letting down everyone in fact, and it sent me into a sudden spiral of negative thoughts. In reality, though, this was the breaking point I'd been allowing myself to drift towards for years.

IN 2013, I'D returned from my last big road trip – a drive from the UK to South East Asia in a Corvette – and on my return I launched a clothing brand with a friend. Anyone who's launched a new business will know that the workload of such an undertaking is immense. I tend to have an all-or-nothing personality and I've always found it difficult to simply coast along, so I threw myself into the new venture with crushing abandon, pushing myself as hard as I could, working month after month without a single day off.

It felt like the right thing to do, but I was pushing myself too hard. As a result, I was only heading further towards depression. I didn't take the danger seriously: I thought I could manage my mental health, I thought I could walk that tightrope above the abyss of depression. And, for a year or two, I could. But eventually, having been so close to the edge for so long, my luck ran out. If my mental health was the overloaded, proverbial camel's back, eventually, the straw that broke it was added to the mix. And in a pattern that's irritatingly predictable before any big road trip of mine, it was a girl who proved to be that final straw.

Jennifer had bounded into my life one autumn day, screeching to a halt outside my workplace in her well-used MX-5, before demanding a ride in my TVR. When a pretty young lady who drives a roll-caged MX-5 covered in 'Speedhunters' stickers makes such a demand, you don't argue. We got on brilliantly, sharing an irreverent sense of humour, a love of crap-yet-worthy cars, and enthusiasm for gloriously daft automotive escapades. Yet, despite wanting to be together, she was still under the influence of a controlling ex-boyfriend, and the terrible timing meant we simply couldn't happen.

We went our separate ways, but over the following months she kept reaching out, drawing me back in and piquing my interest. Each time my hopes would be raised and then dashed, and the stakes between us built to the point where I was risking a major blow to my mental health if things didn't work out for us again. But, in so many aspects of my life, from road trips to MX-5 drivers, I'm generally someone who has no problem playing the long odds, so in the summer before Pub2Pub I took a chance for the last time.

I knew I should have walked away months earlier but, even so, at the time, it didn't feel like I was gambling with my mental health. She'd been missing me, and had told both her friends and me that she was 99 per cent sure she wanted us to be together, so, as we jumped into my Corvette one sunny Tuesday and headed to Cornwall for a few days' climbing together, everything seemed very positive. What could possibly go wrong?

Well, first there was what had happened the previous Thursday, when she'd had to break down a friend's door to save his life after he'd attempted suicide. Then there was the controlling ex, who still couldn't bear the thought of her moving on with me, and did everything in his power to prevent it.

It was a terrible trip. As we drove to Cornwall, Jennifer was bombarded by gloomy, ominous messages from her ex, and her mind was full of images from the previous Thursday night. At the time, her life was like a pressure cooker with no relief valve, and my presence in it had become part of the problem. She wanted to be with me, but the pressures and stresses were too much. She just wasn't able to put them aside.

The following day, we drove back to Plymouth and went our separate ways again.

Like a wounded animal, I stumbled through life for a few more days, thinking I'd got away with it, my mental health not suffering too much damage from this final failure of something I'd invested so much emotional energy in, but eventually it hit me. The final straw had been loaded on board and sure enough, the camel's back broke.

A week later, one of my closest friends was diagnosed with Pulmonary Hypertension – a narrowing of the blood vessels between the heart and lungs for which there is no cure, and which, left untreated, results in an average life expectancy of less than three years. It was as if they – someone who'd never done anything to deserve it – had been handed a death sentence. The spiral into which I'd fallen by pursuing Jennifer became steeper; the climb out the other side, back to normality, seemed impossible. Overworking had left me teetering on the brink of depression, and this double-punch to my fragile emotional being sent me tumbling into the darkness.

I should have seen a doctor. Professional help was what I needed, but I was in too deep to recognise it; I was too close to the coal face. In my life, both in road trips and in work, I was used to battling through issues on my own, and I tried to do just that. However, if you're too stubborn to see a doctor, the only other cure for depression is to take your foot off the gas and coast, allowing your mind and body to slowly recover over a period of months. When you're the co-owner of a business and you feel like you should always be pulling your weight, that's not an easy thing to do.

Relations with my business partner soured as I fought to keep working, even as the darkness invaded my mind. My ability to make it through social events vanished. Anything more than an hour would leave me a nervous wreck, out of my depth in normal conversation, and looking for an excuse to leave. Just muddling through everyday life had become a challenge I simply couldn't cope with. So as far as the future was concerned, I did the only thing I could.

I cancelled Pub2Pub.

It was less than a year before my planned departure, and there was no way I could see myself getting everything ready in time. In the face of depression, it felt impossible.

Suffering from depression is a crushingly immersive experience, and one which is impossible to convey to those who've never experienced it. It isn't the temporary inertia of feeling a bit down on a Monday morning; it's like wading through treacle, dawn to dusk, day after day. It destroys your concentration, your ability to focus, and any enthusiasm you once harboured. Effectively, it hollows you out into a shell of your former self. In the midst of such a condition, all you can do is drift through your days, smothered by the enormity of it.

THAT SATURDAY MORNING in Devon, when I broke down before Laura's wedding, was seven months before Pub2Pub's planned departure date. I didn't have funding in place, I hadn't found a car, and I couldn't even make it through a social engagement, let alone organise one of the most ambitious road trips ever.

At that moment, the dream of Pub2Pub was a dream too far; a dream that could never happen.

03. GENESIS

14th November 2013
50°26'N, 4°03'W. The White Thorn Inn, Dartmoor.

I'D DREAMED UP the idea for the Pub2Pub Expedition a few years before depression had taken over my life. It was shortly after I'd returned from my last big drive – from England to Singapore in an old Chevrolet Corvette – and I was sat on a barstool in my local Dartmoor pub.

You could say that dreaming up increasingly random and unlikely ideas for road trips is a hobby of mine, and on that autumn day in 2013, as the thought of whether it would be possible to drive from the northernmost bar on the planet to the southernmost drifted through my mind, I was on form.

Later that evening, I pulled out my maps, fired up the computer, and began to investigate.

Whilst in the pub, I'd assumed that the northernmost bar would probably be tucked away in some unreachable Inuit settlement in the far north of Canada, and as for the southernmost bar, well, who knows? As a result, I hadn't got too carried away with the idea as its viability still seemed slim at best. However, as I researched, a route formed before me. The northernmost bar turned out to be located in an abandoned Soviet mining settlement called Pyramiden, on the Svalbard archipelago, hundreds of miles to the north of Norway. And the southernmost? Well, there are certainly bars in the research stations of Antarctica, but the southernmost, legally licensed premises I found was on South America's southernmost tip: Tierra del Fuego.

So I had my start and finish points, but how to get between them? As I flicked through the pages of my well-worn atlas, the route became clear. From Svalbard, I'd head to the Norwegian mainland, travel down through Europe, ship the car across the Atlantic from Southampton to New York, breeze across the USA, drop down through Central and South America, then grab a beer at journey's end near Cape Horn. It all sounded so simple when put like that; it even looked simple on a map. However, the reality of making it happen was considerably more complex, especially when battling demons in the infinite abyss of depression.

IT WAS THE January before Pub2Pub's planned departure. Six months to go. In an effort to recover my poor mental health, I'd dropped down to only working a day or two a week at the business, spending the rest of my time doing as little as possible. As I was now spending quite a bit of time doing not-a-lot, Pub2Pub drifted back into my thoughts again. I'd already done some basic research a few years earlier by mapping out a route, completing the costings, researching red tape, and getting a feel for the obstacles and dangers. However, since being struck down by depression, I'd had no inclination to push on with trying to make the trip happen. In my mind, it was dead. The enthusiasm and excitement that travel plans involving unusual cars once generated in me was gone. I hadn't felt it in months. But when you're sat at home with nothing to do other than wait to get better, you're liable to revisit old ideas. And for me, this was maps and dreams of the open road. So one evening, rather than sitting around feeling sorry for myself, I put some Pink Floyd on the stereo, poured an Ardbeg whisky, and dusted off my maps. Specifically, the map of Europe I'd bought in preparation for Pub2Pub years before. I unfolded it and started tracing potential routes for the trip's first leg, taking a pen and marking points of interest as I went: the Nürburgring, the Koenigsegg factory, that car graveyard in Sweden I'd read about once, the place in Germany with all the preserved mining machines. From the depths of my unresponsive mind, I dredged up half-forgotten recollections of places that had been stored away for some future road trip.

As so often happens, these points of interest formed themselves into a line; a ribbon of attractions that snaked across the map like a sign. I kept on researching and recalling places from previous research sessions years ago. I poured myself another whisky. Other than the pool of light that spread itself across the map, it was dark in my living room, but it didn't matter. My focus was on that map, those fascinating places and the fantastic-looking route that was forming before my eyes. And then I noticed something.

For the first time in months — maybe years — I was myself again. Rather than seeing and feeling everything through the smothering effects of depression, I felt back to my old self.

I poured a third whisky and kept on plotting and researching. A future adventure grew across the maps as the night drifted into the small hours.

THE FOLLOWING MORNING, I was back to my normal sluggishness. Depression is often at its worst in the morning. But the euphoria of the previous night, when it had temporarily lifted, marked a step change for me. It reminded me of the person I really was, hidden away beneath the problems I'd been struggling with. It reminded me of this passion of mine; the passion which had seen me cross Asia in a classic Mini and drag an old Porsche across Africa, and it reminded me that despite everything, I was still that person: one who faces problems head on and attempts to overcome them. Was Pub2Pub really dead in the water? The previous night, it hadn't been. It had been real once again.

Through the darkness, I'd started to dream once more.

But it was still just that – a dream. I didn't have the money for it, I didn't have a car in mind, and I didn't have a team. Due to icy conditions around Svalbard, Pub2Pub would have to hit the road in the northern hemisphere summer, which gave me less than six months to get everything ready.

The car was the first piece of the jigsaw to fall into place. When I first came up with the idea for the trip years previously, my vehicular aspirations were rather grandiose, with my beer-fuelled optimism convincing me that the perfect vehicle for Pub2Pub would be a replica AC Cobra. Simple, stunning to look at, and with a big V8 up front, it suited the absurdity of Pub2Pub perfectly, as well as fitting with the 'Rediscovering the Lost Art of Travel' ethos, which I was basing the expedition's style around. However, despite my promises of fame and publicity, none of the manufacturers of replica AC Cobras would give me a free car in return for the promised publicity, not that I can really blame them. I was left in the market for some other stunning-yet-simple V8 sports car, until I looked in my own garage.

I'd owned 'Kermit,' my TVR Chimaera, for six years, and it had been about as close to fitting into the, slightly cringeworthy, 'pride and joy' definition as any car I've had. In the time I'd owned it, it had covered around 2000 miles a year and completed the occasional trip to France or Ireland, but overall, it was very much a 'high days and holidays' car, because, let's face it, who would trust a TVR to do any more than that?

Yes, the marque suffered from a bit of an image problem, centred on a perceived lack of reliability. Playing on this, I'd always joked that mine had been thrown together by a drunken Northerner in a shed back in the late '90s, even though, in reality, it hadn't had much in the way of issues in the time I'd owned it. However, many other owners had had a different experience of TVR ownership, and it was the fragility of TVR's own engine designs (which they built around the turn of the millennium) that did much to bring the company down, through a combination of warranty claims and deteriorating public confidence. And the jokes. When you say you drive a TVR, someone would always make a joke about reliability.

I think this last fact was what sealed my decision to undertake the trip in my own TVR. A desire to set the record straight by showing the world that these charismatic brutes from Blackpool can be just as reliable as any other vehicle. And given that my research had indicated that I was planning the longest journey ever made by a sports car, it would certainly achieve just that. Or maybe it would result in a lot of people laughing at my ridiculous choice of vehicle when they smugly say "I told you so," as I grind to a halt for the umpteenth time – one or the other.

So the car was chosen, and I decided not to modify it for the trip in any way. Kermit would not get the rally car makeover most people deemed essential to toughen it up for the trip. No, I'd service it, make sure it was working as it should, then set off. This had the secondary benefit of comfortably being the cheapest way to hit the road.

And cheap was essential, as with the clock ticking down, I didn't have anywhere near enough money to undertake the journey. In fact, having gone down to one day a week at my business, I barely had enough money to eat. And my costings indicated I'd need to find over £20,000 to make Pub2Pub happen. I'd need to raise some money, and fast.

Fortunately, I already had a few successful sports car-based expeditions under my belt, which gave me some credibility when approaching potential sponsors. This was just as well, as most folks' reaction when you approach them and say, "I'm going to drive this unreliable sports car across the globe, and I'd like your wallet to be part of it," is generally negative at best. However, with the proven track record that my previous trips had given me, I was taken a little more seriously than I might otherwise have been.

First on board was a new website that I'd been doing some writing for, who agreed to put up a decent sum of money in return for the expedition's video content – no doubt expecting to recoup their investment when some catastrophe became the deeply unreliable steed. This was great news, but it came with one proviso – we'd need a film-maker. Fortunately, I knew just the guy: a young and ambitious videographer called Nick.

Not so fortunately, he was covering for me at my business at the time, so poaching him didn't go down too well, but needs must.

So, we had myself, Nick the cameraman, and the beginnings of the money we'd need to make Pub2Pub happen. With things starting to take shape, I began to cast around for further sponsorship – not the easiest task in the world when you're met with laughter at every turn. Despite my track record, I still felt like I was hitting my head against a brick wall, a doubly difficult situation as depression still dominated my life, making every approach to a potential sponsor a struggle, and every rejection a blow.

I received a lot of rejections. My efforts focussed on the drinks industry, and understandably, most of the industry didn't have much time for this dreamer who declared he was going to drive a TVR to a pub in Chile. Most of Scotland's distilleries said no, as did a few breweries. However, there was one brewery which understood the potential in what we were trying to achieve, and a meeting was arranged.

It was a typical Dartmoor day as I headed up onto the moor to Dartmoor Brewery, for a chat with the brewery's manager, Richard Smith. The drizzle swept down and the dun-coloured moorland retreated into the scudding clouds. The TVR was off the road at the time, so the only vehicle I had at my disposal was a boxy, 25-year-old Nissan Micra, which I'd bought a few months earlier to tide me over after selling the Corvette – not exactly a vehicle in which to make an arrival for an important meeting. Feeling like a fraud, I parked the Micra out of sight and strolled across the moor to the brewery, drizzle soaking me, mud coating my shoes. It didn't feel like the prelude to success.

However, Richard turned out to be the sort of person to overlook such first impressions. Jovial and down-to-earth, he'd seen the previous achievements listed in my proposal and considered the idea to be worth a further look. An hour later, we had our first sponsor. With the additional money I raised by selling the Corvette I'd driven to Vietnam, and the income from renting out my flat, it was beginning to look like I'd be able to make it to the end of the trip by the skin of my teeth – providing nothing major went wrong.

As the spring progressed, we also picked up some more team members. Firstly, my old friend Brummy would be joining the adventure – he'd come along on most of my previous trips and had proved incapable of saying no to daft travel plans. However, as he could only get three months off work, he'd only be joining us for the middle section of the trip – New York to Panama.

Also accompanying us for this leg was another friend, Claire, who I'd met at a house party a few months earlier. Despite never having done anything like this before, it was testimony to Claire's sense of adventure that she was willing to put her life on hold and join a bunch of strangers for a trip across the Americas.

Another person who decided to get involved was a friend called Pat, who would be joining us near the top of Norway and travelling as far as he could. Finally, there was Ed. But Ed could only get a week off work, and what's the best thing to do with a week off? Drive from the UK to the northernmost bar on the planet – obviously.

So we had a team. We had enough finance in place to make the trip vaguely plausible, and we had a TVR which, though it hadn't been used much in the previous year, seemed to be working well enough. There was only one thing for it.

Time to hit the road.

04. THE LAUNCH

2nd July 2017
50°33'N, 3°57'W. The Two Bridges Hotel, Dartmoor.

THE ROLLING MOORLAND of Dartmoor is a place of extreme moods. On a glorious summer's day, sat in a beer garden outside one of its many historic pubs, you'd swear it's the best place in the world. Conversely, if you catch it on the wrong day, when the scudding rain cuts through you and clouds smother the landscape, it's difficult to imagine anywhere worse. And as this landscape is the first bit of high ground that weather systems hit as they roll in off the Atlantic, it tends to gravitate towards the latter. Battening down against a storm is a more regular occurrence than beering it up in the sunshine.

So for our Dartmoor launch event, I didn't hold out much in the way of optimism for the weather. In fact, getting to the start line had been such a tough and emotional ordeal for me that launching Pub2Pub through one of those apocalyptic maelstroms that Dartmoor does so well would have felt almost fitting. However, when the day came, I was pleasantly surprised. Pleasant, dappled sunshine greeted us as we headed up to the Two Bridges Hotel one Sunday morning in July.

The weather encouraged quite a turnout of both people and cars to see us off. My parents came down in their 1950s Armstrong Siddeley, Laura rocked up in a Triumph TR6 with her husband. My sister was there in her Mazda MX-5, and then there were the TVRs. A late shout-out from the TVR Car Club – which was also lending the trip its support – had resulted in six more fibreglass beasts from Blackpool joining Kermit for the initial convoy across the moor. And what a sight they made! All sat there, roofs off and paintwork gleaming in the sunshine, their owners no doubt curious to meet the idiot who thinks a TVR is an ideal overland steed.

As well as the cars, the assembled people hinted at some of the interest the Pub2Pub project would generate over the coming months. Various well-wishers dropped by, keen to wish us luck on our journey. The local BBC news crew attended, interviewing me as I leaned on Kermit and attempted to come across as anything other than a deluded fool who didn't have a clue what he was taking on.

There was a definite buzz in the air, but I dealt with it dispassionately. I'd been busily working towards making the expedition a reality for so long that the launch felt like a continuation of that work – a battle to do what needed to be done in the face of depression's best efforts. Previously, this had involved long hours trying to find the energy and motivation to plan the route or attract sponsorship. Now, the effort was focussed on chatting to strangers, smiling, and organising the send-off. As Laura's wedding seven months ago had showed, to sufferers of depression such mundane socialising can be just as much of a struggle as the more obvious challenges – such as driving across the world in a sports car.

At 11am, the pleasantries were over and it was time. We formed our convoy of a dozen classic cars – first the TVRs then the other marques. Kermit led, along with the Micra, which was to accompany us on this first leg to the Arctic and back. With engines revving, and under the gaze of the onlookers and the BBC, we got the journey under way as we roared forth onto the twisting tarmac of Dartmoor, our charismatic motors finally unleashed ...

Straight into the middle of Dartmoor's biggest-ever cycle race.

Yes, 4000 lycra-clad cyclists crowded the narrow lanes, slowing our progress almost to walking pace. Where we'd usually be motoring along at 40mph, we found ourselves crawling across the hilly landscape, going nowhere fast.

Our convoy's objective was a pub about 30 miles away in Exeter, where we had a table booked for lunch. However, the convoy soon fell apart as each car alternated between sitting behind the slow-moving cyclists and – when it was safe to do so – overtaking, only to become stuck again 50 metres up the road.

So yes, it wasn't exactly the grand convoy of magnificent automobiles sweeping unstoppably across one of the UK's greatest landscapes that we'd been hoping for.

Fortunately, Kermit took the hour of crawling, interspersed with bursts of acceleration, in its stride, and an hour after we'd left the Two Bridges Hotel, we reached the pub for lunch. A couple of the other TVRs were there already, and the rest of the convoy slowly dripped in until only one car was missing: our Micra running-mate. I gave Ed – the driver – a call.

"Hey, Ed, you're missing lunch. What's wrong?"

"The Micra just totally overheated. I had to pull over three times, and the third time it wouldn't start again for ages. Now I'm stuck at a petrol station just off the A30."

"Damn, that's not good. Send me your location. I'm on my way."

We were one hour and 30 miles into our 27,000-mile odyssey, and already one of the cars had ground to a halt. I left the slightly bemused well-wishers to their lunch, and set off to the car park where the wounded Micra was waiting.

I parked Kermit next to it and we opened the bonnet. Now, this car's engine had never been the prettiest thing, but at least it had always worked. Well, almost always, anyway. There was that time I tried to drive home after buying it unseen, and promptly ground to a halt with the water pump leaking like a tap.

Still, I guess you should kind of expect that when you buy a car off eBay for £216, from a not-quite-with-it Cornishman whose parting words as you drive off are: "if you find any weed under the passenger seat, it wasn't mine," before reaching in through the window and removing some weed from said seat.

Despite this inauspicious start, though, once I'd changed the water pump, the Micra had given good service over the previous eight months, and had even undertaken a trip to France – proof that I wasn't being completely deluded in hoping it would get to the Arctic and back.

However, when I opened that bonnet, things didn't bode well. Brown stains covered most of the engine, where the dirty coolant had sprayed out through the pressure cap and gaskets. The radiator was cold to the touch, showing it hadn't been doing its job for quite a while. And to cap it all off, when we finally got it started, it didn't sound happy in the slightest.

We refilled the coolant and I escorted the Micra back to the pub where everyone else was tucking into their meals. As I followed it, the acrid smell of an engine slowly cooking itself grew, and by the time we reached the pub, the radiator was once again cool to touch, and the coolant almost all gone. The poor Micra sat forlornly in its parking space, water spraying from its exhaust. The head gasket had blown, allowing water to enter the pistons and escape through the exhaust.

We were in trouble.

We had five days to get to the Norwegian city of Tromsø, 3000 miles away. However, the Micra was going no further. Our friends crowded around the car, swept up in the drama of the moment, hiding nerves behind jokes, and smothering the gravity of the situation with banter. I refilled the radiator to check again what I already knew. As the engine puttered away unhappily, the water flowed from the exhaust.

Lizzy, an American friend, asked first: "so, what are the options?"

I thought for a moment before answering. I could feel my depression returning, brought on by this failure so early in the trip. I felt on the verge of being crushed by the turn of events. Hadn't I done enough already?

"Well, the car needs a new head gasket, and the head will probably need skimming too, after being so badly cooked. And there's no chance we can get that lot done on a Sunday afternoon."

Brummy had started to flick through the car's workshop manual and chipped in.

"Well, there are only 51 steps in the workshop manual. How difficult can it be? Take the top off the engine, poke it with a spanner, throw it back together. Come on, Ben, I thought you were good at this stuff?"

"You thought he was good at this stuff? You've clearly never seen Ben working on a car before," said Pat.

"Yeah, I'm with Pat on this. Don't ever put money on me fixing a car," I added. "Brummy, remember that cylinder head sealant stuff we took to Vietnam but didn't need? I wonder if we can get any of that before the shops shut. It's probably too far gone, but it's the only chance we have that I can think of."

"There's a Halfords just up the road," said Pat. "We'll head up and grab some." And so, only a few hours into the trip, Pub2Pub's first rescue mission got under way.

While Pat and Brummy were off shopping for car bodging supplies, I wandered back into the pub, where about a dozen friends, family, and well-wishers were finishing lunch. Though I joined them, I found it difficult to chat and remain upbeat. As I'd struggled to manage my depression over the previous months, I'd been looking forward to hitting the road. At that moment, the pressure of making the trip happen would be lifted, and would be replaced by hours of motorway driving as I headed north. As one of the best ways to come back from depression is to do virtually nothing until your body begins to recover, I felt sure that once I hit the road, I'd enter the recovery phase. Instead, I'd been thrown a curveball; a problem with no solution. Even as the rescue mission was underway, I felt certain it would be futile, given how badly the gasket was leaking. And sure enough, the expensive liquid, which claimed to be able to fix minor head gasket leaks, proved ineffectual.

The Micra was dead.

However, it's amazing just how serendipitous events can be when your back is against the wall, and our luck began to change as far as the Micra was concerned. While having lunch, I'd glanced at my Facebook news feed and spotted an advert posted by a friend that morning: 'For sale – Nissan Micra. W reg, full service history, 80,000 miles, located in Surrey. £300.'

It was advertised by Kris – an old university friend who I'd not seen in a decade. I messaged him saying I'd give him £250 for it and collect it in three hours. A deal was done.

In a further moment of good fortune, American Lizzy was due to drive back to London that day and had space for another person, so Nick jumped in the TVR with me while Ed joined Lizzy in her early '90s Honda Civic – complete with official, freshly-applied 'Pub2Pub' stickers. A few hours after our first 'support vehicle' died, we hit the road with our second, en-route to collect our third.

I've had more confidence-inspiring beginnings to a road trip.

As we pulled onto the motorway in convoy, my mind had one single thought on loop: "please, please, please don't break down, Kermit."

As fate would have it, though, it wasn't the TVR that offered up the next breakdown.

To raise further funds for the trip, I'd just sold a Renault 4, which I'd bought while visiting Jennifer in Slovenia a year earlier, and a friend had offered to drop it off with the new owner, who lived near London. As I roared through spitting rain on the M4 motorway, I spotted a familiar beige shape on the hard shoulder, its bonnet open. I dived across onto the hard shoulder and stopped next to it. Simon, the driver, was leaning on the Renault's front wing, looking on stoically.

"What happened?"

"I was cruising along, it started running rough, and then cut out. It won't start now."

"Does it turn over?"

"Yeah, it cranks okay, and occasionally splutters, but it won't run. I'm guessing it's a fuelling issue. The AA are on the way – they should be here in about half an hour."

"Can I help in any way?" I asked, feeling bad for putting Simon in this situation.

"Not really, the AA will get it to my house and then we'll sort something out from there. You should push on. You've got a car to buy and a trip to complete."

"Thanks, Simon. I owe you a pretty decent bottle of whisky."

The last time I saw that beige Renault, which had been synonymous with the issues I'd had with Jennifer the previous summer, it was receding in my rear view mirror as I pushed on with Pub2Pub. A chapter in my life closed.

It was another eight months before I was finally able to buy Simon that bottle of whisky though.

NIGHT HAD WELL and truly fallen when we finally arrived at Kris' house in Surrey, where a red Micra K11 sat outside – two parts bland '90s hatchback, one part beacon of hope. We blitzed through the paperwork, got it insured, and then set off for Dover, arriving at two in the morning. Pub2Pub had been under way for 15 hours and we'd already had two breakdowns, and were on our third support vehicle. The TVR however, was running like an absolute dream.

TVRs are unreliable, right? Wrong.

You couldn't make it up!

05. NORTH

03rd July 2017
50°58′N, 01°51′E. Calais, France.

THE EARLY MORNING sunlight flooded the ferry's car deck as the watertight doors opened. We hadn't slept, apart from the hour or so we snatched in the cars while waiting to board the ship, and our minds were muddled by the interplay between coffee and fatigue that was to define our morning. Fortunately, it didn't promise to be a particularly taxing morning – as long as the latest addition to the Pub2Pub convoy proved more dependable than its predecessor.

Our first objective was the city of Bruges, about an hour up the road from the ferry port. It was a gentle introduction to the 6000 miles we'd need to cover in mainland Europe over the coming three weeks, and as we cruised reliably along the French and Belgian autoroutes, I had my first opportunity to relax and let my thoughts settle.

Up until the moment we set off, I'd tended to view hitting the road as the ultimate goal – once we were rolling, I reasoned, everything would become easier. However, the car-related issues had dented this confidence somewhat – instead of the formality of a routine drive to Norway, we'd already been forced to attempt repairs, and even source another car. This wasn't shaping up to be the mindless cruise across Europe that I'd envisaged, and the issues with the Micra had focussed my mind as far as the TVR's reliability was concerned. It hadn't covered that many miles over the previous year, and I was treating the European leg of the trip as a shakedown for the tougher challenges it would face in the Americas. Now, however, with one car already terminally broken, if anything happened to the TVR, it wouldn't look good in the slightest; it would imply that my preparations for the trip were negligent at best. And as this was the first trip for which I'd obtained proper corporate sponsorship, this wasn't something that would sit well.

As we cruised onwards and I gradually got used to having the back end of a Nissan Micra K11 filling my windscreen, I found it difficult to relax.

Fortunately, if there's one place where you can relax, it's the historic centre of Bruges early on a Monday morning. We parked our cars and wandered the streets for a few hours, before most of the tourists had risen. Though fatigued, spirits were high, and, for the first time in the course of Pub2Pub, so was our confidence that our cars might make it to Norway, our second Micra having performed perfectly on its trip across Flanders.

And Bruges itself didn't disappoint. The perfectly preserved town centre kept our fatigue at bay as we explored and grabbed some breakfast. But we couldn't linger too long because that evening we were due at a party in The Netherlands, that was being held in our honour.

The Glym9 garage is a British motoring enthusiast's retreat in The Low Countries, which takes the form of a rather TVR-centric man-cave. Behind the unassuming garage door that leads into the workshop, all manner of quirkiness awaits, including a bar, slot-car track, a selection of guitars and amplifiers, and, overshadowing all else, a trio of TVRs in various states of restoration, ranging from a flat-packed Tuscan project to a near-completed Chimaera. Basically, it wasn't far from petrolhead heaven – especially as they'd got the beers in. As I was driving, I couldn't take too much advantage of this, however, but it was still nice to chat into the evening with our newfound Dutch friends, sharing our enthusiasm for quirky fibreglass sports cars.

From the party in Holland, we carried on north. And doing so reminded me of something I already knew: for one of the smallest continents on planet Earth, Europe isn't half big. We rolled on across the Low Countries then emerged into Germany, from there heading north into Denmark. Hours rolled into hours. Day morphed into night then back into day. Vast, sweeping bridges took us across the straits of Øresund into Sweden, where further long hours on the road brought us to a windswept campsite on the Swedish coast. Here, the sun dropped into the waters beyond the reeds which bordered our pitch. The days had been long and uneventful, the efficiency of Europe's road network sucking any semblance of adventure from our reliable progress.

But I knew this would change when we crossed the border into Norway.

There are certain landscapes that stay with you forever. Rather than having their gravitas diluted by the passing of time, they stand apart. Travelling to new places and experiencing new horizons only serves to emphasise their greatness. They are the special places. The places you live for.

Norway is one of these places.

An improbable stretch of soaring mountains and serrated coastline, Norway was the overwhelming highlight of our journey north. The drive from England to Norway's border, near Oslo, had felt routine; the subsequent drive to the airport in Tromsø – from where we'd be boarding a plane to Svalbard – was a sensory overload in comparison.

The landscape begun to hint at what lay ahead as we rolled north through Sweden, rippling in anticipation of the scenery ahead. Uniform pine forests took over from the farmlands, and swept up from the road into the hills, soon yielding to a tree line which marked the beginnings of the mountains.

As the landscape grew more precipitous, the road followed the path of least resistance across it, flowing through the valleys and being assisted by bridges and tunnels when nature dictated. After a full day on the road, we approached the town of Trondheim, and were lifted up onto an exposed plateau. There, for the first time in the trip, we wild-camped, through a night where dusk merged into dawn, and the sky was full of insects.

As we continued north, the drama contained within the landscape increased. Mountains thrust ever skyward and the coast swept in from our left and began to dominate, the road twisting along the shore, rising and falling with the contours carved out by glaciers millennia ago. But nature wasn't always the dominating influence on our journey because for centuries man has been doing his best to ease progress though this most impenetrable landscape. River valleys were crossed by solemn bridges whilst often, at the end of a fjord, the sheer rock wall would be punctured by a tunnel that led through the mountain to the next vista, each more spectacular than the last.

The first snow appeared by the road as we climbed up onto a windswept plateau that marked our arrival at the Arctic Circle. It was just after midnight and the sun was hovering behind the mountains. We stopped for pictures before pitching our tents for the night, rising the next morning to carry on further into the Arctic. For hundreds of miles the landscape continued to inspire us with its grandeur, until, five days and nearly 3000 miles after leaving the UK, we arrived at Tromsø and boarded the flight to Svalbard.

And I can tell you, after that long haul, the prospect of a few days out of the driver's seat, on an island with virtually no roads, was pretty appealing.

06. THE ISLAND

09th July 2017
78°14'N, 15°29'E. Longyearbyen, Svalbard.

THE FIRST THING that hits you when you arrive in Svalbard is the air. It has a clean, almost acidic, crispness to it, which makes breathing a pleasure. It's like tasting a glass of chilled eau mineral after a lifetime of lukewarm, limescale-ridden tap water. You breathe in and out, savouring this unexpected delight as you descend the steps from the plane and stroll to the airport terminal. And as you do so, you take in the surroundings.

A great fjord swept across the vista that was laid out before us, hemmed in by the dun-coloured mountains that rose sharply from its shores. In some places, this earthen wall was penetrated by glaciers that rolled down to the sea from Svalbard's interior, for glaciers cover 60 per cent of the island's area. And if there was one thing as crisp as the air we were breathing, it was the sunlight that bathed us. It flooded our world, bleaching the glaciers white, and jewelling the rippled waters with a thousand sparkles.

I'd never been anywhere that felt so free of dust and pollution before; a place where the air felt somehow even more transparent, the chill breeze more pure. I savoured it as I passed through the tiny airport, before dropping down to the campsite that nestles on the shore below. Arctic terns dive-bombed us as we walked, while rookie thoughts of polar bears lingered in our excited minds.

WE'D ARRIVED AT the edge of the world. Longyearbyen is over 800 miles beyond the Arctic Circle, with a similar distance separating it from the North Pole. However, gulping in the crisp air as glaciers tumbled all around us towards the crystal sea, the Pole might as well have been just over the next hill. And the more time we spent taking in our surroundings, the more it felt like we weren't at the edge of the world after all. No, Svalbard is a whole *other* world. A world where polar bears outnumber humans and the sun doesn't rise for almost a third of the year. A world devoid of roads, where only boats and snowmobiles serve to bring people together. A world that exists on the edge of our knowledge. Located on the front line of the war against climate change, its delicate High Arctic climate is a barometer for the planet. In the past, Svalbard's main contributions to the world have been purely profit-driven with natural resources to be plundered, first through whaling, then mining. Today, the islands look to the future this plunder has created, through cutting-edge research focussed on conservation and climate change.

It was 8°C as I pitched my tent, and a cool breeze blew in off the fjord, buffeting across the treeless tundra and finding its way through every gap in my clothing. The flysheet, rustling coarsely as it flapped in the breeze, threatened to make a bid for the North Pole as I attached it. Once the tent was pitched, I wandered into the campsite's only building, in search of coffee. Nick and Ed soon joined me, and with the stunning views rushing in through every window, it wasn't long before we decided to head out for a closer look at the other-worldly place into which we'd just alighted.

It's a 15-minute walk into town from Svalbard's campsite, and it gives you a good impression of the area's history. For much of the past hundred years, that history was steeped in mining, and the industrial relics that were left behind still line the road into town. Aerial tramways, which once carried coal several miles from Longyearbyen's mines to the docks, hung silent, the buckets swaying slightly in the breeze. The wood and wrought-iron construction of the conveyor system, while chunky, looked unequal to the landscape that the mining had scarred, and was slowly decaying. It takes a lot to survive here.

The gradual deterioration of Svalbard's industrial heritage that led us into town formed an interesting juxtaposition, for as we followed the linear relics of the past, they deposited us in the present. Modern day Longyearbyen: a town of around 2500 people, which is very much of the 21st century, but with a twist, because let's face it, life 800 miles from the North Pole is never exactly going to be like Surrey.

It tries though. There's a supermarket, restaurants, outdoor and fashion shops and even a cocktail bar – the northernmost in the world, of course. We dropped in and I ordered some drinks – brewed by the world's northernmost brewery, naturally.

"Hi, three Spitzbergen IPAs please."

"Sure, pints I'm guessing?" the barman replied, with a definite British accent.

"Of course. Erm, you don't sound very Norwegian ..."

"Nope, I'm from Bradford. I'm here for a bit of summer work. I did the same last year too. How about you?"

Despite being a little taken aback by this barman at the end of the world hailing from Yorkshire of all places, it's a good reflection of the cosmopolitan nature of Svalbard today. Most of Longyearbyen's residents are either students from across the globe studying at – yes – the world's northernmost university, or tourists like us, revelling in the unique landscape. So while Norwegians obviously predominate, it's very much a global crowd that inhabits this outpost of humanity.

After exploring the town – a fairly untaxing undertaking that takes less than an hour – we dropped into another of the town's bars, imaginatively named 'Svalbar.' There, we were able to eat burgers and chips for a moderately painful £25 a head, before making our way back to the campsite, where an enormous husky greeted us in hope of food. The sun hung low in the sky now, and sundogs – refractions caused by ice crystals in the atmosphere high above – floated to either side. The Arctic terns continued to swoop down upon us while the glaciers continued their slow progress to the sea. It was an incredible place. And the following day, Nick, Ed and I would be leaving it to board that boat and head north to the abandoned Soviet mining settlement of Pyramiden where the northernmost bar – the real starting point of our odyssey – was waiting.

After that pint in Pyramiden, the adventure was truly under way, and the only way to go was south.

07. THE ARCTIC

11th July 2017
69°39'N, 18°56'E. Tromsø, Norway.

FROM ALMOST ANYWHERE else on the planet, a trip to Norway's far north feels like a journey deeper into the wilderness. However, dropping back down from Svalbard, it was the area's sense of development that grabbed our attention first. On Svalbard, a population of 2700 inhabits an archipelago twice the size of Belgium. However, our return to the mainland saw us alight in Tromsø – a happening young city of 70,000 hardy souls, still over two hundred miles north of the Arctic Circle.

Yes, from anywhere else, Tromsø feels like an inconsequential outpost of civilisation, but arrive there from Svalbard and it might as well be New York.

Following our beer in the world's northernmost bar, and our subsequent flight back from Svalbard, we had two weeks left to complete the journey back to the UK, the deadline being set by transatlantic shipping schedules – we had to deliver Kermit to the Port of Southampton in late July, for onward shipping to the New World. This meant that while the time pressure wouldn't be nearly as overwhelming as it was on our journey north, we couldn't exactly hang around, so plans were rapidly made to hit the road south – though not before a quick team change. Ed, who'd only been able to take a week off work, would be taking the quick route home by flying back to the UK. In his week away, he'd driven all the way to the top of Europe and visited the world's most northerly bar and let's face it, weeks away don't get much more memorable than that. Replacing Ed at the helm of the £250 Micra, which, at this stage in the trip, I'd owned for a grand total of eight days, would be Pat. A keen caver and resourceful outdoors person, Pat had been keen to join the trip for months, and would be staying with Pub2Pub as long as possible for the journey across the Americas. He also had a particular affinity to Norway, and it was a rather excited person we found waiting for us in Tromsø.

As we'd learned on our northbound journey, Norway is big. Of the 20,000 miles of driving which now lay between us and the southernmost bar, 1300 were in Norway. Add in the distance we'd have to cover in Sweden and Denmark, and not far off a tenth of our trip's entire distance across the globe lay in Scandinavia. It's not a place to be underestimated – especially in the north, where motorways are non-existent and the towns are few and far between.

The first few days of our journey south passed through somewhere I'd wanted to visit for years; an almost mythical landscape which couldn't seem further from the rolling green of Southern England if it tried. The serrated summits of the Lofoten islands were the jewels in Arctic Norway's crown.

From the mainland, the Lofoten islands stretch for 50 miles into the turbulent ocean, which dominates their character, for the character of this spectacular archipelago is defined as much by what lies hidden as by what draws the eye so compellingly. Every thrusting summit is mirrored by the bottomless ocean to which its slopes fall; each urgent gust of wind seems to hint at a squall just over the horizon. As a result, the landscape feels permanently balanced in its drama.

And what a drama to drive through, midway between the jagged summits and the plunging watery depths! The mountains here are some of the most spectacular around and would impress in any landscape, let alone one where they rise so theatrically from the churning seas. And then there's the road, which snakes so improbably as it follows the path of least resistance through the terrain, tunnels and bridges allowing it to link together the delightful fishing villages that dot the more sheltered bays. The improbable mountains, the hardy wooden settlements, and the feeling that you're driving along a narrowing spit of land into the turbulent Arctic Ocean; could a more compelling place for a road trip exist?

Yes. Yes it could. The weather saw to that.

As we approached Lofoten, the clouds swept down to meet us. The gusting wind rocked our cars as we drove and the horizontal rain built to a full-on deluge. Sheer rock faces rose from the black waters for a few hundred feet before disappearing into the overcast, hinting at views we could only imagine. The villages were deserted, the road a stress-inducing blur of spray and blinding headlights. And as for our convoy, well, it's not often that someone is cruising along at the wheel of their pride-and-joy sports car, feeling jealous of the people ahead in their warm, dry, £250 Nissan Micra, but this was one of those moments.

The weather improved a little as we progressed along the island chain, making camp just off the road before catching a ferry down to the mainland the following day. As we sailed south, we looked back to the islands, which had greeted us so dramatically, and saw the mottled-black sky begin to lift off the summits in a well-timed farewell.

As we pushed on, the churning weather remained our constant

companion, smothering the mountaintops and often making the driving more of a chore than a pleasure. When it rained, my world was reduced to a streak of wet tarmac, leading up to the Micra's cloud of spray. And when it was dry, I eyed the sky eagerly, looking for a blue chink in the sky's steel-grey armour. As the first few days of the long drive south drifted past, I wondered whether opting to take the TVR was a step too far, as the inclement conditions emphasised its lack of weatherproofing and refinement. Not that it seemed to care, of course. Despite having covered 4000 miles in not much over a week, it roared on unconcernedly. In many ways, it had already become my home and travelling companion. Alone in the cabin, I had plenty of time to think as the miles rolled by. And as those miles rolled into days, my confidence gradually grew. Kermit already seemed to have a sense of inevitability about it; an aura that it was going to see this adventure through. It wouldn't let me down.

On our third day of driving south, we crossed the Arctic Circle – our journey's first latitude milestone. Ahead of us, many more milestones awaited. The Equator, the Tropics of Cancer and Capricorn. It was a long road ahead but even so, this first waypoint came with a nice sense of achievement, albeit a slightly contrived one given that we'd passed the same spot on our way north a week earlier.

The following day, we went to Hell. No, not that Hell. The other Hell, which happens to be a small village near Trondheim. It wasn't my first visit, as almost ten years earlier I'd driven there in a Fiat 126 city car to see in the New Year. Why? Because having decided the little Fiat was the 'car from Hell,' a few beers made it seem logical to drive it there. As the sun came out, we pulled the TVR onto the station platform and parked it beneath the famous 'Gods Expedition' sign, which adorns the goods shed, where I'd parked the Fiat years earlier. It was a great opportunity to look back on what I'd achieved in the intervening time. I'd crossed Africa in a Porsche, and Asia in a Corvette. I'd negotiated the Indian subcontinent in a three-wheeled auto-rickshaw, ridden the length of Vietnam on a $200 motorbike, and almost sunk a Jaguar in the Baltic when driving across the ocean's frozen surface. For all those years, I'd been pushing myself, trying to keep myself living life to the fullest. On many occasions it hadn't been easy, most recently when struggling with the depression that characterised the entire build-up to Pub2Pub. In fact, in many ways, I'd shaped my whole life around facilitating these trips, on both a personal and professional level. But as I parked Kermit in the same spot I'd parked the tiny, terrible Fiat almost a decade earlier, I looked back and smiled. It had totally been worth it.

Here I was, on the road once again, living out yet another dream that I'd spent years fighting to make a reality. As I mulled this over, I realised that, without a doubt, all the sacrifices I'd made to live my life so fully, in the way I'd dreamed of, were all worth it.

LEARNING FROM OUR experiences further north, we probably could have predicted what our journey through the mountains of southern Norway would be characterised by. That's right, the driving rain. But we headed up into the mountains anyway, slaloming along roads which twisted across the tortured landscape. You might think that all the bad weather would have soured our impressions of Norway somewhat, but it felt strangely appropriate. The latent power of the cliffs and valleys were mirrored by the very visible power in the skies above. Would we have preferred a series of rare, blue-sky days? Of course we would, but we probably wouldn't have been left with quite the same respect for the landscape and its ability to make you feel small. It was like Norway was testing us. And, as if we'd passed the test and earned its respect back, when we dropped out of the mountains near Oslo to set up camp on our last night in the country, the sun came out. Our surroundings were bathed with a golden light, our reward for the trials now behind us, as the Swedish border loomed ahead.

08. CONTRASTS

20th July 2017
56°27'N, 14°39'E. Kyrko Car Graveyard, Sweden.

THE LOW SUN flooded the forest with a rich, golden light. The fir trees and silver birches crowded in tightly around us as we walked. The silence was broken only by the crisp warble of birdsong. Greenery covered the forest floor, grass and moss, encouraging us to stay on the path as we headed deeper into the forest, anticipating our first glimpse of what had drawn us to this obscure corner of Sweden.

And then we saw it.

Next to the path, the remains of several classic cars lay rotting beneath the trees. Time had taken its toll on the vehicles. Over 40 years of exposure to the elements had left them twisted and rusty. Most were missing vital parts. Doors, windows, bumpers and trim had been cannibalised to keep other more fortunate vehicles on the road. Some were unrecognisable, while others retained enough shape for us to identify them: VW Beetles, Saabs, Volvos, Mercedes. In total, there were 150 cars in the forest, slowly decaying away to nothing.

We explored further. The whole place had an eerie sense of unreality about it, as if a classic car show back home had been hit by a nuclear holocaust and then abandoned. Vehicles that are usually only seen in museums, or polished to their Sunday best for a local car show, were strewn around indiscriminately, slowly dying. The interiors of many of them had filled with leaves and pine needles, which were slowly rotting away their floorpans. Where once there were cushioned seats, now only rusted springs remained. I doubt another forest exists anywhere in the world with quite the same tetanus risk.

So, why would so many cars come to litter an obscure Swedish forest? As with so many of the more interesting stories this world has to offer, it all comes back to the obsession of one person – in this instance, a chap by the name of Ake Danielsson. Following the Second World War, Sweden had found itself in an economic boom, and car ownership rocketed. Old cars became disposable goods to a degree unheard of up to that point in time and, being essentially worthless, began to be abandoned at random around the countryside. Ake, for reasons best known to himself, gathered them, collecting them in the forest we were exploring. Being a terminal collector who would put most car enthusiasts to shame, by 1974 Ake had amassed a collection 150 strong, and had a handy side-business selling secondhand parts from his unique stash.

Ake passed away in 2000 but his collection remains as an outsider tourist attraction and a unique monument to one Swede's obsessive focus. As we roamed the poignant forest, as the sun set and the air took on a chill freshness that seemed to embrace us, we couldn't think of a better monument to the eccentric 'Ake of the Bog.'

The following morning, we headed to the product of another eccentric Swede's single-handed determination to follow his dream. This dream also featured cars and ambition, but the results of the two goals were very different. Because let's face it, you can't get much further from a bunch of old cars rusting away in a forest than a visit to hypercar heaven – the Koenigsegg factory.

Hidden away on the outskirts of Ängelholm, on an old, Cold War-era airbase, there is no sense of drama as you approach the factory. The aircraft hangar and attached office block where some of the planet's most exciting cars are designed and built could be any old medium-sized engineering business. But for the sign next to the front door and the glimpse of a bright orange hypercar through the small showroom window, externally, the factory is an exercise in the mundane. However, thanks to the uncompromising engineering-led focus of the company's founder – Christian Von Koenigsegg – the cars are anything but mundane. In fact, it was one of the few places we visited on our journey where our trusty TVR wasn't the most gloriously extrovert vehicle around.

We met Koenigsegg's marketing manager in the showroom and took in the two cars on display. Everything about them was infused with a single-minded pursuit of performance. We're talking about a company where the budget-friendly base model still puts out 927 horsepower and comes with a seven-figure price tag. A company that, in 20 years, has gone from not even existing to beating all comers by setting a new production car speed record of 278mph. There aren't many places that can make a TVR seem to be lacking in drama or power, but park one outside the Koenigsegg factory, and it may as well be a Ford Fiesta.

Possibly the most impressive thing about Koenigsegg is the way they leave no engineering stone unturned in their quest for performance. They were the first manufacturer to produce carbon fibre wheels, and are close to another world first – perfecting an engine where the camshaft is replaced by hydro-pneumatic valve activation, allowing for infinitely adjustable valve timing. Most impressively, many of their recent creations don't even have a gearbox, instead using a lockable torque converter to effectively make the engine a direct drive, assisted by electric motors which torque-fill to ensure peak power is only a flick of the right foot away. This system can get their latest car – the $2.5million Regera – from zero to 240mph in under 20 seconds. That's the sort of statistic that's hard to get your head around. And just like the almost diametrically-opposite dream that led to the car graveyard just up the road, the entire business exists solely because of the vision of Christian Von Koenigsegg, Sweden's answer to Enzo Ferrari or Ferruccio Lamborghini.

As we left the factory, a Koenigsegg Agera sped past us, undergoing final testing before being delivered to a very rich customer. Never has my TVR felt more low rent than at that moment.

On the plus side, Kermit's old-school, shock 'n' awe V8 engine definitely sounded better than the young hypercar's million-dollar motor. I still found myself wishing I'd worked harder at school, though.

09. AUTOBAHN

21st July 2017
55°00′N, 13°30′E. The Baltic Ocean.

THE SUN APPEARED to fizzle out as it dropped from the perfect blue sky to the sea. Barely a wave was in evidence on this sheltered corner of the Baltic, and the sunset was mirrored perfectly on the water's surface. As always when I watch a maritime sunset, I looked out for the 'green flash' as the light disappeared, but as always, none was forthcoming. The spectacle was still worth it though, its clean drama offsetting the cool breeze that the vessel's forward motion was generating.

Although only a few weeks into the trip, we'd already spent a lot of time onboard various vessels and this voyage across the Baltic's pinched western reaches from Sweden to Germany marked our fifth trip across the waves. I enjoyed the enforced inactivity of the time we spent on boats. Freed from having to drive, or the routine of camping, it was about the only time I was able to do next to nothing with a clear conscience. As I sought to put my depression behind me, doing nothing without guilt was a very useful tool.

To beat depression, you have to reduce the pressures you're under to a minimum, be patient, and wait for your mind to bounce back. It's not a quick process and it can be a frustrating one with plenty of ups and downs complicating the road to recovery. But it's the only way: put simply, it's something you just have to do.

Obviously, in the build up to the trip, when I was frantically raising funds, researching the route and prepping the car, I wasn't really in a position to take my foot off the gas. I had to keep pushing as hard as I could, and when you're suffering from depression, 'hard' isn't nearly as hard as you'd hope. In fact, the build up to the trip had been a kind of catch-22: the efforts I made to get to the start line were counterproductive as far as my mental health was concerned, and it was once the trip was under way that I had any chance of making some sort of recovery. The long hours in the car, along with the inescapable idleness of the ferry crossings, was actually pretty good therapy. The time spent with my mind just ticking over was exactly what the doctor ordered − or would have been, if I'd had the common sense to see one, instead of being a typical bloke and battling on ineffectually by myself.

Unfortunately, the positive effects of the downtime were offset by the inevitable stresses of the trip. Would the money last? Would we get the car to Southampton in time for it to be shipped to New York? And then there was the route. Would it be blocked by some sort of political uprising or natural disaster? Ahead lay 20,000 miles across a range of hotspots for earthquakes, volcanoes, political unrest and red tape – the coming months didn't represent the most relaxing of prospects.

The darkness was total when we rolled off the ferry into Northern Germany and headed on into the night, taking advantage of the quiet autobahns. It was a hypnotic few hours, following the burning red tail lights of the Micra while trying to stay awake.

Morning saw us basking in the first light of day in the – quite literally – sleepy town of Templin, near Berlin. Templin has two very different claims to fame. The first is that it is the childhood home of the German Chancellor, Angela Merkel, whose family moved to the area when she was three months old.

But that's not why we visited.

No, we were there because of religion. Or more precisely, the faux-religion that is the Church of the Flying Spaghetti Monster. This light-hearted riposte to the likes of Christianity has been doing everything it can to be considered a 'proper' religion, and illustrate the apparent absurdity of organised religion in the process. In Europe, the one place that its attempts have yielded the most visible progress is in Templin.

As you enter German towns, you'll often see signs detailing the times of the various weekly religious services held there, enabling you to make sure you're not late to connect with your chosen God. And yes, you've guessed it – as you enter Templin, there are signs displaying the Flying Spaghetti Monster, inviting you to join the service praising him at 10am every Friday. Admittedly, the church is actually a bloke's front room, but still, you've got to admire whoever managed to get the signs on display, and irreverently poke fun out of organised religion in the process. At least, *I* felt I had to admire the achievement. Pat felt a little different.

"So we've driven through the night to come and look at some signs? There isn't even a church, for God's sake! This was the worst idea ever, I can't believe you dragged us here."

Evidently, Pat didn't share my slightly daft and irreverent taste when it came to choosing places to visit. But on a 20,000 mile journey to grab a beer at the far side of the world, detouring across Germany to check out some quirky signs seemed to make perfect sense. To me, anyway.

Even so, there's only so long you can look at a bunch of signs before you've ticked the experience, and so as Templin began to wake for the coming day, we were already gone, speeding down the autobahn to Ferropolis.

THE RUSTING FRAMEWORKS of girders and conveyor belts towered over the lake as we approached, mottling the heavy grey sky. From a distance, the colossal machines merged together and the resultant clutter made it impossible to spot their individual shapes. It was like an industrial junkyard from an Orwellian dystopia.

We passed old warehouses as we arrived. One of the buildings had a mural painted across its front, portraying mine workers. Four solemn, weathered faces looked on from the area's past with a steely determination that glorified their hard lives.

The towering jumbles of metalwork were resolving themselves into individual machines now. Enormous strip-mining machines, with rotating buckets and conveyor belts designed for only one purpose – removing coal from the rich deposits that were once scattered across the area. There were five of the excavators, though now they stood as silent monuments to a previous age. The open cast mine that surrounded them had long since flooded, its coal reserves depleted. And without coal to mine, what use could such machines have? In completing the job they were built for, they had destroyed their *raisin d'être*. A patina of age and neglect had overtaken them. Rust streaks ran down their metalwork, their paintwork was flaking, and their control room windows were cracked.

The largest of the five machines measured over 100 metres long, 30 metres high and weighed just shy of 2000 tonnes. It stood on a gloriously oversized set of caterpillar tracks, but it would never move again. It was a monument of 20th-century engineering, but the world had left it behind.

I parked Kermit next to it, and the morning drizzle began to fall.

The five machines were laid out in a circle, and within the circle was a concrete area that was used for festivals and events during the summer. It's a spectacular transformation, refugees from the industrial age forming a unique backdrop to the recreation of today: where once the pursuit of wealth through natural resources dominated, the pursuit of pleasure now calls the shots.

However, there's a moroseness about Ferropolis. Visit on a rainy weekday morning when the place is deserted and you can't help but sense a tinge of sadness, because despite the modern repurposing and changes for the better, the place is still an industrial graveyard. Here, some of the largest land-based machines man has ever made fulfilled their purpose around the clock, and people earned livelihoods and cared for them, but there is now only silence. The bustle has gone. As the rain fell and the cloudbase came down to obscure the highest metalwork, it was difficult not to feel slightly melancholic; nostalgic for a world you never saw. We lingered for several hours, strangely reluctant to leave, as if to do so would be disrespectful.

Ferropolis. What a strangely compelling yet conflicting place. If you're passing, I recommend that you to drop in. It certainly leaves a much stronger impression than the Flying Spaghetti Monster signs further north.

10. THE RACETRACK

23rd July 2017
50°19'N, 06°56'E. The Nürburgring, Germany.

IT WASN'T LIKE any other forest we'd been to. The densely packed woodland swept across the hillsides in the usual familiar fashion, but here, nature wasn't in control. This wasn't a forest you came to relax in. However, for those of a certain persuasion, a visit is an almost religious experience, as snaking through the endless trees is one of the most revered names in motor racing – The Nürburgring.

This 14.2-mile track bares comparison with any of the other famous crucibles of motorsport. Its peers are Monaco, Le Mans, Spa and Daytona. And in many ways it towers above them all, for it stands alone in the scale of the challenge it offers. No other track is so long nor so hard to learn as the Nürburgring's legendary Nordschleife. And no other track has struck the same fear and emotion into the drivers who have attempted to master its turns. The story of the track is rich, with legends both created, and so sadly lost.

It was here that Juan Manuel Fangio completed one of the greatest drives ever seen: by pushing his aging Maserati hard after a disastrous pitstop, he beat the challenging Ferraris and secured his fifth world title. It was on these unforgiving turns that Stefan Bellof manhandled his Porsche 956 to a lap record of six minutes 11 seconds – a record that would secure him a place in the history books by remaining unbeaten for 35 years.

But for every legend that has been born at the Nürburgring, there is another that has been cut short, for it is a track which can never be mastered. The racing occurs so close to the limits of what is possible that occasionally, inevitably, the line is crossed. And when this happens, the tree-lined slaloms of The Green Hell are as unforgiving as they come. Racing legend Peter Collins was killed here, and in 1976, Nicki Lauda's life was almost cut short when a crash left him trapped in a burning car. It is a place with no margin for error; a place where you must be fully confident in yourself and your vehicle if you're to complete a flying lap safely.

So, it made perfect sense that it would be the first place where I got to drive the Micra. We'd noticed a few days previously that despite it being my car and despite the fact that it had covered over 5000 miles since I'd bought it, I'd still never actually got behind the wheel. A lap of the Nürburgring seemed like the obvious solution.

The racetrack is open to the public on many evenings and weekends for what are poetically called 'touristenfahrten' – tourist laps. For a few dozen Euros, you can fling your car around The Green Hell, and as a result, this is one of the places on Earth where petrolhead culture runs thickest. Tricked-up Porsche 911s, roll-caged classic Volkswagen Golfs, and track-prepped MX-5s are a common sight on the area's roads, the density of the sightings increasing as you approach the track, peaking at the car park which surrounds the aptly named Devil's Diner, where you start and finish your lap.

Nick jumped in the back of the Micra while Pat and I took our places in the front seats. Though I hadn't driven the car before, it didn't feel too unfamiliar, and it was certainly one of the least intimidating cars I've ever looked across the bonnet of. I've driven my fair share of small, mundane hatchbacks over the years, and they all follow the same template – minimal power, soft suspension leading to colossal amounts of body roll, and a stubborn keenness to understeer, balanced by the hilarious oversteer which you can trigger with the correct application of weight shift.

Neither Pat nor Nick had been to the 'Ring before, and as we queued to join the track behind a hard-as-nails modified Mercedes, I don't think they really knew what they'd let themselves in for. On previous visits to the track, I'd learnt that counter-intuitively, the faster you go, the less scary the track is. When I first lapped the Nordschleife ten years previously in my Porsche 944, I'd found my first attempts at a gentle lap terrifying, as the traffic approaching from behind was going so much quicker than me that there was almost no time to get out of the way. It was only once I started going at seven or eight tenths that the intimidation subsided and the fear lifted. Well, except for that moment when I barrelled into Hatzenbach a bit too quickly and ended up taking it broadside. But that's a whole different story – as far as the Micra's lap was concerned, it was going to be flat out.

The barrier lifted and we accelerated glacially onto the circuit, the Nissan's lack of a rev counter meaning I had to guess when to make my gear changes. Arriving at the first corner – my first ever in the Micra – I assumed the grip levels would be similar to my old K10 Micra, the one that had expired an hour into the trip. I assumed wrongly, however, and found the tyres had slightly more to give, meaning I pushed harder into the next turns, triggering a predictable understeer that could be neutralised by a slight lift of the throttle on corner entry.

Meanwhile, I noticed Nick had gone silent, while Pat had begun to protest that I was clearly trying to kill us all. In reality, I was just trying to avoid giving the Micra a Porsche 911 to its posterior.

And it was a very real risk. I might have been pushing hard, but there's only so much a 74-horsepower shopping trolley can give, and we were certainly one of the slowest vehicles on the track. Car after car flew past us disdainfully: Porsches, Mercedes and BMWs – the German home crowd was well represented. Then there were the motorbikes, which flashed past like guided missiles, and the Dodge Viper, all spoilers and aggression and, let's face it, the reciprocal opposite of our Tesco-spec Nissan. Despite our best efforts, as we wheezed down the straights and almost toppled over in the corners, we were definitely the slowest car there.

Until we were about two thirds of the way around, that is.

Approaching Carousel – the most iconic of all the Nordschleife's corners – we found ourselves gaining on a rather serious-looking '90s BMW 3-series. The car was covered in stickers, rode very low, and was fitted with a roll cage which took up most of the rear window, while a large rear spoiler removed the rest of its driver's rearwards view. However, the most significant thing about the BMW was the fact that due to some unseen mechanical malady, it didn't seem able to do much over 60mph.

I stepped up the pace, intent on passing at least one vehicle during my slowest-ever lap of the 'Ring. But while the BMW may have been glacier-like in its performance, the Micra wasn't that much faster. For mile after mile I gradually gained on my target. In corners there wasn't much in it, but on the straights I could make up the metres. We kept up this game of cat and mouse as the end of the lap neared, but with less than a mile to go, as the three of us in the Micra bounced up and down with excitement, we finally drew level and passed the BMW, as I shouted, "Dude, I actually had you."

And with that we rolled off the track and back into the car park at the Devil's Diner. It wasn't a moment too soon for Nick, who was finding that one of the most efficient ways to get motion sickness is to look through a camera viewfinder as the car you're in is flung around a race track.

With 14.2 miles and 160 corners complete, I clambered out of the Micra and rejoined the more familiar world of the TVR. And on we rolled.

11. THE HOME RUN

25th July 2017
49°15'N, 3°55'E. Reims-Gueux circuit, France.

IF THE NÜRBURGRING has become a monument to the modern-day excesses of petrolhead culture, then the Reims-Gueux Grand Prix circuit is a memorial to its past. Once, it bore witness to the competitions of yesteryear: epic slipstreaming battles from the gladiatorial age of motor racing, where death was never far away, and the roars from the packed grandstands had mirrored those rising from the redlining motors on the starting grid, as scores were settled and legends made.

But the world moved on, and the track fell silent in the early 1970s. No longer a place of competition, the roads returned to a steady flow of Renault 4s and 2CVs, and slowly, the dust settled. Pit lane garages were stripped and abandoned, grandstands slowly decayed beneath a patina of neglect. But the bulldozers never arrived; the redevelopment never came, and after a while, this farmland to the west of Reims became a place in which to reconnect with the past. A place where the golden age of motorsport still speaks to you from across the ages.

I rolled down the main start-finish straight, the grandstands and race control tower growing larger in my windscreen. The vista suited the TVR, which often feels like a '60s British sports car that happened to be built in the '90s – the walnut dash, classical instruments, and howling V8 could have come from the same era as the mouldering buildings we were approaching.

I parked next to the long vacated pits. They were surprisingly small, harking back to a less commercial age, but the slogans adorning the buildings showed that commercialism had encroached in Reims' later years. BP, ELF, Zenith, and, predictably, Coca Cola logos were crudely painted onto the white walls. They seemed to speak of a more innocent age, before million-dollar drivers, interactive TV, and design teams measuring in the hundreds took over.

We climbed the steps to the top of the race control tower. The sweeping view encompassed the stripped-bare concrete bulk of the grandstands and the start-finish straight. The tarmac now only sees service as a public road but the buildings surrounding it make it easy to imagine the area's poignant past. The grid of dashing hopefuls and their gleaming machines, the bustle of mechanics, the blipping throttles, and enthralled crowds waiting for battle to commence.

However, there is something missing, for obviously I can't recall a past I never knew. My imaginings are tinged with questions and rendered in black and white rather than colour. It's an era I'll never know, and can only half picture. The more I explored the tired structures, the more gaps I found in what my limited imagination could fill in. Like Kermit, Reims can only hint at the past, it can't take you there.

I sank into the TVR's classical interior, fired up the big lazy V8, and rolled over the start-finish line, bound for Chantilly.

WE SAW HIM coming from a long way off. A well-used silver Porsche 928 is a rare-enough sight in a French service station, but this was something else. The paintwork was flecked in stickers: Motul, Recaro, The Porsche Club, and various other French companies whose logos were new to me. The car had a purposeful stance, sitting five centimetres higher than standard, and the tyres were more mud-focussed than you'd usually expect to see on a Porsche. A full-size spare wheel was bolted to the roof, a rollcage had been fitted inside the car and stone protectors covered the headlights.

Clearly, this was one sports car that had been put together with more than just a trip to the French Riviera in mind. This was emphasised by the world map on the door, complete with a line showing the route taken by the 928 when it circled the world a year previously, passing through Europe, Russia, Japan, Canada, and the USA in the course of its 22,000 mile odyssey.

Philippe Delaporte parked his well-proven machine next to Kermit, climbed out excitedly, and finally, we shook hands. We'd known of each others' exploits for many years, through our mutual Porsche-based adventuring, and my previous trip across Africa in a Porsche had even provided some of the inspiration for Philippe's spot of globetrotting in his 928. Despite this, the moment he pulled up in the French autoroute services marked the first time we'd met.

In his 60s, slightly portly, and with a greying tuft of hair marking his head like an exclamation point, Philippe is one of those people who has a definite presence; a larger-than-life persona that dominates whichever situation he finds himself in, but makes those around him feel completely at ease in the process. And he was excited, because let's face it, it's not every day you meet a fellow Porsche-driving adventurer.

After getting to know each other, Philippe showed us around his Porsche, and we were certainly impressed by the lengths he'd gone to, to prepare the car for its adventures. As well as the obvious signs, such as the roof-mounted spare wheel, there was a depth in the preparation that impressed me deeply. The shock absorbers had been replaced with harder-wearing Koni items, while an 8mm alloy sumpguard protected the engine. All the vehicle's service parts had been replaced for his big trip, from the radiator hoses to the wheel bearings, while the removal of the rear seats allowed the back of the vehicle to be completely redesigned around a second spare wheel and extra fuel tanks. The dashboard was covered in extra navigational equipment, the roll cage towered over the bespoke seats, and a safe was fitted in the old spare wheel recess. Everything about the car had been done to make it as functional as possible on a world tour and look good at the same time.

Meanwhile, over in the TVR, life was rather different. My journey promised to actually be a fair bit longer than Philippe's, but to any casual passer-by my car was a flimsy joke in comparison. Kermit's original suspension was already worn out and my preparations appeared to be non-existent – which is a more-than-fair observation, as compared to what Philippe had done before his trip, they were. Hell, I didn't even have a spare wheel for the TVR yet, and if I didn't already have a track record of making similar trips in such under-prepared vehicles, I'm sure Philippe would have simply laughed at me. Instead, he diplomatically complimented me on how I embrace the adventurous aspect of such trips by using such standard vehicles. But the reality is somewhat different.

Before all the big road trips I've made, I would have loved to have been able to apply the attention to detail that Philippe did, but the reality of how these trips happen seems to prevent me from doing so. Money is always marginal at best, so all preparations are done on a shoestring. Affording garage help in preparing my cars is something I've almost never been in a position to do. Likewise, expensive modifications are a no-no; everything has to be done on the tightest budget. And because I tend to dream up and undertake these trips fairly independently, while also working a full-time job, the time constraints of the planning – and the 1001 other tasks that need to be done to make them happen – mean my time for car preparation is pretty limited. And that's before you get onto the fact that depression had made even reaching Pub2Pub's start line an incredibly close run thing, never mind extensively preparing the car. So, as I say, while to Philippe my approach appeared to have a purity to be commended, the reality is somewhat different. Bringing my trips to fruition has always been so marginal that luxuries such as having the car properly prepared have had to remain a distant dream.

We took the cars in convoy to Chantilly, an elegant old town just north of Paris, which is home to a magnificently restored chateau and a somewhat more modest pizzeria, to which Philippe took us for dinner, and many stories of global adventuring took us into the night. Being an absolute gent, Philippe insisted on picking up the tab – something we didn't complain too much about, as our expedition finances were about as convincing as our vehicle preparation.

THE SKY WAS still black as the ferry approached the harbour at Dover. The White Cliffs were almost invisible, and we perceived them as little more than a whitened blur in our peripheral vision.

We were almost home.

It was 24 days since we'd hit the road on Dartmoor, and in those 24 days, we'd driven over 6000 miles, passed through eight different countries, and been to a bar within 800 miles of the North Pole. By anyone's reckoning, it was quite a road trip we'd just experienced, but to us, it was just the warm-up. And while we were thankful that the warm-up had gone well, and that my confidence in the TVR hadn't been destroyed by some catastrophic breakdown, we had no reason for overconfidence.

In total, over 20,000 miles still lay ahead, through all the rough roads, red tape, and bureaucracy that The Americas could muster. We'd completed the first continent, but the expedition's success would live or die on our performance in the coming months. When Kermit reached the American continent, it would be facing one of the hardest challenges ever attempted by a TVR.

Despite this, and despite the acute lack of preparation and my lingering depression, I knew I could do this. An irrational, almost religious belief in the ability of myself and the car to get to the finish line had taken hold of me: we were going to do this.

I passed through Southampton's port security and dropped Kermit off in the compound from which it would be shipped to the New World, on a vessel loaded with brand new Jaguars and Range Rovers for the export market. After a few minutes of paperwork and a handover of keys, for the first time since I'd bought it six years previously, Kermit's fate was out of my control. I'd see it again 14 days later in the Port of New Jersey.

As I left the compound, I glanced over my shoulder and saw it sitting there amid the sea of shiny new Range Rovers, looking like a scruffy terrier who'd just gatecrashed Crufts.

"See you in a few weeks, mate," I said quietly to myself, already thinking ahead to the next leg of the adventure.

www.veloce.co.uk / www.velocebooks.com
All current books · New book news · Special offers · Gift vouchers

INTERMISSION

Havana   Varadero

CUBA

Santiago
de Cuba

Cayman Islands

12. CUBA

04th August 2017
23°02'N, 81°26'W. Varadero, Cuba.

THE SUNLIGHT WAS beating down so hard that the whole world seemed overexposed. Palm trees towered into the bleached, blue-white furnace of the sky, the air was still, and the humidity drained our energy almost instantly as we left the airport buildings. Four-wheeled relics from another age sat waiting in the car park, a vibrant mix of '50s Americana and more recent Soviet metal, which spoke of the shifting allegiances of this feisty little island. Locals in ill-fitting casual clothes huddled in any shade they could find, dozing their way towards the evening. But of all our senses that had come alive as we walked out of the airport into Cuba, it was the smell that struck us most. A warm, musty aroma of rotting plant matter, which, after ten hours in the hermetically-sealed world of an Airbus, seemed thick enough to chew on. Not that you'd want to, of course.

After dropping off Kermit in Southampton, we had two weeks to wait before we could collect it from the Port of New Jersey, and we figured what better way to kill some of that time than by spending a few days in Cuba? After all, flying to New York via Cuba was barely more expensive than flying direct, and who wouldn't want to spend a few days in this enigmatic country? So we made it happen, with Nick and I flying out with Claire, and Pat joining us a few days later.

Our budget flight across the Atlantic had deposited us in a town called Varadero, which turned out to be about as far from the edgy intensity of Havana as you can get. As the taxi dropped us outside our high-rise hotel, we found our home for the coming days was a rather sprawling beach resort, a kind of Cuban answer to Spain's Costa del Sol. Still, there were compensations for ending up in such a place: the sand was so fine it felt like liquid between our toes; the Guatemalan-made beers were so cold it was like drinking ice cream, and the rum? Well, the rum was everywhere. And then, of course, there were the cars.

Everyone associates Cuba with the old American cars that still prowl the streets there. However, before I visited I'd assumed that instead of being a particularly common sight, they would be a relative rarity, the myth of which was perpetuated by the fact that every visitor went out their way to come home with a clichéd photo of an old Chevy. But nothing could be further from the truth. Interesting classic cars were everywhere. And not just the Americana of legend. There was also Soviet stuff from the '70s and '80s, and even the mighty Daewoo Tico, imported from Peru in the '90s. It's a car lover's paradise, and much to the irritation of Claire and Nick, I spent far too much of my time in Varadero crossing roads and generally going out of my way to get a closer look at some old Polski Fiat or postwar Plymouth.

Without the cars, I think I would have been bored of Varadero within a few hours – not that I could escape even if I wanted to. As well as having to wait for Pat to arrive, there was the small matter of our bags, which had decided they didn't fancy crossing the Atlantic with us. Each day our hotel would call the airport, and each day we'd be told they hadn't arrived, so we settled in and waited. Our routine typically involved a stroll down to the beach in the morning, before the day heated up too much, at which point we'd hide in the air-conditioned hotel room for a few hours before venturing out in search of some evening beers, and marvelling at the passing Ladas, Moskvitches and Chevrolets as we drank.

After three days in Varadero, even the cars were starting to lose their appeal, primarily because I'd already seen them all and was starting to recognise their owners as well. Fortunately, however, we found ourselves in possession of both our luggage and Pat, so we were able to head for the big city – Havana.

Our transport for the two-hour journey? A 1950s Chevrolet soft top, of course.

HAVANA IS A rough diamond, a gritty gem of a city that seduces you with its sheer *joie de vivre*. Many of its buildings are an exercise in decay, fighting a constant battle with the encroaching rains, mildew and vegetation, which the city doesn't have the resources to win, but they give the city its unique character as it elegantly struggles against the onset of time.

We took a couple of rooms in a property just off Plaza Vieja, whose enterprising owner had realised that the tourist trade is one of the few ways to make good money in a country where everyone, from doctors to dustmen, survive on Cuba's official salary of $25 per month. Our host also happened to have a '57 Ford Fairline with straight-through pipes on its gravelly V8, and hence was alright in our book.

So, in a compelling mix of living history and V8 noise, our time in Havana began. It was a very pleasant place to while away a few days as the TVR made its way across the Atlantic. We roamed the town, dipping in and out of the street café culture, and soaking up the uniqueness of a city beyond the reach of globalisation, where no McDonalds or Starbucks intrudes, no advertising clutters the views, and The West feels much further away than the 90-mile sea crossing that would see us in Florida.

We gazed out across that sea when we went for a cruise down the Malecón, living out a cliché by riding in a slice of classic Americana. But it wasn't just any old American car; no, we set forth on our cruise in the only Studebaker in the country, still running its original 3.3l V8 engine though kitted out with the radiator from a Mercedes Sprinter van and an old Soviet carburettor. It may not have been a contender for any best-in-show awards back in the States but there's something delightfully satisfying about seeing the lengths to which people have gone to keep their cars on the road in the face of a near-continuous trade embargo by their powerful neighbours to the north.

Despite the mongrel nature of its engineering, the mighty Studebaker drove well, as I found out when I got behind the wheel: smooth and dignified, but with a rather tricky column-mounted gearshift that took some getting used to. Not that that mattered – getting behind the wheel of a magnificent Studebaker on Cuba's famous Malecón ... what a memory!

The other car I drove in Havana wasn't quite as glamorous, in fact it was possibly one of the least glamorous vehicles the world has ever seen – a Polski-Fiat 126. Powered by a rear-mounted, air-cooled 650cc engine, which endows the shoe-sized vehicle with the performance of a sloth, the little 'Maluch' isn't many people's idea of a dream car, but it's tiny size and simple engineering suits the cramped one-way streets of Havana perfectly, and I spent a fun 20 minutes flinging it around the town. I'm a sucker for ostensibly rubbish cars with a big dose of character, and the feisty Fiat certainly fits the bill – as well as bringing back memories of the time I drove one to that village called Hell, years before.

From a Western perspective, one of the most interesting things about the cars we'd encountered was their price. The cheapest car in the country – the Polski Fiat – will still set you back at least £6000, while the Studebaker was reckoned to be worth around £60,000, making it the most valuable vehicle I'd ever driven. Even our host's '57 Ford was worth over £20,000. It all comes down to supply and demand, and the lack of vehicle imports has made a car an irreplaceable family heirloom to be treasured and passed down over the decades; I'm very relieved I didn't crash while on the island.

* * *

AFTER SIX DAYS in Cuba we boarded a flight to New York, psyched to be getting back on the road, but full of respect for the country we were leaving behind, after our all-too-brief visit. Very few nations have had a tougher recent history than Cuba. From the 1959 revolution, which gave Fidel Castro control of the nation, through the US-backed Bay of Pigs invasion in '61, and the full-on missile crisis of '62, Cuba's modern history started with a bang. One that led to isolation and difficulty at every turn, firstly at the hands of a US embargo, and more recently with the collapse of the Soviet Union, which cut off Cuba's remaining funding. Every year in living memory has been tough for this place, but Cuba's spirit somehow remains undimmed. No other country has shown such defiance and resilience in the face of overwhelming odds.

What a tough little island.

13. FRIENDS REUNITED

17th August 2017
40°41'N, 74°08'W. The Port of New Jersey, USA.

SITTING IN THE TVR for the first time since it had arrived in America, it felt like I'd returned home after a few weeks away. Living with the machine day in and day out across Europe had made it more than just a car. I'd committed to spending eight months of my life with Kermit, moving location every few days, and it was already a constant in my life, replacing one that was previously bricks and mortar. It was where I stored my immediate worldly possessions, it offered shelter and solace, and after so many hours together on the roads of Europe, it dripped with comforting familiarity. I'd become accustomed to everything about the car – the feel of the meaty alloy gearstick resting in my hand, the chatter that rose up through the steering as the road surface changed, the laid-back driving position, and the mumbling growl of the engine as we cruised along. But the familiarity had to end somewhere, and as I cruised out of the port of New Jersey, having collected the car after its transatlantic voyage, I realised that 'somewhere' was just beyond the end of the bonnet.

The tyres droned coarsely as we rolled along the rough grey concrete of the New Jersey Turnpike. Unfamiliar vehicles were all around us. Muscular pick-up trucks, and semi-trailers laden with attitude towered over us as we cruised along, and yellow Lincoln Crown Victoria taxicabs sped by, rushing from Newark Airport towards downtown Manhattan. The road signage adopted that simple bluntness which characterises the US style, while the no-nonsense feel extended to the way the impatient New Yorkers drove: tight and aggressive. But I registered all this only vaguely, as I was guiding the TVR almost on autopilot, my attention very much elsewhere.

Ahead of us, flickering in and out of view behind buildings, the lower Manhattan skyline formed our horizon, while to our right, the iconic outline of the Statue of Liberty rose from Upper New York Bay.

I was transfixed by the famous view, familiar from so many images and films. Huddled tightly along the waterfront, the skyscrapers sparkled against the blue sky as the afternoon light played on their glazed frontages, which appeared to merge into one as they shimmered together. Only one building seemed to break away from this glazed mass, standing behind the front row and towering above it: the 1776-foot tall One World Trade Centre, which symbolised this great city's resilience.

The view to my right was no less compelling, with the Statue of Liberty rising from its plinth, gazing southwards across New York Harbour towards the open oceans beyond. But the statue's allure stems not from its sheer size, for it appears smaller in real life than in so many movies, where its towering presence is often used as a metaphor of America's power. No, it stems from familiarity, for those same films that emphasised the statue's importance have also rendered it larger than life in our minds.

What a place to find yourself after driving out of the port, covering your first miles on a new continent as the plan you've been working on for years becomes real. With Manhattan ahead and the Statue of Liberty scrolling past to my right, life was good. Very good.

WHILE GETTING READY to set off across the United States we lived in an apartment in Hoboken, New Jersey, just across the river from New York City. Despite a history which mirrors some of the UK's more rundown inner cities – a decline in shipbuilding and industry triggering a rudderless drift towards dereliction – today Hoboken is a rather pleasant, though unspectacular, place. It has its claims to fame (it's the birthplace of both baseball and Frank Sinatra) and its trademark sights (the view across the river Hudson to the Manhattan skyline), but nowadays, Hoboken seems happy to take the easy life, relaxing in the shadow of its more famous neighbour, while absorbing some of its prosperity.

We ended up staying there for a week, our time passing in an agreeable mix of sightseeing, relaxing, and preparing for the coming journey across the Americas. And a fairly important part of the preparations involved finding a second car: with the group having swollen to six people, and the Micra having remained in the UK, we clearly weren't all going to fit in just the TVR. So Claire, Pat and Brummy set out to track down a suitable steed, while I worked through the temporary import paperwork, which eventually resulted in the TVR being able to make that drive past the Statue of Liberty towards the New York skyline.

So what car would you choose to buy for such a trip across the New World? A big butch Jeep? An old Cadillac? Maybe a Crown Victoria taxicab? These sensible options were all mooted, and they all paled into a grey world of dullness in comparison to the vehicle which was eventually purchased in a slightly seedy used car lot in Jersey City. Yes, Kermit's long-term travelling companion turned out to be a Hemi Dodge Charger, powered by a 5.7-litre V8. Because let's face it, if you're going to go on a great American road trip, you may as well do it properly.

Built in 2006, this retro-modern piece of Americana ticked every box you'd expect from an old-fashioned American icon. A butch-yet-simple exterior, paired with a huge-yet-flimsy interior? Tick. A brutally torquey motor, matched with a simply terrible automatic gearbox? Yes, that too. And a gloriously ridiculous Trump-orange paint job, complete with 'Daytona' stickers and a chalkboard-black bonnet? Of course. Why would anybody want their Dodge any other way?

The one thing the enormous Hemi had in bucket loads, however, was attitude. Its styling seemed to consciously shun the sophistication of its European equivalents, instead majoring on a whole heap of Detroit aggression. And that's before you fire up the engine, which, again, was all about attitude, roughly grumbling away to itself before making a noise like a gurgling hippo when you accelerate away. Or maybe it sounded more like a drain emptying. Or a TVR with one of its pistons missing. We never did quite decide on the most accurate way to describe it.

Say what you will about the Dodge though, it managed to carry four people in comfort, and it made for a nice counterweight to the TVR, being as American as Kermit is English.

WHILE WE WERE waiting to collect the mildly offensive Dodge from the dealership, we busied ourselves by taking in the sensory overload that is New York. Each morning, from our base just across the River Hudson, we'd take either the water taxi or subway over to the glistening city to roam its canyons, summit its heights, and soak up the atmosphere of one of the world's greatest cities. Everywhere we went, we felt like we'd been there before, because New York is one of those places you've known all your life, and every new avenue seems to flicker like a part-remembered film reel. Brummy, in particular, lapped up the cinematic connections.

Wandering Central Park – that famous, manicured take on wilderness surrounded by prime apartment blocks – the talk was of the scene in *Die Hard 3*, where Bruce Willis races across the landscape in a yellow cab. Further south, we found ourselves outside the *Men in Black* headquarters – or more accurately, the subway vent that masquerades as said headquarters. And then there was the apartment block from the sitcom *Friends*: a pigeon crapped on me from a ledge as I stood outside it – definitely one of my more esoteric claims to fame.

Not every sight in New York instantly triggers a memory from the world of film, though – some sights bring to mind the ebb and flow of history. And, most powerful, in New York, it's what you don't see that speaks the loudest.

New York's glorious skyline is missing something. In many ways, the city that existed before September 11, 2001 is still there, but its self-assured confidence and air of invincibility died with the old skyline. It is no longer the hard-nosed centre of the world. Now, adversity has brought out its human side. Because the emotions everyone feels when they look upon its altered skyline have permanently changed.

Nowhere is this more obvious than at Ground Zero, where the foundations of the fallen towers are now marked by two waterfalls hewn from black marble, which flow into the ground until they are lost from view. Around the waterfalls, the names of the victims are engraved, and people slow as they pass, gazing into the water being lost to the abyss, scanning the names of those lost, and above all, remembering.

The new World Trade Centre now towers above the solemn memorials to its predecessors. It stands defiant, but it can't quite erase the gap in the skyline; it is impossible to look at it without catching the hint of what was there before. And perhaps that's the point. For all the office space and amenities it offers, this is a building whose primary purpose is remembrance. It's a 1776-foot tall poppy that screams 'never forget.'

But for all these reflections on the past, New York is a city that bustles in the present. And in the United States of 2017, when it comes to the present, there is one subject of conversation which seems to animate people more than any other: a certain Mr Donald Trump. Everyone has an opinion on him. The college lads at the pizzeria we frequented in Hoboken hated him, but a few blocks away in The Heights, the Latin American guy who served me my burger and fries pointed out to me, 'These terrorist attacks in Europe are making Trump look like such a clever guy for shutting the borders. The whole world is looking at us real jealous right now.'

Nowhere were the opinions more impassioned than opposite the tasteless, gold-plated exercise in egotism that is Trump Tower on Fifth Avenue, where a permanent protest was in evidence. Hand-made placards were adorned with slogans such as 'Racist coward, get out of NYC,' or 'condemn KKK terrorists,' but my favourite demonstration was far less ambitious. An industrious New Yorker in his late fifties had scrawled 'An NYC salute to Trump' on a piece of corrugated cardboard and stood facing the building, flipping the bird continuously on the off-chance Donald happened to be looking out.

After seeing that guy delivering his message to the most powerful man in the world, the further tourist sights of New York couldn't really compete. Times Square lacked the humour and irreverence, while the view from the top of the Rockefeller Center – though immensely impressive, looking out as it does over the rooftops of one of the most dramatic landscapes on earth – seemed impersonal in comparison. To me, nothing could sum up the character, confidence, and resilience of this city better than that guy, silently holding up his middle finger at Mr Trump for hours on end.

IT TOOK A week, but eventually the big, old Dodge was ready to be picked up from the used car lot. Kermit had already been cleared through customs a few days earlier, so with the Dodge keys in our hands it was time to get rolling on Pub2Pub's next leg, which just so happened to be one of the most dreamed-of road trips in the world – from sea to shining sea, clean across the USA. That's New York to San Francisco, via some of the finest sights the massive nation has to offer.

With the Manhattan skyline forever etched in our rear-view mirrors, we fired up our Anglo-American convoy's 10.7 litres of V8 muscle, and hit the road to the most powerful city of them all – Washington DC.

14. THE CAPITAL

18th August 2017
40°07'N, 74°54'W. The I-95, New Jersey.

THE SKY BILLOWED upwards. Clouds were stacked in bulbous tiers, haemorrhaging rain. The downpours came and went suddenly as we drove, and in between them the sun punched through and flooded our world with contrast. The spray was thick as we travelled westbound on the I-95, the vehicles around us throwing it up in huge sheets. In the tiny TVR, Nick and I felt vulnerable, sitting lower than the wheels on the huge lorries thundering along the concrete, and likely invisible in the mirrors of the standard-issue pick-up trucks, the drivers of which would often have a camera phone pointing at us. We followed the Dodge through the melee, the conditions doing little to dampen our relief at being back on the road.

It had been over three weeks since I'd dropped the TVR off at

Southampton, and having smashed out so many miles across Europe in the weeks before, the sudden loss of momentum had felt strange. As nice as spending time in Cuba and New York was, it felt like a diversion; like we were simply killing time. We'd committed to the long drive and to be back in the groove, making progress once again, was great.

We passed through three states in as many hours, leaving New Jersey when we crossed a bridge into Delaware, before entering Maryland as we neared our day's objective – Washington DC.

Because we needed to keep costs down, we decided to camp during our visit to Washington. While finding a decent campsite in reasonable proximity to the capital might sound rather unlikely, we were in luck, thanks to the US National Park Service.

Wherever you find a national park in the US, you'll also find a campground, and they all offer pretty much the same deal. For about $24 a night, we'd get a pitch just large enough for our group, a firepit, a picnic table, and access to a toilet block. From the forests of Washington to the deserts of Arizona, the pattern didn't change, and these campsites were a lifesaver for us, providing cheap accommodation in what had the potential to be one of the most expensive countries of the whole trip.

The campsite in Washington went by the name of Greenbelt Park, an area of woodland just out of town that was somewhat overrun by biting insects when we were there. Fortunately, however, there were various ways in which we could escape this menace. In the evenings, the smoke from a campfire, combined with the distracting properties of a case of beer would suffice, and in the daytime, we headed into town. From our tents, a half-hour walk followed by a 20-minute train ride took us away from the bug-filled forest, and into the centre of Washington DC.

The train travelled underground for its final run into the capital, so on the morning after our arrival, blinking and disorientated, we emerged from the station into a world about as far removed from our campsite as could be imagined. The heart of a superpower.

Everything about Washington DC has been scrupulously planned. From its name, which honours the first president of the United States, to its location, which was chosen by that president and bridges the age-old gap between America's North and South, nothing is an accident here. The focal point of the city is the National Mall and it's here that the city's planned purpose is clear: to provide a symbolic and functional centre for the United States. It's the pride of a nation, laid out for the whole world to see.

The Mall's defining space is an open sweep of grass that measures almost two miles from the Lincoln Memorial to Capitol Hill. Forming the focal point for this grand public space is the Washington Monument, a spectacular obelisk which commemorates the former president by soaring almost 170 metres into the sky. From the monument's base, the Mall sweeps away to Capitol Hill in a carefully planned expanse of grass, and lining the edges are museums housing the high points of American achievements in every field imaginable, from aerospace to art.

This space is the public face of America at its most manicured and perfect. Its purpose is to convey a message of pride, dignity and benevolent power to the 26 million people who visit it every year.

As the heat built across the Mall's unshaded lawns, we sought out cooler temperatures in the Smithsonian National Air and Space Museum, our entry delayed slightly when the guard's scanners clocked a penknife in Nick's bag, which they weren't happy about, for some reason.

"It's only my camping cutlery," Nick protested. "It's a fork and the bluntest, least pointy knife in North America. What do they think I'm going to do, viciously attack someone with a camping fork?"

But the museum guards were adamant and so the cutlery was abandoned in a bin in front of the building. Once we were in, it became clear that nowhere is the United States' contribution to the world more visible than in this unrivalled collection of history.

As you enter through the museum's high glass doors, if you have more than a passing interest in aviation, you'll glance around in awe. Overhead hangs Chick Yeager's Bell X-1 – a bright orange winged rocket which was the first aircraft to break the sound barrier. It hangs near The Spirit of St Louis; the aircraft in which Charles Lindbergh completed the first-ever solo nonstop transatlantic flight. A glance upwards also reveals the Bell X-15, which still holds the absolute speed limit for a manned aircraft at Mach 6.72. Then you bring your eyes level once again and notice the Apollo 11 re-entry capsule, and a Mercury orbital spacecraft.

All this in one room! We were in the presence of the crown jewels of America's aerospace industry, and nobody could fail to be impressed by the achievements of the priceless machines on display. They come together as a demonstration of just what the United States can achieve when it throws its considerable resources at a challenge, and as someone whose fascination with aviation was a defining feature of my childhood, my visit felt like an almost religious pilgrimage. My childhood heroes weren't footballers or film stars – they were pilots. People like Chuck Yeager, Guy Gibson and Douglas Bader, who'd blazed a trail through the sky and left the impressionable young Ben dreaming of doing the same. Wandering the museum with Brummy and Claire, I felt the person I used to be drifting back and my enthusiasm may have overflowed a little as I talked about the exhibits.

"That's a P-51 Mustang. D model. It's got a 27-litre V12 up front with a twin-stage supercharger, licensed from Rolls-Royce and built by Packard. 1600hp at 2400rpm. And that one, that's a Spitfire Mk.7. You can tell by the extended wingtips, which reduce the wing loading so it performs better at high altitude."

"It all makes sense! I can definitely see why you're single now," was Brummy's considered reply.

"Yeah, fair point," I replied, wandering off in the direction of an interesting-looking late model Messerschmitt Bf-109.

OUR TIME ON the Washington Mall and in the Air and Space Museum had been a fine advert for the United States. It drove home the dignified power that the nation wishes to be synonymous with, and demonstrated the technical prowess it is capable of. Roaming the Mall further, the heartfelt memorials to those who died in war promoted a deep-seated love of freedom and a capability for sacrifice. The Lincoln Memorial celebrated the man who'd finally abolished slavery in the 1860s, and it was on its steps that Martin Luther King gave his 'I Have a Dream' speech. Everywhere you look, you can't escape the well-manicured air of stately pride and history.

That is, unless you swing left at the Washington Monument and head over to the surprisingly small house in the distance: The White House.

Once again, we couldn't escape the fact that we were visiting the America of Donald Trump, and the bemused lack of respect for the guy certainly coloured our impressions as we wandered up to the railings and took in the famous view of the White House. And as a building that symbolises the office of the President of the United States of America more than any other, we couldn't just view it objectively. No, to us it was a trigger which made us think about the sheer ridiculousness of the person who holds that office today. He wasn't there on the day of our visit; he was spending time at one of his golf clubs instead. And as we dwelled on this latest twist in the history of this great nation, the carefully crafted, timeless dignity of Washington was hit by a broadside of reality. Because for all the great deeds and achievements of the past, today this historical legacy is in the hands of a leader who appears incapable of living up to the gravity of the office.

Get well soon, America.

15. ECLIPSED

20th August 2017
39°00'N, 76°51'W. Greenbelt Park, Washington DC.

THE MORNING AFTER taking in the sights of Washington DC we got our tents packed away and left early. We had a long drive ahead: almost 700 miles, and we needed to complete it by lunchtime the following day. 1:40pm the following day, to be exact. Why? Because the countdown was on for one of the natural world's most spectacular sights – a total eclipse of the sun.

I'd learned of this piece of celestial history while researching the trip years previously, and had gone to great lengths to ensure we'd be in the area of totality at the right moment. We hadn't already covered 6500 miles across ten different countries and crossed several oceans just to miss an eclipse because we slept in. We needed to get the hammer down and hightail it across to Tennessee pronto. The only problem was that on the route we'd chosen, it turned out that getting the hammer down was pretty much impossible.

SKYLINE DRIVE, FOLLOWED by the Blue Ridge Parkway, is one of the classic American road trips, flowing for over 500 miles through the mountains of Virginia and North Carolina. The smooth tarmac, forested splendour, and elevation changes would make it a driver's dream, were it not for the speed limits. We're talking a frustratingly sloth-like 35mph on Skyline Drive, which rises to a heady 45mph once you reach the Blue Ridge Parkway. Just what our straining-at-the-leash V8 motors were designed for. As Bob Denver sang of country roads on the TVR's stereo, we dropped the roof and crawled up into the mountains.

It was exactly what you'd expect from a US forest near the Eastern Seaboard: a densely packed sweep of oak and chestnut trees, vividly green in their high-summer state. The road rose and fell but the terrain was never so precipitous that it felt daunting, while the woodland crowded in tight around us, only occasionally opening up to reveal a view of the flatter world towards the horizon.

But the driving felt wrong. This was the sort of road that would have a 60mph speed limit back home, and being so restrained, sitting in third gear at 35 with the engine barely above idle, felt unnatural. And with the slowness comes a vulnerability to boredom and distractions, to such a degree that makes you wonder whether this immensely twisty road is actually any safer as a result.

On the plus side, you see a lot more wildlife at 35mph, and in our first hour on Skyline Drive we spotted both deer and, more unexpectedly, a brown bear, lazing contentedly by the road. As it looked our way, I suddenly wished we'd left the roof on, as having slowed to a walking pace, we were basically a rolling, V8-powered buffet.

Fortunately, the bear was too overcome with lassitude to act on it.

It was mid afternoon by the time we'd completed Skyline Drive, and the prospect of covering another 500 miles of speed-restricted twistyness in time to catch the eclipse seemed remote. So we swung out of the mountains onto the faster-paced I-81 and motored on towards our goal.

THE AMERICAN SOUTH had contracted a serious case of eclipse fever. As we followed the interstate towards the area of totality, traffic was only going in one direction – clearly Central Tennessee was the place to be. There was a carnival atmosphere on the road and everyone was getting involved. The petrol stations were cashing in by selling eclipse glasses, T-shirts, and a selection of other tacky souvenirs. Farmers had taken the initiative by turning fields into giant viewing areas, offering parking at five dollars a car. And on the local radio stations, the talk was of little else. The country music station helpfully advised us not to stop on the freeways during the eclipse and to keep pets indoors so they don't look directly at the sun (despite the fact they manage pretty well on non-eclipse days), and gushed forth with excitement that stemmed from the fact that for 118 seconds that afternoon, the eyes of the world would be on rural Tennessee.

A change of frequency saw us listening to one of the Christian radio stations, where a charismatic preacher with a surfeit of enthusiasm proclaimed the eclipse to be the beginning of the coming rapture, when the god-fearing believers will ascend to Heaven, leaving the broken earth to those less worthy. His proclamation, delivered in a rising and falling cadence, which drew you in almost hypnotically, was sufficiently compelling that I almost headed for the nearest church. Almost, but not quite.

With an hour to go, we pulled off the I-40 near Cedar Point and parked in The Rose Garden Restaurant. A small church sat opposite and about a dozen people stood outside, holding up banners suggesting we save ourselves by joining them before it's too late. However, the restaurant's ice creams looked like a more compelling life choice, and so, having ordered a round of them, we fought back against the baking heat as the light slowly began to dim.

It was a gradual process, the interplay between the two celestial bodies played out in a slow, teasing manner which steadily built anticipation in the Tennessee car park. But the sheer grandeur of the moment was clear. 240,000 miles above us, a ball of rock over 2000 miles across was hurtling through space at 40 miles per minute, its shadow being projected onto the earth's surface as it passed between us and the sun. And as we waited, that shadow was racing towards us across Nebraska and Illinois at about three times the speed of sound. It was truly theatre on the grandest scale imaginable, the simplest interplay between the two discs creating a drama which was at once both humbling and empowering.

The darkness was coming quicker now. Streetlights began to glow in defiance and the sky was cleared of birds. The trees and bushes, which bordered the nearby railway line, began to buzz with insect life and some unwelcome mosquitoes appeared in the air, which had become noticeably cooler.

And then, the almost infinite masses were aligned and the full darkness of totality hit as the moon's shadow, only 70 miles wide, swept across us. The sun's corona shimmered around the moon's black disc and as our eyes adjusted to the sudden darkness, stars began to appear in the blackness around it. And all around the horizon, through a full 360 degrees, a distant light glowed, reaching us from the world beyond the shadow. It was a surreal sight, like the late dusk light was spanning the entire horizon, creeping in beneath the umbrella of darkness under which we found ourselves. The chirping of crickets reached fever pitch, but was drowned out by the very American whooping and yelling which filled the chill air.

"Yee ha! Wow, that's amazing," shouted the portly chap from Florida who stood nearby, while other loud cries of "Oh my God, that's incredible" and "Would you just look at that" filled the air, reminding me just how much more dignified life is when you apply a bit of British reserve.

As we were almost exactly on the line of totality, we were under the shadow for nearly two minutes, but eventually the low dusk light that surrounded us on the horizon began to build in the west as the eclipse raced off towards the Atlantic Coast. And then, in a fleeting moment which stirred us all, the most memorable moment of this incredible experience occurred. As the sunlight rushed through the moon's rugged topography, for a few brief seconds the ring of light shimmering from behind the moon was jewelled with a diamond, as the first rays reached us.

It was beautiful.

Then, as the moon continued its orbit, light flooded into our world once again, the sun reacquired its blinding power and things no longer seemed to be standing still. It was the end of another one of those moments that I'd been planning for so long – I'd discovered that an eclipse was due during my planning 18 months earlier, and had overcome all the obstacles to get the expedition to the right place at the right time. Like that surreal pint of beer on Svalbard, or the moment when I rolled out of the Port of New Jersey to be greeted by the Manhattan skyline, it was an experience that I knew would come to define the trip, and make those dark days battling depression to make this dream happen worth it.

As we left the restaurant, I noticed the crowd assembled by the church were no longer willing us to join them. I guess the lack of a rapture was a bit of a blow.

16. HUMAN EXTREMES

22nd August 2017
37°40'N, 87°54'W. Morganstown, Kentucky.

IT WAS A searingly hot day in Morganstown, Kentucky. We pulled over at a gas station to grab some cold drinks. A dusty, L-shaped forecourt stretched around a small shop. Three well-used pickup trucks were there already, seemingly near the end of their lives. We parked next to them. A few old petrol pumps stood amid the dust, rusting slightly like relics from the past. We strolled past them, to the shop entrance.

Either side of the door there was a cheap, tacky-looking plaque, upon which the Ten Commandments were embossed. A faded and slightly frayed Confederate Flag hung above the door. In the shop window, there was a sticker celebrating a political allegiance which we probably could've guessed at, reading: 'Trump Digs Coal.'

We entered the shop. It was dark inside and the TV in the corner was screening Fox News. The shelves were stacked with all the usual things you'd expect to find in any Deep South service station – crisps, rope, oil, and

Continued on page 81

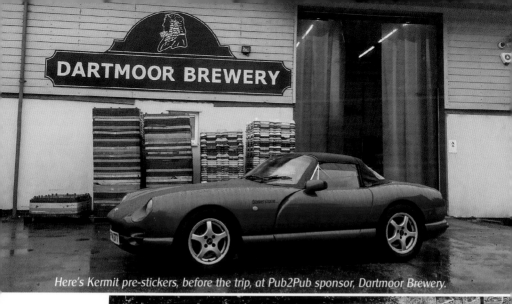

Here's Kermit pre-stickers, before the trip, at Pub2Pub sponsor, Dartmoor Brewery.

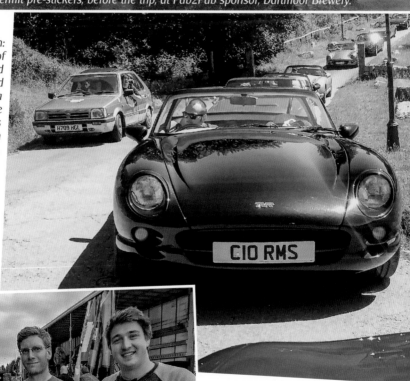

The launch: a convoy of TVRs and the doomed Nissan Micra leave the Two Bridges Hotel on Dartmoor.

Before the Glym9 party in The Netherlands. L-R Ed Johns, me, and Nick Hughff.

Crossing the Arctic Circle while heading up through Norway, en-route to the northernmost bar.

Rolling across Arctic Norway beneath the midnight sun.

The second Nissan Micra, bought a few hours after we left Dartmoor, makes it to Norway.

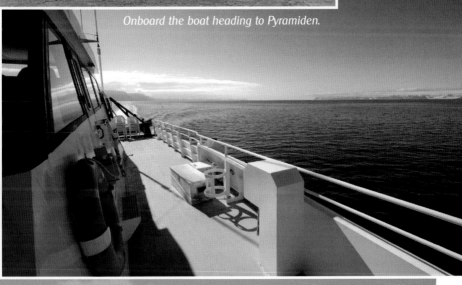

Onboard the boat heading to Pyramiden.

Looking across Pyramiden to the glacier opposite.

Anti-clockwise starting top left: Sea cliffs near Pyramiden; The northernmost bar, located in Pyramiden's old hotel; Looking back towards Norway's Lofoten Islands as we take a ferry to the mainland; Making friends with the locals in southern Norway; Ed and me by the Pyramiden town sign.

Kermit resting in the pit lane of the Reims-Gueux Grand Prix Circuit.

Exploring Germany's mining past among the open cast mining behemoths of Ferropolis, near Berlin.

The Koenigsegg factory showroom.

Me, Philippe Delaporte, and the two overlanding steeds in Chantilly, France.

Roaming the streets of Havana, Cuba.

Me at the wheel of a Studebaker on Havana's waterfront.

The Dodge Charger and Kermit on the campsite near Washington DC.

The solar eclipse, seen from Tennessee.

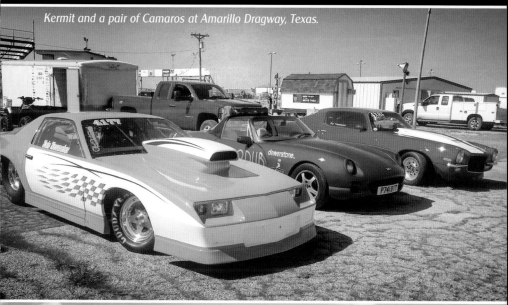

Kermit and a pair of Camaros at Amarillo Dragway, Texas.

A local lights up the tyres at Amarillo Dragway.

The Cadillac Ranch, Texas.

The symbol of Utah: Delicate Arch, Arches National Park.

Leaving the tarmac to explore the Valley of the Gods, in Utah, USA.

Posing for a photo by Monument Valley.

Camping in the Valley of the Gods.

The team stops for a photo outside Area 51, Nevada. L-R Claire Scully, Brummy, me, Nick Hughff, Pat Hillier, Alex Williamson.

Exploring a dried up lake bed just outside Area 51 in Nevada, USA.

Death Valley. Braving the 50°C heat to drive to the lowest point in North America, 86m below sea level.

The Little A'le'inn, in Rachel, Nevada.

Smoke from a multitude of forest fires drifts across the 3000ft sheer face of El Capitan, Yosemite, California.

Making coffee at sunrise in Joshua Tree National Park, California.

Dawn in Joshua Tree National Park, California.

Kermit and Johan's 'Herbie' replica in the Arizona desert.

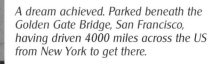

A dream achieved. Parked beneath the Golden Gate Bridge, San Francisco, having driven 4000 miles across the US from New York to get there.

Kim walking into the sunset by the Pacific Ocean, at San Blas, Nayarit, Mexico.

BIENVENIDO A TEQUILA

Dropping into the town of Tequila, near Guadalajara, Mexico.

The Pyramid of the Inscriptions, Palenque, Mexico.

a few magazines about guns. Ammunition of various calibres was available, with a handy guide on the wall helping you choose the right rounds for your weapon. Opposite, another flag took pride of place, this one displaying the stars and stripes and the slogan 'POW/MIA – not forgotten.' I selected a ubiquitous can of Coca Cola from the fridge and wandered over to the till, behind which the shopkeeper stood staring at the TV, while talking to Nick in a thick, Deep South drawl.

He was a mousy kind of guy, who appeared to be in his mid sixties. Outdated glasses and a scruffy grey beard defined his thin-set face, while long greying hair streamed down his back from beneath his 'Vietnam Veteran' baseball cap. He wore a dirty black T-shirt which covered what I assumed to be his life's work – a more-than-ample beer belly, against which his wiry frame offered a sharp contrast. Next to the belly his belt was adorned with a holster containing the largest handgun I'd ever seen. I listened to what he was saying as I joined the queue to buy the cold drink.

"These people, they come in here to use the rest rooms, but don't buy anything," he said. "I'm gonna put a sign up to stop them, but I bet they won't read it. It's always foreigners. Korean, Mexican, those people. Always the same."

He spoke in the manner of someone who had long seen himself as the victim, and I guess he was. An embattled relic of the past, powerlessly existing in a world which had moved on from the rose-tinted world he cherished. The simple, black-and-white America of his youth had gone; morphed into something else which had left him behind.

He continued to address Nick, who was treading very carefully.

"I see you took a photo of my flag out there? That's not gonna get put anywhere, is it?"

"Oh, no. Don't worry, these photos aren't going anywhere," replied Nick.

"Better be the case," he replied. "People take photos of my Confederate Flag. Post them around. Then the niggers come and try to get rid of it. Yeah, those niggers come to mess with my flag, but I got my gun, I'll shoot them."

Silence hung in the air. Nick didn't really have anything to say to that.

"I don't care. Means less niggers," he added, as if it somehow justified his stance.

Silence returned to our conversation and through it, we noticed the noise from the TV which hung on the wall. Fox News was showing a report on the Charlottesville Riots. Our new friend voiced his opinion:

"These people, they're makin' the US look real bad, real stupid. Trump though, he'll sort them out. He's doing good."

We retreated outside to enjoy our cold drinks in a somewhat more open-minded environment. However, a few minutes later, our gun-toting friend reappeared.

"Y'all want some pot-bellied pigs to take back to England? About this big?" he asked, gesturing that the pigs he had in mind were about two feet long. "I breed them over there. Horses, too. Anyone messes with them, I'll shoot them."

We politely declined the offer and retreated back to the cars. He watched our progress, but then noticed the TVR and offered me some advice as we parted.

"You need to put mothballs in the gas tank of that mother. Turns 87 gas into 100 octane. Race fuel. Used to do it back in the '70s, when I raced. Makes the petrol burn hotter than acetylene. Melts the carb if you're not careful. But you'd win the race."

As I was obviously on the verge of coming around to the idea of wringing out another few horsepower by packing my sports car's fuel tank full of pest control devices, he offered me one last tip as we left: "Gotta cut them up, put quarters of mothballs in your tank. That'll have your little car running real sweet."

As we pulled off the forecourt and continued across the rolling Kentucky farmland, Nick and I shook our heads disbelievingly, and asked each other, "did that really happen?"

BECKY GREETED US warmly as she opened the door.

"Hello, it's great to meet you! You've made good time. Don't just stand there, come in. I'll get you a coffee. But first, don't leave your cars there on the road. Bring them around the back, they'll be safe there. I've cleared the drive for you."

Becky was already providing a free roof over the head of a friend who was recovering from a cycle-touring accident, and had offered us somewhere to stay too. All six of us. All strangers. It was a way of life to her, and she often provided accommodation for any tired cycle-tourers who were passing by – we just happened to have been passing by in a slightly less environmentally friendly fashion.

Becky was an occupational therapist while her husband – who was away in Connecticut – had started life as a plumber, and through hard work had made good of it. In the garage was a Corvette C5 with a 340hp motor, made at the factory just down the road in Bowling Green, and parked on the road was their equally fast Chrysler wagon. They were living the American Dream, and for two nights, we were part of it. And we were so glad we were, as their southern hospitality did everything to dispel the negativity of the earlier encounter at the gas station. We were welcomed into these strangers' house with all the coffee, biscuits and orange juice we wanted, and were looked after like long-lost friends during our time there.

And it wasn't only us who were well looked after: the Dodge had been having some teething troubles, with rattles coming from the front brakes, a permanently-lit engine warning light, and a rather irritating habit of cutting out in traffic. It went into a garage for a once over, and came out with the brakes sorted, but not the running issues.

On our last evening in Kentucky, Becky insisted on taking us to a pizzeria. At the end of a wonderful evening, when we tried to pay our share, she would have none of it.

"It's on the house," we were told with a knowing wink. We were her guests, and we had no right to pay.

The following morning, Becky left at 5:30am to go to the gym. We let ourselves out, and drove on towards the state line.

So that was Kentucky. A place where the extremes of human nature live side by side.

17. GUNS AND THE QUARTER MILE

24th August 2017
36°12'N, 89°15'W. I-69, Kentucky.

THE ROAD TOWARDS Memphis went on forever. It's rare to find yourself on a dual carriageway that provides much in the way of interest, but this was something else. A plumb-straight line of boredom, with broken woodland, warehouses and the occasional truck dealership on either side, it provided nothing to interest the mind and so the mind was prone to wander. Sometimes it would wander to the car. I knew my TVR very well now, having covered nearly 8000 miles together in the previous seven weeks, and such over-familiarity can be a negative, for it breeds paranoia: is the engine running differently? Is that a new vibration? Could it be that the low grade fuel is slowly destroying the valves? Just how much octane booster should I be adding to the 91 octane gas anyway?

While you must always pay attention to the car on a trip like this, over attentiveness can wear you down, leaving you unable to relax. So, if your mind is going to wander, it's better that it wanders in more positive directions. And the views through the gaps in the trees and past the retail parks were enough to fuel my imagination, for they brought me back to a half-remembered world of my childhood.

A pickup truck rolls down a dirt track next to a creek. A police car sits motionless on a country road. An old Camaro rusts beneath a tree. These are the views you see beyond the dull world of the interstate; views which hint at the illicit adventures that seemed impossibly glamorous to me as a child. Out there, beyond the confines of this tarmac, moonshine was being run. Bright orange Dodge Chargers were oversteering crudely around dusty corners, doors welded shut for stiffness, the Confederate Flag on the roof. Swampy creeks are being jumped by bandits in Trans Ams. Every sighting of a policeman seemed like a scene from a part-remembered TV series from my childhood, for this is the America I grew up with. The world of Hazzard County, and Smokey and the Bandit. A world I was seeing for the first time from behind the wheel of my very own V8, while on the adventure of a lifetime.

WE STOPPED IN Memphis for the night and gradually came to the realisation that none of us were actually that bothered about dropping into Gracelands. And let's face it, if you're not up for Gracelands, what are you even doing in Memphis as a tourist anyway? We took heed and carried on west. Another long, empty day on the road, rolling along the I-40 in our curious convoy, past pickups and semi-trailers, dining on the junk food which fuels the American road trip.

In Oklahoma City, we fancied a break from the long straight road. So what options are there for some downtime in OKC? Well, there's a museum dedicated to the terrorist attack that took place there in 1995, the National Cowboy Museum, and an Indian Cultural Centre. Unfortunately, none of these options really floated our boat, but my pre-trip research had turned up another option. It turns out that Oklahoma City is the perfect place to let off some steam, second amendment-style. Yes, grabbing a gun and blazing away at a target in some surreal concrete basement is a popular pastime in much of America, and as curious British tourists, it would have been rude for us not to give it a go.

The signs at H&H Sporting Goods proudly proclaim that they have the largest selection of firearms in the state. And when I found myself lost in the secondhand machine gun aisle shortly after wandering in through the front door, I didn't feel in a position to argue. The place was National Rifle Association heaven. For a few hundred dollars, you can walk out of the store with a handgun. Need something bigger? No worries, $300 will pocket you – figuratively – a 12-gauge shotgun. But what if you want to go all-in? In that case, you'll be wanting to splash out $9000 on the catchily-titled FN M249S. This semi-automatic bad boy is accurate out to 1000m, has a shortened barrel and collapsible butt for close-quarters combat, and can take a linked ammo belt should the standard 30-round magazine prove a little effeminate for you.

To this roaming Brit, it was a whole other world, and one which doesn't seem to make much sense. I'm sure the taxidermied heads of slain animals that lined the shop walls would have agreed if they could talk.

While the guns seemed outrageously cheap for such potent pieces of kit, it wasn't actually that cheap to make use of one of the 42 available shooting ranges, working out at $23 to empty a handgun into a paper target. With so long to go on the trip, I was still pretty paranoid about finances and so I elected to sit out the shooting. However, everyone else laid down the cash and got their gun off. The more I lingered in the shop, the more I found the relative normalisation of gun culture in this part of the world to be utterly surreal. Couples would wander in to spend some quality time together by romantically emptying a few magazines. Professionals popped in and out quickly, relaxing after a hard day in the office by blowing the crap out of a target. And as it turned out, Nick and Pat were both closet shooters back home in England and took their gunshooting rivalry pretty seriously once they were both packing heat.

Still rather bemused by the fact that theoretically, I could pick up a secondhand 0.44 Magnum – the most powerful handgun in the world, according to Clint Eastwood – for under a thousand dollars, I didn't really fit in. I didn't feel lucky, punk.

A BUFFETING BREEZE blew across the flat Texan countryside, taking the edge off the heat. Weeds were pushing up through cracks in the neglected concrete along which we rolled, while the edge of the hardstanding had slowly decayed, giving way to the seemingly endless grasslands. But the surface on which we were driving wasn't important. There was only one piece of real estate that mattered here and it was a quarter of a mile long. Every few minutes, the sound of tortured rubber and howling engines would drift over from it for a few seconds at a time, before silence returned.

Drag racing is big in Texas, and given we had a couple of powerful V8s at our disposal, and a heady banter had developed as to which was faster, we dropped into a Sunday morning 'test and tune' session at Amarillo Dragway to settle the score. On our arrival, we realised just how seriously they take their drag racing in the Texan Panhandle. Huge motorhomes were lined up with car trailers hitched up behind them and race cars shaded by their awnings. And race cars, they all were. Pure-bred, big-budget builds made with a single objective in mind – obliterating the quarter mile.

In comparison, we'd brought a couple of blunt spoons to a gun fight.

I parked Kermit between a pair of ancient Chevy Camaros. Both had rear rubber which would make an Indycar blush, matched to skinny front tyres whose sole purpose seemed to be keeping the front splitter off the ground when the car wasn't running at full throttle. Both had interiors in which comfort had been switched out for a roll cage and a racing seat, and a dashboard festooned with more dials than a '50s fighter jet. The fancier of the Camaros – which its shrinking violet of an owner had named 'psycho' – was also fitted with a brake parachute and a framework extending from the back of the car, to prevent it from doing a backflip if the driver was over-enthusiastic with his launch.

But if this all sounds a bit high-tech, don't be fooled. Beneath the bonnets of these behemoths lurked the usual low-tech, huge capacity V8 and supercharger combination which, even today, gives the American muscle car its derisive, pre-technology character.

Beyond these two extrovert Chevys, the cars just got crazier. There was a mid-'60s Corvette which sported a massive bonnet scoop to feed its near 1000hp motor. This beast's side exit exhausts seemed purpose-designed to pump smoke into its opponent's faces, and its styling was dominated by a polished aluminium rear wing which would put a Cessna to shame. There were also pickup trucks with load beds full of nitrous which could run the quarter mile in under ten seconds, and even a few top-fuel dragsters, the noise of which seemed to split the air in half when they launched.

Suddenly Kermit's four-litre, 240hp V8 felt rather inadequate.

And in many ways it was, because I was there to race the expedition's Dodge Charger, which sported a 5.7-litre Hemi V8, putting out 350hp. Adding to my woes, my TVR's clutch had recently begun to slip at high revs, meaning I wouldn't be able to take full advantage of what power I did have.

It promised to be an interesting race.

There is a refreshing casualness to hitting the quarter mile on a Texan Sunday morning, with only two questions being asked. Are you wearing trousers? And if you're running a pickup, is the load bay free from dead animal carcasses, or whatever else the average Texan usually keeps there? Yes on both counts? Great, then you're free to race.

You don't even need to wear a helmet if you don't anticipate breaking the 14-second barrier.

Having passed the stringent tests and paid a few dollars, the next step was a technical inspection to ensure beyond all doubt that the cars were safe to race. I rolled up outside the workshop where the inspections are carried out.

"Why's the steering wheel on that side?" asked a rather portly chap, leaning on an oil drum by the entrance.

"We brought it over from England," I replied.

"Okay, go have some fun and race it then," he said. And that was that. Show time. I've given taxis a more thorough inspection before letting them drive me home.

A pillar of lights marked the start point, and beyond it, the rubber-streaked tarmac stretched away into the distance. Before lining up, we were invited to warm our tyres with a spot of wheelspin on a purposely-wetted area of tarmac. Never one to look a burnout-gift horse in the mouth, I obliged, lighting up the rear tyres of my classic British sports car for Queen and Country, before proceeding to the start line. To my left, Brummy pulled up in the big orange Dodge.

This was it. The pride of Britain was at stake.

I held the car at about 3000rpm, ready to drop what was left of my clutch and race away. No way was I losing to that big yank tank. The starting lights came on. Three reds, one after the other, followed by a green. Any second now, they'd go out and we'd be off. I noticed movement in the corner of my eye.

It was Brummy. He was on the gas already. He'd gone on green, while I was waiting for the lights to go out, as they do in Formula 1 races.

Convinced he'd jumped the start, I dropped the clutch anyway. The rears started to spin slightly, but the traction on the rubber-coated surface was next level stuff and I got a great start. Hitting 5000rpm, the clutch began to slip, and I grabbed second, punching through the gear change in a fraction of a second. Brummy may have been well ahead, he may have had traction control and an automatic gearbox meaning all he had to do was stamp on the gas, and he may have had 110 horsepower more, but I wasn't out of this yet. The speed and revs rose. A few seconds after the start, I was going up to third – never an easy change to make quickly with the Chimaera's meaty T5 gearbox. But I nailed it. And I was gaining.

But the finish line was coming very quickly now and the Dodge was digging deep. At lower speeds, the fact that the TVR weighed something like 800kg less than its opponent meant it could accelerate faster, but as aerodynamics came into play, the advantage lessened. And as we crossed the line, throttles wide open, engines roaring and scenery rushing by, that big old Dodge was 0.2 seconds ahead.

"Loser," was Brummy's first word, as we parked.

"I'm sure you jumped the start," I replied. "In Formula 1, the race starts when the lights go off."

"Well, this isn't Formula 1, is it? And you're still a loser."

"But this was about who has the faster car and the TVR was definitely faster over the quarter mile than the Dodge. If I didn't screw up the start, it would've destroyed you."

"Which bit of loser don't you understand?" Brummy asked. He had a point.

If you take the driver's relative incompetence out of the equation, the TVR covered the quarter mile in 13.7 seconds, while the Dodge did it in 14.2. And against normal cars, that's a pair of pretty respectable times, even if they don't measure up in the nitro-assisted, doughnut-tyred world of Texan grassroots Sunday morning drag racing.

My overbearing mechanical sympathy and desire to preserve the clutch meant I turned down the offer of a rematch. If I kept running the quarter mile only for the car to have some issue near the expedition's finish line in deepest Patagonia, I'd regret it hugely. So instead I accepted the continuing mockery of Team Dodge. It was a small price to pay for giving Kermit every chance of surviving the trials and tribulations of the 15 countries that still lay ahead.

THE OCTANE CONTENT of the rest of our time in Texas was considerably lower. We camped in the Palo Duro Canyon State Park, a thousand-foot deep gouge in the Texan countryside, which is very popular with the RV and camping chair crowd. In hindsight, overnighting here probably wasn't the best choice for the Pub2Pub Expedition, as alcohol wasn't allowed into the park and rangers prowled the campsite on the lookout for anyone breaking the law. Of course, we applied British ingenuity to this traumatic rule and the back of the Dodge became the focal point for our rather British moonshine equivalent – decanting cans of Coors into mugs and water bottles, to which the rangers wouldn't give a second glance.

It was almost like being 16 again.

We also took in a few of Amarillo's tourist attractions in between our bouts of drag racing and illegal drinking. Firstly, the modestly named 'Big Texan Steak Ranch,' which stands proudly on Route 66 and does exactly what it says on the tin – serving up big Texan steaks. The largest, weighing in at 72oz (that's 1.8 kilos) is free if you can finish it, along with the heady pile of potatoes and salad it's served with. We opted for more modest options, washed down with beer, while taking in the kitschy, theme park-like interior of the place, which reached its apogee with a taxidermied bison head, whose beady eyes stared down at us as we ate.

The other attraction in the Amarillo area is pure Americana – The Cadillac Ranch. In a cornfield just out of town, a line of ten Cadillacs jut from the earth, their bonnets deep underground while their bewinged rear fenders point skyward, as if they have somehow crashed to earth in formation. The art installation is heavily graffitied in gaudy colours and seems to exist as a challenge to the conformity of traditional American life. Effectively, it stands as a question mark in the face of stifling convention.

It also stands next to the main road out of Amarillo, heading west, and so it marked the end of our time in the beef capital of Texas, as we pushed on towards the state of New Mexico.

18. HOW THE WEST BEGAN

28th August 2017
37°49′N, 106°18′W. New Mexico.

THE WIND-RUFFLED GRASSLANDS undulated away to the infinity of the horizon. Other than the occasional fence or small barn, nothing broke their uniformity. The sky above mirrored their vastness and was dominated by late afternoon thunderstorms that mushroomed upwards into the jetstream, unleashing far-off rumbles of thunder as they broke, deluging the plains.

New Mexico. It was basically like driving across Outer Mongolia. But with less camels. And actual tarmac roads, which always help when you're on a road trip.

It was the sheer size of the landscape that became seared deepest into our memories. We were looking at about 500 miles of driving to cross the state, and for most of those miles, the smooth tarmac and those endless rolling plains were our only company. So we drove on for hour after hour.

The sun arced overhead and descended, setting in front of us and leaving us in a dark night of far-off strobing lightning and the occasional pool of man-made light, which always had an air of futility, glowing weakly against the blackness of the landscape. One of those sad pools of light turned out to be an RV park where we spent the night, too tired to do much more than pitch our tents and crawl into them. But the next morning saw us reanimated, for we were hitting the road to one of America's great landscapes. A place of legend, a backdrop for countless films, and in many ways, the symbol of the American West.

Yes, we were heading for some of road tripping's most hallowed ground: Monument Valley.

It's one of the Americas' most iconic views. The road runs arrow straight for miles, fading to nothing in the distance, where the towers rise. Proud bluff towers of the deepest red sandstone, which are an unofficial symbol of a nation that sees itself reflected in their characteristics: timeless, tough, impregnable, and slightly above and apart from the world they rise from. And thanks to Hollywood, we'd seen them so many times before. For this is the landscape in which Forrest Gump stopped running, it's where Tom Cruise went rock climbing in the second *Mission Impossible* film, and it provided a backdrop for *Once Upon a Time in the West, Easy Rider*, and one of the *Back to the Future* films. Hell, they even managed to shoehorn the landscape into *2001 – A Space Odyssey*.

But why is Hollywood so fascinated by this sweep of charismatic desert? When you cut away all the silver screen conditioning and see the real Monument Valley for the first time, you'll know. And you'll pull over and marvel at it, while simultaneously shaking your head at the tourists who insist on braving the traffic to take selfies on their iPhones while sitting in the middle of the famous road.

But I can understand the desire to record the moment, for it is truly one of the great landscapes. Its impact may be diluted slightly by the familiarity born from decades of overexposure and the towers, having been built up in your mind over the years, may not be quite as colossal as you'd imagined, but still, what a spectacle. I joined the iPhone-wielding masses in grabbing a picture of myself enjoying the view. But instead of a selfie on the tarmac, I had my picture taken gazing across the landscape, while leaning against the little sports car which I'd just driven there, all the way from England. And then I jumped back into the driver's seat and roared on across the vista, my Blackpool steed sending its exhaust note echoing among the terracotta towers.

Yeah, that was one of those moments when life felt pretty damn sweet.

The sweetness didn't abate that evening as we drove out into the desert to make camp in the modestly named Valley of the Gods. A dirt track took us there, contouring us past the crumbling towers of rock which rose from the dun scrubland. All around us, in the middle distance, rose escarpments which merged together to seal us into the valley. There are worse valleys to be sealed into though. Given its name, the hardy people who'd discovered this place clearly thought the world of it, and as we pulled over and set about preparing to wild camp, we could see why.

The lowering sun seemed to flood the landscape with fire, drawing deep reds and oranges from the cliffs and earth. Several sheer pillars of rock stood near our camping spot, blazing in the sunset, while the few low clouds which hung over the valley reflected the explosion of colour as the sun fell. But far away among the escarpments which marked the edge of our world, dust storms were raging. We watched them twist and turn at the whim of the winds, being blown around the craggy summits and sometimes exploding with crimson when the sun hit them, the low rays saturating our world with drama.

And then it was over. A deep blue dominated above, fading slowly to black. Stars appeared, the first few puncturing the twilight almost apologetically, before hundreds more packed out every inch of the heavens. And then it was time for bed, because all the beer was gone, and the conversation had crossed into the realm of the ridiculous hours ago.

WE WERE BACK on the road early the following morning, heading north through Utah. Following a deeply important spot of cultural research in Moab's Brewery (the Pilsner proving the people's choice, with the Dead Horse Amber IPA coming highly commended too), we carried on to the Arches National Park. A place that leaves you asking: "just why? Why does this little corner of Utah have so many natural sandstone arches crammed into it?" I can't think of more than a handful of natural arches in the whole of the UK, yet this national park, only one third of the size of Dartmoor, has over two thousand of them. Seriously, how?

A geologist would describe how millennia of wind and rain have sculpted the sandstone blocks into the extraordinary shapes which are the norm in this trippy landscape. They'd talk of upthrusts and fault lines; of erosion and the hardness of Entrada and Najavo sandstone. But to me, the geographical reasoning can add little to the spectacular landscape and the rich-hued sculptures by which it's defined. The evocative names of the features hint at their uniqueness: the Petrified Dunes, the Tower of Babel, Tower Arch, and the Parade of Elephants. And then there's the feature whose name sums it up to perfection. The feature that is so unlikely its slender outline has graced postage stamps and today appears on Utah's license plates. This feature is in many ways a symbol of Utah, and is called Delicate Arch.

Standing 18 metres tall, the arch teeters improbably on the edge of a sandstone bowl and looks for all the world like the striding legs of a frozen cowboy, rendered in a rich gold that turns orange with the sunset. We hiked for 40 minutes to reach the arch, and then there it was, a gateway of perfection. Nature doesn't often overachieve in the artistic stakes to this heady degree, but when it does, it's always worth the effort to see the results.

Another day, another amazing memory. Our road trip across the US was certainly putting on quite a show.

AMID THE SOARING granite walls of Zion National Park, Alex was waiting for us. A friend-of-a-friend, we'd first met Alex in New York, where he was making a killing on the markets. An ex-pat, he worked long and hard hours for the big stacks of cash he was making and when it came to his downtime, he'd go all in. He was the living embodiment of work hard, play hard. And that's why, when he decided to fly over and join our trip for a few days, he splashed out by renting a bright yellow, 425 horsepower Chevrolet Camaro SS convertible. With logic like that, he'd fit right in.

However, on the morning we left Zion, we weren't a full convoy anyway. Pat had to leave at the crack of dawn to drop his girlfriend off at the airport, so Kermit and I spent the day rolling with the bumblebee Chevy. And as hire cars are well known to be the quickest vehicles on the road, it was no surprise when we found that Alex certainly wouldn't be hanging around in his supercharged holiday rental.

What was a surprise, however, was the fact that the TVR could keep up, not losing out too much in the performance stakes, even in a straight line. Despite being way down on power, my fibreglass Blackpool steed weighed over half a tonne less than the Chevy, which gave it a fighting chance of keeping up as we climbed through the hilly countryside of western Utah.

I got the impression that Alex took the presence of a tatty, 20-year-old TVR on his bumper as a challenge and began to work the Camaro harder and harder as we swung through the flowing turns that were leading us towards Nevada. It was refreshingly fun after so long following the Dodge down the interstate at a fairly sedate pace. We pushed on for mile after mile until we rounded a corner to see a member of the state police coming the other way, in his don't-mess-with-me, nudge-barred patrol car.

The flashing blue lights in the grille and on the roof lit up as he passed us, and in the rear view mirror I saw him throw the heavy police car into a layby, spinning it around aggressively to come after us in pursuit. Romantic thoughts of running for the state line didn't last very long and having slowed down, we were soon caught and pulled over. Our new American friend parked the patrol car behind our vehicles and came towards us, the blue lights still strobing across the scene. Once again, we were living in a movie.

He fitted the popular image of a rural American police officer, sporting a starchy brown shirt, deep brimmed hat, aviator sunglasses, and a liberal sprinkling of official bling – the sheriff's badge, shoulder insignia, and the gun and handcuffs that glinted from the waist belt. I opened the door and began to climb out as he approached the car.

"Don't get out of the car," he said, but it was already too late.

"Terribly sorry," I replied, trying to sound as English as possible.

"Do you have any idea how fast you were going back there?"

"Oh, I guess we might have been going a little over the limit, maybe 60, 65 miles per hour. I'm incredibly sorry," I said, giving it the full Hugh Grant.

"73," he replied. "Where's this car from, anyway? Is it even allowed in America with the steering wheel on that side?"

"Of course, don't worry about that. We've brought it over from England on a temporary import. That's why it's still on UK plates. We picked it up from the Port of New Jersey a few weeks ago."

"Let's see the papers and your driving licence please."

"Sure, here you go," I replied, pulling the documents out from the folder I keep them in.

"So where are you going anyway?" he asked, as he thumbed through the wedge of paperwork he'd just been presented with.

"Chile," I replied. Then, feeling at risk of appearing flippant, I figured I should probably explain further.

"We're driving from the northernmost bar on the planet, to the southernmost. We were in Europe last month, heading up to the top of Norway where the northernmost bar is. We're crossing the US this month, and then it's down into Mexico and Central America, before we push on to the southernmost bar in Patagonia."

"How are you finding the US so far? Any issues with having the steering wheel on the wrong side of the car?"

"No, it's fine. We're really enjoying the US," I replied. "The people are great. And Utah is the highlight so far. We'd never been here before, so didn't know what to expect, but we've been blown away by the landscapes."

Our new friend then proceeded to chat with Alex in the Camaro for a few minutes, before addressing us all: "If I process this now, it's an automatic $200 fine for each of you. And if you'd been doing another three miles per hour, you would have been in for an automatic court appearance on Monday. Now, you're heading to Nevada today, aren't you?"

"Yes, in a few hours."

"Right, as this is your first transgression I'm going to let you off with a warning. But you all take it easy and drive sensibly while you're on our roads. We won't tolerate any more speeding from you here."

Thanks no doubt to our bumbling Englishness, we'd got away with it, and our progress on the last few miles that Utah had to offer was best described as 'stately.' But still, at least we finally got to admire the scenery, as the mountains of Utah gave way to the flat deserts of Nevada.

19. ALIENS

2nd September 2017
37°39′N, 115°45′W. Rachel, Nevada.

IMAGINE FOR A moment, an empty landscape. The sort of place you'd expect to find a sign that reads 'the middle of nowhere.' Except, obviously, there's no sign, because the landscape is so empty.

I'm inclined to bet that you're currently imagining Nevada. There, you'll find flat, empty plains that go on for miles. Small hills, which are not only too small to add any drama to the landscape, but also prevent the landscape from acquiring the subtle drama that stems from monotonous flatness. And the ground itself? Well, it's not a grassland, for grasslands support farming and imply that something actually happens there, in the form of precipitation. No, for the middle of nowhere, only a barren semi-desert will do. Small, hardy shrubs growing from the stony wasteland. To me anyway, that's the definition of disinterest – no irregularities or dramas to draw the eye. Just rolling wasteland for mile after mile.

Yes, that's Nevada.

And as you drive across it – more sedately now, having just came within three miles per hour of a court appearance – you realise why people's imaginations are fuelled by the desolation. You can see why artists retreat from the outside world to places like this, searching for expression. The landscape is a blank canvas for your mind to run amok on. No wonder that over the years Nevada has provided a haven for outcasts, cults, dreamers, and fans of alternative living, because there's an other-worldly feeling that here, anything goes. The edges of reality are blurred and the blank canvas that your mind is freed to fill becomes populated with outrageous ideas which, out here, could just be reality. Is it so farfetched to imagine dinosaurs just beyond the horizon? Is that actually a UFO sweeping silently overhead? And what's over the next hill? An abandoned nuclear test site, or maybe a top secret military base?

For us, it was the latter, because we were approaching that repository for so many conspiracy theories and flights of imagination – Area 51.

It's not really secret, though. What goes on there may be hushed down, but even nomadic tribesmen in the Kalahari probably know of its existence, so great has Area 51's legend grown. You can see it on maps, read about it in books and watch documentaries which speculate about what exactly goes on there. Hell, even the road past the base is called the Extraterrestrial Highway, and has signage indicating the speed limit is 'Warp Factor 7.'

I wish they'd had those speed limits in Utah.

We rolled along the highway to the dustbowl town of Rachel, where a grand total of 50 people live between the dust and the sun. Sounds small? It is, but it's also the largest settlement for miles around. Except for the enormous and highly secretive military base just over the hill to the west, obviously.

Rachel feels frozen partway between its optimistic founding and its seemingly inevitable deterioration into yet another desert ghost town. Space is clearly not an issue and the debris of human existence sprawls across the area. Slowly rusting, patinated cars and trucks are scattered all around, along with the odd bus and shipping container. Caravans in varying states of abandonment collect dust alongside the mobile homes in which most of the residents live. The petrol station closed years ago due to lack of business – the nearest gas is 50 miles away now. It's a strange, transient place, but there is at least one reason to visit.

The bar.

The Little A'le'inn is what could be described as an acquired taste. As the only bar on the Extraterrestrial Highway, it's a theme bar of the most unique decor – alien kitsch. A sign on the front of the building encourages you in with the message 'earthlings welcome,' and once inside, you'll find walls covered with grainy black and white photos of UFOs and alien autopsies. Alien heads dangle liberally among the clutter, while above the bar hangs a forest of countless dollar bills, signed by visitors from around the world and who knows, maybe other worlds too?

Given the strangeness of what we were attempting on our odyssey, it seemed like the perfect place to stop, pitch our tents and grab some food and a few beers.

Lingering in front of the inn as the sun disappeared behind Area 51, we had our first true desert sunset of the trip. The air's lack of humidity and slight dustiness resulted in a gradual pink tint rising up from the horizon, before the inky blue that had swept over our heads plunged down to smother the colour from our world. We gazed skyward taking it all in, the beer flowing freely as we wondered who else was out there.

I turned in reasonably early that night, but a few of the guys from Team Dodge stayed up rather later, filling me in the following morning over breakfast.

"So, did I miss much last night?" I asked.

"Well, funny story," replied Pat.

"Go on."

"So you remember that guy who was drinking at the bar last night? The guy who wasn't quite right? Well, we got chatting to him and he was giving it all that, claiming he used to be a chef at the White House, that he'd cooked for presidents and been abducted by aliens."

"Sounds legit," I replied.

"Yeah, well he ended up getting blind drunk, then suggested he take us to Area 51."

"While smoking a massive joint," Nick added.

"And you agreed?"

"Yep," Nick said. "We'd had a few beers, too. It seemed like a brilliant idea at the time."

"So, we all piled into his pickup and he took us out across the desert to the entry gate. He was absolutely hammered. And then he started doing doughnuts on the tarmac right in front of the guard tower, about 20 feet from the barrier," Pat said. "He reckoned it was fine though, and said they do it all the time for fun. Apparently, you can do whatever you want outside Area 51 and they won't touch you. However, put so much as a foot under the fence and they'll take you down."

"We were bricking it by this stage," Nick added. "And after the doughnuts, he's like, 'There's a shotgun in the back, let's do some shooting.' So he takes us off into the desert, and we started shooting old tin cans. His dog wandered off into the night, and I was so scared of shooting the dog by accident."

"He would've killed us if that happened. Definitely killed us," Pat added.

"He nearly killed you, Pat, when you turned around and pointed the loaded shotgun at his pickup," Nick pointed out mischievously.

"It was fine."

"You had your finger on the trigger and everything," Nick said.

"So I leave you alone for one evening and you end up almost shooting up a stoned local's dog and pickup truck just outside Area 51's front door?" I said.

"Oh yeah. You're jealous, aren't you?" said Pat.

"Maybe a little bit," I replied.

After our chat, as we were preparing to leave, Nick and Pat headed over to the drunken guy's house to say goodbye. Inside, on the wall, was a photo of him with George Bush, complete with a personalised message of thanks from the man himself.

So it turned out that part of the story was true. We never did get to the bottom of the alien rumours though, despite taking our three sporty steeds up to the security barrier which marks as close to Area 51 as you can get without becoming a target, before hitting the road south out of Rachel.

A FEW PAGES ago, I asked you to clear your mind and picture the emptiest place imaginable. A place so empty that anything could be just over the horizon. A place called Nevada. Well, Nevada obviously decided it needed an exception from this emptiness which proves the rule, and that exception was where we were heading next. A place whose juxtaposition of toweringly tasteless kitsch amid such a pure desert environment is almost comical.

A place called Las Vegas.

And Las Vegas is the last word in everything I don't look for in a place. It's brash, superficial, and strangely soulless, a tacky exercise in extravagance and showing off. While I can see the appeal if you're into that sort of thing, or you thrive on gambling, it's really not my kind of city.

But even I have to admit that, wandering the strip, surrounded by the towering casinos and bathed in neon light as the taxis and limos hustled by, it's an impressive place: a theme-park demonstration of where capitalism can lead if morals lapse sufficiently to allow it.

And occasionally, it surprises you with subtle beauty. Like when the choreographed fountains outside the Bellagio Casino begin to dance, or when the hand-painted roof of The Venetian tricks you into believing it is, in fact, the sky, as the gondolas ply the canals beneath them.

But for every hit, there's a miss. The replica of the Eiffel Tower, for instance? I mean, what on earth were they thinking when they came up with that idea? And then there's the giant slipper you can pose inside, the miniature replica of New York, and the fake volcano which erupts on the hour, every hour. Who thought any of this was a good idea?

But the people who came up with this stuff have got preposterously rich off the back of their flights of fancy, and who am I to judge them? I was the one saving money by eating peanut butter sandwiches rather than splashing out on fast food every day, while their casinos were making them millions every year. Maybe they were onto something, after all.

20. THE VALLEY OF DEATH

03rd September 2017
36°28'N, 116°51'W. Death Valley, California.

THEY'D NAMED IT 'Furnace Creek' for a reason. The mercury was reading 126°F in the shade when we arrived. That's 52.2°C. Which to put it another way, is within 4.5°C of the highest temperature ever verifiably recorded on Earth. Coincidently, that was also in Furnace Creek, way back in 1913.

We could see how the landscape we were in came to be called Death Valley. Just leaving the shade of the cars almost killed us. Amazingly though, the TVR was fine with the heat, its engine temperature remaining comfortably below boiling point. Yet again, it was showing itself to be the plucky underdog, determined to prove the doubters wrong.

If you happen to find yourself in Death Valley in midsummer, I have one piece of advice to offer you: if you value your sanity, don't camp. With completely still air and an overnight low of 38°C, it proved to be one of the most uncomfortable nights of my life, sweating through the small hours in a poorly ventilated tent. With the ground beneath the tent having been heated by the sun all day, it was like laying on a hot-plate and sleep was all but impossible. Seriously, don't camp. Just don't.

The following morning, before the temperature got too deeply into the forties, we headed south out of Furnace Creek to visit Badwater Basin, which sits in the shadow of Funeral Peak. If we'd gone north, we might well have ended up at Hell's Gate instead. Based upon the area's naming strategy, the early immigrant pioneers must have really hated the place. Given it got named Death Valley after 13 gold prospectors died while attempting to cross it in a wagon-train, they had pretty good grounds for this.

Badwater Basin is the lowest point in North America, sitting 282 feet below sea level. It's an uninspiring spot – a smudge of soggy salt in a barren landscape of dust and broken rock – and it possesses none of the elemental beauty of more celebrated salt flats. The thin crust of salt sits on a bed of mud, which often breaks through the salt, destroying the illusion of purity that salt flats often portray. It's as if Death Valley, in its quest to prove as unappealing as possible, has decided that even beauty is off-limits. People really have no place here.

Which, ironically, is a big part of the attraction.

YOSEMITE HAD TAKEN Death Valley's unwelcoming atmosphere as a challenge, and conspired to outdo it. If all of the United States is a movie, during our visit, Yosemite was very much of the disaster genre. Smoke from the forest fires that were raging across the national park blew across the road as we drove, a dense acrid fog that whirled around us, making visibility so bad it sometimes slowed our pace to a crawl. We passed through landscapes where only the bullet-hard granite had survived. Every tree was a torched stump; the undergrowth reduced to ash. Sometimes an elevated vantage point would give us a view across the park, dotted with flame fronts.

Forget Hell's Gate in Death Valley: we'd passed through the gates to Hell for real when we entered Yosemite National Park, and the blown ash crushed beneath our tyres. The most celebrated wilderness in the country had gone from a rolling land of lake, forest, and rock, to a rather surreal disaster area, and a stickered-up TVR on a grand tour felt like just about the most disrespectful vehicle it would be possible to drive through such a place.

We arrived at a petrol station. There was no immediate danger and the smoke was thinner, but the power supply had been taken out by the fires, so they were unable to pump any gas. People held their T-shirts over their faces to try to escape the smoke. We waited for half an hour before power was restored, enabling us to fill up and continue.

Yosemite Valley itself was free from fires, but the smoke was still drifting through. The sun was reduced to an opaque disc, floating in the pink-tinged eddies of grey ash. The 900-metre-high sheer face of El Capitan rose defiant into the pollution. A few months earlier, the climbing world had been wowed when it had received its first-ever free-solo ascent, but today it cast a sombre shadow across the valley, for its famous outline was the symbol of a world struggling to survive.

Our original plan had been to camp at the base of El Capitan, on the climber's campground there. However, the smoke would have been an unwelcome companion, so we headed out of the park, dropping into yet another National Park Service campground on the road to San Francisco. As this was our first camp site with bear boxes – to keep food safe from the forest-dwelling neighbours – it was surprisingly easy to convince Nick that due to his tent positioning he'd probably see a black bear before he saw morning, and as a result, he was deeply paranoid as he crawled into his tent on the edge of our camp that night.

SAN FRANCISCO WAS one of the expedition's really big waypoints. It wasn't just another destination; it marked the end of our traverse of the United States. And let's face it, what more alluring American road trip could there be, than a trip clean across the country? It's a classic journey, glamorised by everyone, from Steinbeck to those flat-out guys who gave the world the Cannonball Run, and when we rolled into San Francisco, we'd have completed it. Before reaching the city by The Bay, our time in the Americas had been all about heading west; afterwards south became the only way, until the land ran out.

There's only one way to do arriving in San Francisco justice, and that's by crossing the Golden Gate Bridge. Which is exactly what we did, 80 years and two months after the mile-long span had first opened.

You approach the bridge through the rolling coastal hills, which slip down between the Bay and the Pacific, slowly narrowing around you until the road emerges from a tunnel and the bridge is suddenly there, dead ahead. Traffic was heavy as we drove, and drizzle fell. I kept close to the back of the Dodge, making sure our convoy wasn't split up. And then we rolled onto the bridge itself. Finally, I was crossing this great symbol of America in my little English sports car. I changed lanes and pulled alongside the big Dodge. With windows down, smiles and thumbs up were exchanged, and cries of "we've done it" flew through the air between the cars. We revved our big engines and a cacophony of exhaust noise from our motors echoed around the bridge. From the celebrations, you'd think we'd already reached the southernmost bar, but such an observation was to sell ourselves short. It was another milestone achieved. Another moment of progress which showed the naysayers that they were wrong to doubt the reliability of the TVR.

Famous bridges are almost always a slight anticlimax to drive across, because if there's one place you can't fully appreciate a bridge's scale and delicacy from, it's in a car on the roadway, trying not to crash. So while our crossing of the bridge brought us close to those famous towers and their iconic 'international orange' paintwork, the experience also left us keen to drop down to sea level for the full-fat view. And so it was that we parked our steeds at Fort Point for the inevitable photos. And a fine backdrop it provided, the bridge showing itself to be an improbably slender structure that wears its uniqueness with pride.

As I gazed up at that bridge so far from home, I looked back on what the TVR had already achieved. Even without the ocean crossing, it had covered over 10,000 miles in the previous two months. Its clutch was slipping a little, and the rear shock absorbers had given up the ghost, but other than that, it was fine. From the chill air of the High Arctic to the heat of Death Valley, from the aggression of Amarillo Dragway to the monotony of Arkansas, it had taken everything in its stride. Certainly, the toughest challenges still lay ahead, but the omens were good.

At that moment, there was no other car I'd rather be standing next to than Kermit, my 20-year-old Blackpool beast. It was proving the perfect companion for the trip.

21. THE BAY TO OBISPO

07th September 2017
37°47'N, 122°24'W. San Francisco, California.

SAN FRANCISCO IS a city that drips with laid-back American cool. There's the unmistakable patchwork grid of streets which tumble down to the water. Then there's that icon of the American can-do spirit that spans the Golden Gate Bay to the north, its shadow reaching for the dark outline of Alcatraz. And it's all infused by the fresh breeze blowing in off the Pacific, the air's salty tang proving refreshing after so many weeks inland. This is a city that is all things to all men.

For us, it was a brief lunch stop down on Fisherman's Wharf.

Another city passed through, another city marked up for a more thorough visit sometime in the future. Because based on the quality of the crab meat, San Francisco was definitely worthy of a longer stay. It was just a shame we didn't really have the time to do it justice.

Heading south through California, our original plan was to drive the famous Highway One – The Big Sur. This coastal road clings to the Santa Lucia mountains as they rise from the ocean and is a famously good drive, which I'd completed in a Ford Mustang years before. With the roof down and the blue of the ocean matching that of the sky, I'd sped along the hallowed tarmac over soaring bridges and past secluded beaches that were packed with elephant seals. This time, however, nature wasn't feeling so kind. A year before our arrival, torrential rains had triggered a landslide so vast, it still hadn't been cleared. The Big Sur was severed, so instead of heading for the coast we rolled down to Laguna Seca and stayed on yet another National Park Service campsite, though this one had a more unusual view than most – the sweeping tarmac of Turn 11, Laguna Seca Raceway.

We awoke close to the cloudbase, breathing in air moist with drizzle. In the paddock below us, all the paraphernalia of a motorcycle track day had assembled. The ubiquitous RVs, this time towing trailers full of race bikes, packed out the tarmac. We mingled amongst them, clutching overpriced cups of coffee as people gazed skyward, trying to second-guess the weather. If you're a bike kind of person, the paddock must have been heaven, which meant it certainly was for Claire. And given that I'd bored her with my knowledge of all things aviation back at the Smithsonian in Washington DC, she exacted her revenge here.

"Look over there! That's a Yamaha RZ500. Crazy things, it's got a two-stroke and is pretty much my dream bike. Ooooh, and a Panagale! Some of the stuff here is unreal."

I had no idea what she was talking about. My knowledge of track-day bikes is equalled only by my knowledge of Bulgarian politics, which is to say, it's non-existant. When Claire got all excited about a Triumph 675S, I could almost feel a coma coming on.

As the cloud lifted, a few rays of sunlight started to show themselves, coaxing a few of the more adventurous riders out onto the track. We headed over to the famous 'corkscrew' corner to watch. As riders cross the blind crest just before the corner, the view that opens out in front of them is one of the most unique in motor racing. The tarmac plummets, dropping suddenly by about 18 metres as it twists aggressively left then right. It's one of the most celebrated corners in motorsport and a challenge all the riders aspired to master, as they refined their lines through the twists.

It was such a shame I couldn't join them in the TVR, but once again we had to push on, this time to the laid back town of San Luis Obispo (SLO), where we were due at a party at the local German car garage that evening.

So why was a party being thrown there in our honour? Well, as often happens on these trips, an improbable cycle of Chinese whispers was responsible. It started when we met a guy called Joep in the Glym9 garage in the Netherlands, on the first full day of the trip. Joep knew a guy called Tucker in California. Tucker worked at the German car garage in SLO and suggested we drop by for beers and some spannering if we fancied it. And given what we were attempting, beers and spannering promised to make our onward journey somewhat less daunting, not least because the Dodge's power loss issues were gradually getting worse. It had now started to cut out momentarily while cruising down the Interstate and if the problem wasn't to stop us for good somewhere in Latin America, it would need sorting before we left the US.

We rolled up to German Auto of San Luis Obispo and immediately felt we were among fellow enthusiasts. Outside the garage, a pair of 1980s BMWs baked in the sun, the cracked lacquer and faded paintwork showing them to be honest daily drivers. In the parking lot, a pair of old Porsches awaited attention – a 911 from the 1980s and a similarly aged 924. Clearly these were people of taste.

We wandered inside the workshop and found Tucker next to a track-ready R32 Volkswagen Golf.

"So you made it then?" he said, handing each of us a beer.

"Yeah, it's been a bit of a drive, but we got here in the end."

It was Friday, and the people who worked at the garage were slowly laying down tools for the weekend. Various people dropped by to say hello as we chatted. Anthony, a pilot, showed up in his highly modified Porsche 911 convertible, and we spoke for a while about our shared appreciation of older, air-cooled 911s. And then a guy called Dylan showed up – the first dyed-in-the-wool TVR enthusiast we'd met in the States. Others appreciated the Chimaera, taking photos and asking questions, but Dylan was the first person we'd met for whom a TVR was genuinely their dream car – not an ideal situation, given it was about 40 years since TVRs had last been sold in the States.

Dylan's interest in the TVR was so absolute that I crossed one of my lines – I offered him a drive. So, with Pat in the passenger seat, he headed off out of the garage for his first taste of right-hand drive, manual gearbox action.

He did surprisingly well actually, returning it in one piece and with no bits missing. You can't really ask for any more than that.

While we were having beers, we brought the faltering Dodge into the workshop so they could look into the running issues. However, the diagnostic equipment couldn't get to the root of the issue, so we planned to take it to another garage the following day. That suited us in the TVR just fine, as waiting for us at the garage was a full set of replacement shocks, freshly sent over from the UK, another job for the following day – replacing Kermit's saggy rear dampers. But first things first. The party at the garage lasted another few hours before we headed to the beach to camp.

Saturday dawned bright and the Dodge was delivered to a garage which understood such vehicles, before we headed back to German Auto with the TVR to get stuck into changing the shocks. Soon, the car was up in the air on axle stands leant to us by the garage, the rear wheels were off, and Pat and I each set about one side of the car.

Getting the original shocks and dampers off wasn't easy though, as after 20 years in situ they seemed rather keen to stay put. The bolts were rusty, and getting the tools onto them and loading them in a way that meant, they, hopefully, wouldn't shear, was quite an undertaking. Add in the fact we were working in direct sunlight with the temperature in the mid thirties and it wasn't a whole lot of fun. Soon we were smeared in grime, with sweat running off us as we wrestled to get the bolts undone.

And then I glanced up and saw an air-cooled 993-model Porsche 911 pull up. It was Anthony, who I'd met at the party the night before.

"Fancy taking it for a drive?" he said.

He didn't need to ask twice.

YEARS BEFORE, IN the far-off days of the African Porsche Expedition, I was very much a 'Porsche' person, and my realistic dream car – the car I wanted to park in the garage next to my 944 – was a 993. The last of the air-cooled Porsches' has quite a ring to it, and the model is a bit of a legend as the ultimate, most sorted, and most developed of all the classic, rear-engined Porsches. I never did get one – my road tripping addiction has an annoying habit of hoovering up all my money – but I always wondered what I'd missed out on. In fact, when I bought Kermit, I'd nearly gone for a Porsche 911 instead, but the curiosity as to what I might be missing out on by sticking with the German marque was too much, so I went with the Blackpool Brit.

Behind the wheel of the silver Porsche, memories of the Stuttgart DNA came flooding back. Everything felt precise; engineered. In comparison, a TVR feels 'built.' And there's a difference – a microwave is engineered; a sideboard is built. One is a precision tool, designed as precisely as possible, while the sensation of precision and functionality is less overt in the other. And the Porsche's engineering made it a pleasure to drive – the gruff, torquey flat-six revving rabidly, the gear change precise, the steering balanced. As I got to know the Porsche, I came to see it as something with a depth of engineering that I respected greatly, but it didn't have the almost human charisma and failings which give a TVR its character. A Porsche is a fantastic tool, but a TVR is your best mate.

I'd always wondered, but now I knew I'd made the right decision in opting for the TVR. Which, by the time I'd finished my jaunt around coastal California in the soft top Porsche, had new rear springs and dampers fitted. I found Pat in a nearby café, dripping in sweat and looking rather exhausted. He'd done well. And I'd been a bit cheeky swanning off in a Porsche when I should have been pulling my weight.

Sorry Pat.

BACK AT THE campsite that evening, someone who looked like an exile from a '70s rock band was staggering from pitch to pitch, looking rather agitated. He approached us.

"You've gotta run guys, save yourselves. There's a storm coming, it's gonna destroy all of this. Get outta here while you still can. Get to Arizona, away from the sea."

"So what are you still doing here?" Brummy asked.

"Warning people. Someone's gotta warn everyone. Don't you understand, guys? There's a storm coming. Save your women and children." His voice tailed off as he disappeared into the night.

We were a bit too preoccupied to take him seriously. Beers had been drunk and a large lump of kelp, which Nick had brought back from the beach, had, for some reason, been jammed up the Dodge's exhaust pipe and had then snapped off inside. I never did figure out why anyone thought sticking seaweed up their own exhaust was a good idea, but beer can make even the daftest ideas seem like flashes of genius – Pub2Pub's origins on a barstool in an English pub stood testimony to this. Anyway, given that the Dodge was due back in the garage the following day, and as it was Nick and Pat who'd put it there, it was them who got the job of retrieving it, as we sat around drinking beer and directing sarcastic comments in their general direction.

Then the '70s reject returned.

"Hey, y'all wanna hear some ghost stories?"

"What sort of ghost stories?"

"Y'know. Ghost stories," he replied, as if the extra emphasis would make everything clear. "Scary ones. I'm gonna be telling some over by my car in half an hour. It's the blue Mustang over there. Y'all should come over and join."

"Sure, maybe," we replied, as Pat lay on the ground, prodding around inside the Dodge's exhaust with a tent pole, trying to lever out the kelp while shouting "come on, ya bastard" at it.

"Pat, you're pushing it further in. It'll be in the cylinder head soon at this rate," said Brummy.

"No, I've nearly got it. Come on. Ah, dammit. Nearly had it."

"Maybe if we gaffer-taped a tent peg to the pole, we could hook it and drag it out that way?" suggested Nick.

"Come on, it's so close."

Yeah, it was one of those evenings.

THE NEWS FROM the garage wasn't great.

While the exhaust was now 100 per cent free of seaweed, the Dodge's computers weren't 100 per cent free of issues. The cutting out was down to a break in communication between the gearbox and engine control units, and our hope that it was down to a loose connection in the wiring loom came to nought. It needed a new gearbox control unit. And as this was a Dodge Hemi-specific part, it wasn't exactly the sort of thing you could just pick up in a parts store. In fact, after a chat with the local Dodge dealership, it turned out that the nearest one was in Salt Lake City, over 1000 miles away. Oh, and it was going to cost $900 and take two days to arrive.

So that was that. Team Dodge were facing a forced stay in San Luis Obispo. We left the ailing car in the garage and headed to the Frog and Peach Pub with Dylan to pass some time.

But that day was to be my last in SLO, as we had a new team member flying in to Los Angeles to join the trip. Kim's flight was due to land at 3pm the following day and with the Dodge out of action, Kermit was to be the airport taxi. The following morning, as the storm we'd been warned about so vigorously rolled in as a mist of light drizzle, I fired up Kermit and set off alone for the City of Angels.

22. CALIFORNIA DREAMING

12th September 2017
35°09'N, 120°40'W. Pismo Beach, California.

THE MIST SWIRLED on the gentle winds as I drove. Sometimes, it would thicken to rain, on other occasions it thinned to nothing. California's famous Highway One was in no mood to live up to its endless summer, sun-drenched reputation. But soon Highway One was behind me, and with an explosion of sunlight, Highway 101 showed that on that particular Monday morning it could be everything its more glamorous neighbour wasn't. To my right, the millpond Pacific stretched beyond the horizon, shimmering alluringly in the sun with the occasional oil rig nudging up to silhouette itself against the sky. The talus tumbled down to my left, while the road rolled on past deserted golden beaches and well-to-do towns, where every lawn had not a blade of grass out of place, and every drive harboured a spotless SUV.

I was on a high. I was doing what I felt most at home doing – roaring across some far-flung landscape in a car which, by all rights, shouldn't have been there. As fun as the life with Team Dodge could be, it was a rather full-on atmosphere in which to spend weeks on end, and one in which it was impossible to relax. And in my state, with depression still lingering in the shadows, relaxation and alone time were sometimes essential. It was a long trip, and right from the start, when the very act of battling to make it happen had left me feeling destroyed, I'd been having to continuously manage my mental health. I felt I was doing okay, but there was a long road ahead, and reaching the end of the trip feeling closer to recovery than when I'd started was something I'd made a goal of mine.

Soon, I wasn't alone among the talus and beaches anymore. One of California's biggest hitters was all around me, a twisted jumble of concrete freeways and hard-driving motors, with a ballooning wall of smog as a backdrop. The idyllic coast had slammed into the City of Angels. I swung off the 101 at the Hollywood Bowl, and with the roof down, joined the catwalk of capitalism on Sunset Boulevard.

And as I rolled along trading exhaust noise with the white Lamborghini Gallardo that had appeared alongside Kermit, all I could think was 'to hell with depression.' Damn, life felt good.

I was ahead of schedule, so I drifted around Beverley Hills for a while, wondering what glamorous lives hid behind the tall walls, and what far-fetched stories had played out beneath the towering palms. But Kermit didn't fit into the landscape. It was too dirty, too honest. It lacked the clinical perfection of its millionaire surroundings. It was the real deal in a fake world. I drove on down the steep hillsides, picked up the Santa Monica Boulevard and headed for the sea. But not before stopping off at a shop to replenish my low-budget supply of lunchtime bread and peanut butter sandwiches – yet another aspect of the life I was living which contrasted rather starkly with Beverley Hills.

KIM'S FLIGHT WAS delayed by over two hours so there was no urgency about my slow drift down to Los Angeles International Airport. As the urban jungle drifted by, I mulled over what I was getting myself into. I'd last seen Kim four years earlier, when she left for the airport in Kiev, to fly back to the UK. During the two weeks before, we'd driven there in a Corvette, and while Kim's holiday time had run out in the Ukraine, I went on to spend the ensuing four months driving the Corvette to Singapore.

But at times, it had been an awkward two weeks together in the 'Vette, as Kim had followed the pattern that seems to play out before every big road trip I make. Just as with the African Porsche Expedition years earlier, before we'd left, she'd gone for the other guy.

I really should break that pattern one of these trips.

I'd said goodbye to her on that chill April morning in Ukraine, and I hadn't seen her since. That's not to say she'd forgotten me though. She'd missed me and tried to be part of my life again on various occasions, but I'd kept my distance. It would've been inappropriate in the circumstances, and would probably have ended up in a Chernobyl-sized mess.

But as I was making my way across Europe in Pub2Pub's early stages, she'd got in touch again. Her relationship was on the rocks, she was on a career break, and she wanted to join the trip. Conveniently, we had one free seat in the cars and so Kim found herself on a flight to LAX, where a green TVR was parked.

I was waiting in arrivals for over an hour before she appeared, a tired-looking, little blonde slip of a thing, shouldering a well-used backpack that wasn't far off the same size as her.

"Hola. Long time no see. You made it then?" I said in greetings.

"You wouldn't believe the flight I've just had. I thought I was never gonna get here."

"Flying. That's where you went wrong. Driving is way more reliable."

"I hope so. We've got enough of it ahead," she replied, wearily.

We rolled west out of Los Angeles, the sun diffusing through the haze behind us as it set. And as we drove, we had a lot to catch up on. Four years, in fact. But Kim was exhausted, falling asleep before we reached the city limits. I woke her as we climbed up into one of my favourite landscapes − Joshua Tree National Park.

It had been dark for hours, but the air still retained a residual warmth that made roof-down driving a pleasure, and we were in the perfect place to enjoy it. Above us, the milky way swept clean across a sky that dripped with stars. The moon had just risen and the world around us was rendered in a subtle monochrome of silver and black. Our headlights picked out detail in the landscape as we drove. Joshua trees rose from the dry earth in their hundreds, their simple outlines fleetingly painted by our headlights before returning to their ghostly silver state. And then our headlights picked out a coyote, scavenging next to the road. It gave us a guilty stare, before trotting off into the night.

We pitched our tents beneath a group of towering granite boulders and turned in, falling asleep to the howls of coyotes echoing through the darkness, before rising early as the sunrise flooded the desert orange and gold. And speaking of orange, while I was at the airport I'd received a message saying that the garish orange Dodge had finally been fixed, $900 worth of gearbox computer bringing it back to full health. And evidently Team Dodge didn't like being left behind as they were back on the road before sunrise, showing up at the Jumbo Rocks Campground in time for lunch. It hadn't been all plain sailing though.

"You couldn't make it up. We picked it up from the garage and got a few miles down the road and then the check engine light came back on," explained Brummy, over a coffee. "We took it back and it was a stuck EGR valve. They fixed it for free in the end. It really pays to be English sometimes."

"So in its trip across the US, the Dodge has suffered problems with its brakes, its electrics and now its EGR valve? I thought the TVR was supposed to be the unreliable one?" I replied.

"Yeah, but the Dodge still beat the TVR in the drag race though," said Brummy.

"Yeah, keep telling yourself that," I replied.

JUST LIKE THE landscape, life in Joshua Tree has a beautiful simplicity to it. Lethargic days avoiding the heat. Evenings around the campfire drinking weak American beer from the can. Early morning starts to make coffee as the sun comes up. Trips down into town for supplies. It's a wonderful counterpoint to the long days in motion, covering miles. But therein lays a problem. Because as compelling as the simple, lethargic life is, we had a far-flung bar to drive to, and we weren't even halfway yet. So after a few days in the park, enjoying a life free from interstates and roaring V8s, we said goodbye to the Joshua trees and dropped down out of the wilderness, onto the road to Arizona.

23. PHOENIX NIGHTS

16th September 2017
33°55'N, 111°50'W. Phoenix, Arizona.

THERE WAS A party atmosphere in the TVR as we sped through the Phoenix night, with the roof down and the wind in our hair. It was one of those rare occasions when the big V8 was drowned out by the music coming from the stereo, which we'd turned up so loud the whole car seemed to vibrate in time. We were listening to cheesy '90s dance music and it seemed to suit the situation perfectly. Kim and I were sure we were having more fun than anyone else on the freeway as we rolled through the night to meet some locals at a wild west-themed steakhouse. Certainly, we were sure that the guys in the Dodge wouldn't have the music cranked up to 11, and we were pretty sure they didn't have the wind in their hair, either.

The unlit steakhouse car park was full of enormous pickup trucks and Kermit was lower than most of their bonnets – or hoods, depending on who you're talking to. We parked among them and then wandered in to meet up with Johan and his friends, who'd been following us online and had offered us a beer if we passed through Phoenix.

Johan was an interesting guy to chat to. Because let's face it, it's not every day you meet someone who, during the yo-yo craze of the 1990s, had been a sponsored yo-yoer, travelling the world performing tricks, setting records, winning competitions and starring in music videos. But Johan was that guy. Older and wiser now, he owned a yo-yo factory downtown, was restoring a Triumph TR6 with his son, and rolled around Arizona in a perfect replica of Herbie, the Volkswagen Beetle. Yes, it's safe to say that there's no-one else on the planet quite like Johan. We settled into an evening sitting outside in the crisp desert air, chatting over steaks and mountains of French fries, as a country and western band played and the mounted buffalo heads looked on.

The next day, we learned that Johan could fairly hustle his tuned-up Herbie on the twisting Arizona back roads as he took us in convoy to an abandoned mining town up in the hills. Suffice to say, the vibe there was somewhat different to the mining town we'd started the trip from just over two months earlier – for a start, there were no polar bear signs, and the North Pole wasn't just up the road.

We were in Arizona for a few days, as reliability wasn't the only tactic the Dodge was using to slow us down – there was also the slightly baffling matter of registering it. Since we'd bought it, it had been running on a series of temporary registrations. The first of these hailed from New Jersey but was time limited, and so Team Dodge had been forced to get another temporary registration in Nevada, complete with a laminated paper licence plate.

The reason for this is that every state has a different set of rules regarding registering a car. In some states, it's impossible to permanently register a car without an address within that state. Some require a US driving licence to register a car. Some, like California, require a full smog test and some pretty hefty taxes to be paid. Others are far more lax. So, when it comes to fully registering a car as a foreigner of no permanent abode travelling the country, it pays to choose your state carefully.

Brummy in particular, wasn't a big fan of the system: "How can you have 52 states, all with a different way to register a car? It makes no sense. Surely there's one way which works best and it should just be rolled out across the whole country? 52 different systems? I'm telling you, the United States isn't a first world country. It's like being back in the 1950s."

While the Dodge had crossed the States on temporary plates designed to allow an out-of-state buyer to get their new purchase home, it now made sense to register the car properly, as Arizona promised to be the easiest place to do this and Mexico was just over the horizon. Team Dodge set about trying to make this happen, but were ultimately defeated by our lack of an address, and the need for the car to pass an emissions test, which wasn't ideal as the car's engine warning light was back on for most of the time and this alone would cause the car to fail the test. So, they decided to see whether they could cross into Mexico on the temporary plates.

Mexico was looming large in our minds as we rolled down to Tucson, the last city before the border. The USA had been a pretty straightforward place to drive across, but in Mexico, the adventure promised to get a lot more real. The stories of corrupt police, carjackings, drug cartels and off-the-scale murder rates didn't make for comforting reading, and here we were in the most conspicuous convoy known to man, about to roll through the middle of it. I was taking my usual approach to such uncertainties by soaking up as much information as I could and planning to take a sensible approach to minimising the risks – such as not driving at night – as well as embracing my standard saying on these trips: *It'll be fine.*

However, in spite of the dangers that apparently lurked across the border, we had one more danger to survive before we'd be allowed to leave the US. A danger which none of us could have predicted.

WE SAT AROUND the picnic table, eating the fajitas Kim and I had cooked, while working our way through a crate of the weak lager that passes for beer in large swathes of America. Our world was the pool of light from a camping lantern and our head torches, the Saguaro Mountains having disappeared with the daylight. The tents were pitched, the cars were running well, and Mexico was near, meaning the adventure was about to begin in earnest. Life was good.

Clearly having gained a head start on us with the cans of beer, Brummy wandered back from the toilet, but stopped a few feet from the table, suddenly agitated.

"Guys, I shit you not, but isn't that a black widow?"

His head torch had picked up the distinctive outline of nature's most infamous spider, wandering its web just above Claire's knee.

"Shit, it is. It's a fucking black widow," confirmed Pat, retreating from the table, as we all did.

"There's another one here," Nick added.

"There are loads of them."

The night had brought them out from their nests, which they'd made in the metal tubes from which the table was constructed. We counted about a dozen of them, mostly roaming the dirty webs they'd spun directly under the table. They'd been going about their business about six inches above our knees as we ate, drank, and joked.

I can't imagine how close any of us must have come to accidentally hitting one, or even just startling one with our presence. If startled in its web, a black widow's standard response is to lower itself to the ground to escape. Except in this instance, they would have lowered themselves directly onto our legs.

We stood around the table, watching them in a mild state of shock as we slowly regained the courage to reclaim our beers.

"Holy crap, I can't believe we just cooked dinner in a black widow nest," said Kim.

"Yeah, how badass are we?" I replied.

Once the shock subsided, curiosity took over. Our campsite neighbours have quite a reputation and let's face it, it's not every day you come face-to-face with a black widow. We watched them as closely as we dared, which given we'd been drinking beer for a few hours, was probably closer than was sensible. And they took no notice of us as we did so. They knew they had us beaten – the picnic table was theirs.

"Guys, come and see this. There are loads more of them over here," Pat shouted from the other side of our pitch.

True enough, their scruffy webs – spanning bushes and fence posts – shimmered in the light of our head torches as we looked closer. And the spiders were there too, just beginning their night shift.

"Who chose this campsite? Who on earth thought it would be a good idea to camp in the black widow capital of the world?" asked Pat.

"I'm blaming Ben, as usual," said Brummy.

"Yeah, sorry about that," I replied.

We all slept with our shoes in our tents that night, and when we arose, the spiders were gone.

Seriously, just how much more dangerous could Mexico be?

WE HAD A few more things to do before crossing the border. Tourist things. First up was the catchily-named AMARG, at Davis-Monthan Air Force Base. If you've ever wondered what the US Air Force does with its planes once they're not needed anymore, well, they fly them down and park them in a big field in southern Arizona.

Oh, and yes, I'm serious.

What we're talking about here is basically the US military's desert aviation junkyard, where something like 4000 airplanes and helicopters rest, either in long-term storage or waiting to be stripped of their usable parts to keep other aircraft flying. Funnily enough, they wouldn't let us hoon around the site with our V8s so we joined an organised bus tour of the airbase, where the surplus aircraft are parked in long rows, preserved by the dry desert air. Almost everyone else on the bus tour seemed to be of retirement age and we felt pleasantly young as we boarded – something to be savoured these days.

The tour was narrated by a very enthusiastic Vietnam veteran, and for me, it offered another opportunity to bore people with aviation knowledge. Kim was the unlucky target this time.

"Those ones over there are F16 C-models. You can tell it's the C because of the antenna bulge at the base of the tailfin. The A model doesn't have that. And the B and the D models are two-seaters, of course."

Listening to me witter on, I think she regretted joining the trip even more then, than when she'd nearly got a black widow in her lap the night before.

FOR OUR LAST stop before the Mexican border, we figured we'd head underground for a spot of nuclear Armageddon at the Titan Missile Museum – the only preserved strategic nuclear missile silo in the world. Spread beneath the surface of the barren desert, the complex contains control rooms, living quarters, engineering facilities and hundreds of metres of passageways all with one sole objective: to ensure that if the order came, the site's single Titan II intercontinental ballistic missile would lift off, carrying its nine-megaton warhead to some unfortunate, far flung target. And unfortunate is a definite understatement. We're talking a fireball three miles across and enough heat being pumped out to kill anyone within a 20-mile radius who doesn't duck and cover. These things meant business.

Once, the silo we were exploring was one of 18 scattered around the Tucson desert waiting for a spot of mutually assured destruction, but now only the one remains, the rest having been destroyed when their 154-tonne, 31-metre high missiles reached obsolescence.

But Brummy didn't care about any of this, because on the right subject, he can be just as geeky as me.

"Some of *Star Trek – First Contact* was filmed here. The scene where Brent Spiner and Patrick Stuart, who play Data and Jean Luc Piccard, are standing by the rocket after they go back in time. Piccard gives it a bit of a stroke because it's the first human object ever to go to warp and it connects him to Starfleet's history. The ship was called the Phoenix, by the way."

It was probably a very valid comment, but it was little more than a load of white Klingon noise to me. And so ended our tourist trip across the United States, because 45 miles down the road, Mexico began.

We piled into the cars and rolled on to the adventure's next chapter.

www.veloce.co.uk / www.velocebooks.com
All current books · New book news · Special offers · Gift vouchers

MEXICO

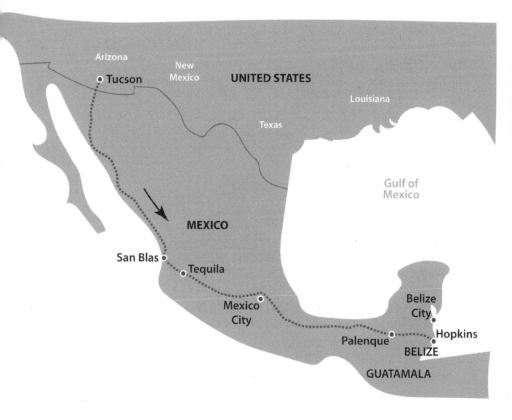

24. A DIFFERENT WORLD

20th September 2017
31°20′N, 110°56′W. Nogales, Arizona.

THE MEXICAN BORDER loomed large in our windows, marking not just our departure from the United States, but also from the world we knew. Up until that moment, nine weeks and almost 11,000 miles into the journey, we'd been travelling through familiar cultures and countries. Nothing had really been that far removed from life back home, except for maybe the polar bear warnings on Svalbard, of course. But now, that familiarity was being left behind. From the moment we crossed the Mexican border until the end of the trip, every country, every landscape, and every culture would be new to us.

There wasn't a queue to leave the US and pass into Mexico, so we rolled straight up to the border post and got down to business. The border guard spoke to us in the TVR first.

"Where are you heading to?"

"Chile. Via a few other places in between."

"And this car, where's it from?"

"England. We shipped it over to New Jersey. It's on a temporary import," I replied.

"Okay, so you'll need to cancel that. Take your documents to the window," the border guard said, pointing to the customs building. "Then you'll need to present your passports over there."

And it really was as simple as that. A few minutes, some stamps and some signatures, and we were no longer in the USA.

As we were getting our passports stamped, we heard the border guard shout across the checkpoint to one of his colleagues.

"Hey, these guys with the Dodge say they're gonna sell it down in Latin America somewhere. Do we care?"

The other border guard, dozing lethargically in the shade, shrugged his shoulders in the most disinterested way possible before returning to his siesta. So that was the answer. No, they really didn't care, and the Dodge was free to proceed. For now, anyway.

For all the rules and regulations they're built on, there is often a surprising degree of irrationality about border crossings, and this particular international gateway was no exception. We'd left the US and now we had to get the cars imported and insured. So that happens on the Mexican side of the border post, right? Wrong – such logic clearly had no place here. To get our cars and hence ourselves legal in Mexico, we'd first have to drive 12 miles down the road to a customs and immigration checkpoint. So off we went, in cars which technically shouldn't be in the country, with no papers and no insurance. On first impressions, Mexico was indeed a very different country.

This was emphasised as we drove our vehicles of questionable legal status out of the border post and into the Mexican side of Nogales. Suddenly, our world changed. The traffic crowded in tightly around us, jostling for position on the dusty thoroughfare. The buildings acquired a weather-beaten character which wouldn't be tolerated in tidy, straight-laced Arizona, and the people became more animated and alive. But there was edginess too. Police were a worryingly common sight and occasionally a pick-up truck loaded with armed officers or soldiers would edge through the melee, generally with a rather large, belt-fed machine gun or grenade launcher mounted on the roll cage. And there we were, suddenly feeling rather conspicuous in our shouty little green sports car. After the spacious order of Arizona, it was like a baptism of fire – though not literally, we hoped.

In many ways, on leaving the US we'd entered a low-level warzone, where the army and the police were taking on some of the world's most powerful drug cartels. By the time we arrived in Mexico, this war on drugs, along with the infighting between the cartels, had claimed over 200,000 lives and displaced several million civilians. So why are drugs such a problem in Mexico? A big part of it comes down to the demise of Colombia's cartels in the '90s, which gifted their Mexican counterparts control over 90 per cent of the cocaine flow into the US. And that made the border area through which we were passing one of the war's hotspots.

Drugs. What are they good for? Absolutely nothing, based on the Mexican experience.

And it's not just drugs. The border is also a hotspot for human trafficking, with people being illegally smuggled into the US in search of a better life. And the shady dealings flow the other way, too. All these drug cartels need guns, and while there are almost no gun shops in Mexico, just across the border is that last bastion of pile 'em high, sell 'em cheap gun culture – the USA. Many guns are smuggled across the border into Mexico for use by the cartels.

So, that's the Mexico/USA border. Drugs and illegal immigrants going one way, while guns and a rather conspicuous TVR head in the other direction.

We rolled on south and were relieved to arrive at the customs and immigration checkpoint without even coming close to being murdered. Situated right next to the main road, the checkpoint was an uninspiring selection of blue, single-story buildings which provided the venue where, all going well, we should be able to make our cars legal in Mexico. What could possibly go wrong?

For us in the TVR, the answer was 'very little'. We'd already purchased our tourist cards and got our passports stamped, so we set about getting the car's paperwork in order. Following a customs deposit and about 40 minutes of paperwork, we were buying insurance and preparing to hit the road. But Team Dodge weren't having so much luck, as their temporary registration lacked sufficient gravitas to impress the Mexican customs officers. If they wanted to keep on rolling south, they'd need to go back to Arizona and get the orange beast properly registered.

"Right, let's go then," said Brummy. "It's two o'clock now so if we move, we can get across the border and back to Tucson in time to get the pre-registration inspection done this evening."

"Do you think Johan would let you use his address for the registration?" I asked.

"We'll give him a call and ask. Come on guys, let's get out of here."

"Good luck. We'll head south for a bit and find a hotel. I'll let you know where we end up," I said.

And then they were off, the Dodge's uncouth, gurgling exhaust note echoing along the 12 miles back to the border.

NORTHERN MEXICO WASN'T quite how we'd expected it to be. The dusty deserts of Arizona stayed north of the border and we found ourselves back among attractive rolling hills, packed with green vegetation. As we got away from the perceived dangers of the border area, we started to relax. But we also realised we were about to break one of our unwritten rules – no driving at night.

The sun set as we rolled into the town of Hermosillo, where we checked into the delightfully-named Hotel Bugambilia, a snip at £20 a night. We figured we'd be there for a few days as we waited for the Dodge to catch up, and it was a pleasant enough place to pass the time, and discover just how ineffective our attempts at learning Spanish had been as we frequented the cafés and restaurants, and of course, the local 'London Pub.' This little taste of home, where Bombardier beer was served in a dark bar with a deeply anglophile décor, was most welcome. It was a shame they didn't stock any brews from our friends at Dartmoor Brewery, but even so, we ended up spending quite some time there.

We weren't alone for as long as we'd expected, as once again, the Dodge guys had taken it upon themselves to catch us up as soon as possible and things had been going their way. They'd made it back to Tucson by 4pm, and had managed to get the car inspected for registration that afternoon. Their luck held and it made it through the emissions test, thanks to the engine warning light deciding not to come on and slow the momentum. Johan had helped out with an address, the registration taxes were paid, and so, as Kim and I were enjoying a late morning coffee during our first day in Hermosillo, Team Dodge were already back on the road, heading for their second attempt at getting across the Mexican border.

And this time, they were successful. They rolled into Hermosillo after nightfall, 24 hours after we'd arrived, and headed straight to the bar. The following day we rolled onwards to the beaches of Guaymas, which gaze out across the bay towards the Baja Peninsula, then hit the road once again, heading to El Fuerte, the old colonial capital.

THE ROADS HAD been good, the miles falling behind us in a blur of run-down roadside restaurants and cheesy rock music. El Fuerte was close now. We pulled off the main road for the final 30-mile run to the town and as we did, I dove into a petrol station because Kermit's insatiable appetite for unleaded was making whether we'd make it all the way to the evening's destination a bit touch and go. I rolled towards the pumps, but they were roped off. No petrol. I had no choice but to cross my fingers and push on.

"It'll be fine," I said to Kim, rather unconvincingly.

"I don't think so," she replied.

"Trust me. I've just done 11,000 miles in Kermit. I know this car," I said.

It turned out I didn't know my car as well as I'd hoped, however. About 20 miles from El Fuerte, the engine began to miss occasionally.

"It's the fuel boiling in the tank," I said to Kim. "The fuel pump sends way more gas to the engine than the engine is actually using, so most of it gets sent back to the tank, which acts as a kind of heat sink. It's so hot that it's probably boiling in the lines, messing up the pressure to the injectors."

The engine's power losses became more and more regular until we spluttered to a halt at the side of the road. Team Dodge were most sympathetic.

"For goodness sake, Ben, why the hell didn't you fill up before?" said Pat.

"I was aiming for the petrol station at that last junction. I didn't know it was going to be closed. It's just fuel vaporisation anyway. Once the fuel system cools down a bit, a few primes of the fuel pump and we'll be back in business."

"Rubbish. You've run out of gas, and now you're just making excuses," replied Pat, coarsely.

"Trust me. Ten minutes of cooling down with the bonnet open, and it'll fire right up," I replied.

Ten minutes turned out to be rather ambitious, but after about 15 it did indeed burst into life. We carried on, the dead straight road undulating up and down across arable land, the roadside verges having been overrun by bushes and long grass. I drove as gently as possible, crawling along at just over tickover in fifth gear, trying to eke out the maximum fuel economy as Kim counted down the miles. And we nearly made it, but with about five miles to go until the salvation of the next gas station, we ground to a halt once again. This time, we were definitely out of fuel.

"See, I told you you'd run out of fuel," said Pat.

"I'd say we have now, yeah."

"So I suppose you're gonna want the Dodge to go and find you some fuel then?"

"Well, if you're offering," I replied.

And so the Dodge headed off to the petrol station just over the horizon, while Kim and I settled in for a long wait.

We were in the middle of nowhere. No buildings were in sight, just overgrown verges and bushes at the side of the road. But from this vegetation there came an endless flow of company. Grasshoppers, about five inches long, came marching out of the undergrowth by the hundred. We had to close Kermit's doors and windows to stop them ending up in the footwells as they swarmed and leapt onwards, intent on crossing the road. Some had already fallen victim to the passing traffic and others lingered on the tarmac, joining their fallen comrades. We didn't mind finding ourselves in the middle of what looked like a biblical plague, however. They took our minds off the situation.

As we were waiting, a vehicle approached: a police Toyota Hilux pickup truck. It pulled up in front of Kermit, and two rather portly policemen climbed out. Each of them wore what looked like a bulletproof vest and had a handgun hanging from their belt. The sidearm seemed somewhat superfluous to the situation however, given the daunting size of the fully-automatic assault rifles they were waving in our general direction.

We figured it was probably in our best interests to co-operate with them.

The language barrier raised itself pretty high as we attempted to communicate, thanks to our faltering Spanish and the policemen's total lack of English. Despite this, however, we managed to explain the situation and turned down their offer of a tow, as our friends were due back any minute. They seemed strangely reluctant to leave us though. Fears for our safety, or eagerness for a tip? We figured it was probably the former, as the town we were heading for was once a popular tourist destination, but the region's drug-related violence had kept visitors away in recent years. Certainly, two Brits in a fuel-less sports car made for an unusual and rather vulnerable sight in the area.

Shortly after the police left, the Dodge came to the rescue with a gallon of gas, and we finally made it to El Fuerte. It wasn't a bad place, but its lack of recent income was very apparent. Away from the old colonial centre – which was very much polished up for tourism – the town had a veneer of neglect. Flaking paint, broken roads and stray dogs dominated once we'd walked a few blocks away from the Plaza de Armas. And then there was the heat. There was no escaping the heat. It was a shame to see this potentially prosperous place so far from reaching its potential, but the policemen's edginess and the size of their guns emphasised the reasons why. After staying for a few days, we felt we'd exhausted El Fuerte, and so we headed back down to the coast.

THE WAVES GENTLY lapped against the sand as we sat in the restaurant. Several pelicans swooped and circled above the ocean, diving down through the surf to catch fish. Bulky and ungainly, they seemed to defy the laws of aerodynamics as they went about their day, unaware of how improbable their ability to fly seemed to the humans on the shore.

We were in the town of Mazatlán, slowly adjusting to life on the road in Latin America. And security was once again high on our minds. Since crossing the border we'd gradually adjusted to the realities of life in this part of the world, and Mazatlán was a good place to mull them over. This is a city which the US Government recommends avoiding all travel to, due to the huge amount of drug related crime. A few weeks before we arrived, seven people had been killed in a full-on shoot out between undesirables and the police. However, during our time there, the only issue we encountered was flooding so bad that it made many roads impassable. Oh, and the mariachi.

I hate mariachi.

I can think of no other noise – because that's all it is to me, just a noise – which intrudes into one's skull as completely and painfully as the overbearing racket of a mariachi band. Only ever played at a volume far beyond what's comfortable, the assault of a mariachi band is the danger you're most likely to be subjected to when in Mexico. And based on my first experience of it in that seafront restaurant in Mazatlán, at the very least it results in a good meal ruined.

Flooded streets, a high crime rate and music which makes the cries of a strangled cat seem appealing? Yeah, it was time to move on.

25. THE RIGHT PLACE AT THE RIGHT TIME

26th September 2017
21°32'N, 105°17'W. San Blas, Mexico.

THE WORLD HAD gradually been getting greener as we progressed across Mexico. Ever since we'd left the deserts of the Arizona border, each day on the road had brought a change in the scenery and by the time we were halfway down the Mexican coast, nature had truly got its game on. The trees soared high overhead and birds darted urgently through the canopy. We'd reached our first jungle, and wouldn't be leaving the rainforest ecosystem behind until we hit the equator in Ecuador. As if to mark the occasion, near San Blas, we saw our first crocodiles, dozing in a swamp, utterly disinterested by the stringy gringos waving camera-phones at them.

In San Blas, something happened that hadn't for at least a week: the Dodge broke down again. Its automatic gearbox got stuck in park and refused to move into drive, immobilising it. This issue ended with us stripping down the centre console and removing the spring loading on the mechanism which locks it into park when your foot isn't on the brake. The centre console trim never did get put back and from then on, some dexterity was needed to reach in and move the latch every time Team Dodge wanted their car to move.

With all its complexity, it was inevitable that the Dodge was going to have its fair share of issues, but none of us really expected it to make the TVR look like the epitome of reliability. Given the TVR's reputation back home in the UK, that was quite an achievement.

Near San Blas, Kim and I went to check out one of the trip's more delightfully named archaeological sites – The Valley of the Throat Cutters. Getting there from the road required about 30 minutes of jungle-bashing, meaning it doesn't exactly feature very highly on most visitors tick lists. Without detailed instructions you'd never find it, but that's all part of the appeal. Much of the fun of a visit is going full Indiana Jones as you struggle your way through the vegetation to reach the site, which occupies a river valley about a kilometre long, where the rocks lining the river are littered with faint petroglyphs. They're not the easiest things to spot and only by running water across them to bring out their contrast can you truly visualise the designs. Outlines of people, animals and concentric shapes, echoing to us through the ages. They've been there for over 4000 years, and that's certainly something to ponder.

But for me, the impact of the subtle petroglyphs was equalled by the impact of their jungle setting. Exotic palm trees reached up into the sunlight, which descended in crisp, sharp shafts through the humid air. Waterfalls gurgled timelessly over polished-smooth rocks, while a chaos of slippery boulders aided us in our frequent river crossings. Ferns grew from the sodden ground and, in lieu of a decent path, progress was made by slipping along the river bank, ducking under vines and branches. And then there was the wildlife. Crickets scattered from our path as we walked, leaping indiscriminately away from danger. Birds brought the forest canopy to life, while huge ants slaved on the forest floor. And most majestic of all was the orb-weaver spider hanging in space, its orange-and-black body four inches in length, its web over a metre across. These spiders don't take any prisoners. Even hummingbirds and bats sometimes fall victim, first to their webs, then to their jaws. This monster may not have had the venom of the black widows we'd met in Arizona, but when it comes to looking intimidating, it had them beaten.

Having got as close as we dared to the magnificent eight-eyed arachnid, we left it in peace and headed on out of the valley. Tequila was calling.

THE BLUE TINT of the cultivated hillsides tells you you're close. The colour comes from the blue agave, a spiky monster of a plant that grows to two metres in height and can weigh over 100 kilograms. Millions of them lined the road, dominating the landscape as far as we could see. Then we came to the town and a sign across the road reading 'Bienviendo a Tequila' and everything made sense.

French wine has its vineyards and Scottish whisky has its fields of barley.

This is Mexico's equivalent – the blue agave plantations that produce the raw material from which tequila is made. Pub2Pub had just arrived in the town where it all happens.

And it made me happy.

Not the drink itself, though. I've never been a fan of tequila and sampling the stuff in the town made famous by it didn't change this. Maybe this aversion harks back to some unfortunate encounter with the stuff back in my student days, but when it comes to spirits, give me a decent Scottish whisky instead any day. But despite this, it needed to be sampled – 'when in Rome,' as the saying goes.

We dropped into a bar and ordered a round of shots from the extensive menu, and to our untrained palates their sharp, sweet taste was something to be downed, rather than sipped and savoured.

It's probably heresy to do this in Tequila, but I moved over to less potent drinks for the rest of the evening. Fortunately, the Modelo beer I found to replace the shots was rather more interesting than the chilled blandness of the Tecate lager which had lubricated our time in Mexico up to that point.

Yes, it's the Modelo that made me happy in Tequila, not the salt, lemon and lime time.

SOMETIMES WHEN YOU travel, you get lucky. You arrive at a place with no inkling that anything out of the ordinary is happening, only to find yourself in the thick of the unexpected. This is what happened when we stumbled into the city of Morelia late one Friday evening, only to find that in the city centre, party preparations were in full swing.

A carnival atmosphere had energised everyone and people were lingering, drinks in hand, soaking it up. Performers in fancy dress drifted through the crowd. A huge stage was being set up in the central Plaza de Armas, while the main street running past the square was being barricaded off, ready for a Saturday morning parade which we were told would measure almost three kilometres in length.

We heard various explanations for the reason behind the celebrations, the most believable being that Morelia was about to celebrate its 189th anniversary.

Saturday dawned, overcast but dry. It was the day the city had been waiting for. As we set off in search of breakfast, people were already out in force, laying claim to the best vantage points on the parade route. The historic buildings that lined the route had onlookers filling the balconies in anticipation, while every window was draped with a Mexican flag. And the laughing, smiling crowds just kept on pouring into the town centre. It was an upbeat, well-ordered version of bedlam.

At ten in the morning, it began. A vee of immaculately polished Harley Davidsons, ridden by police officers, got proceedings under way, somehow managing to move their heavy steeds forward in formation at walking pace without toppling over. A large Mexican flag carried by representatives of various government departments then followed before the parade went up a gear. 50 firefighters in spotless protective gear, marching as if they'd been practising all year. A dozen trucks, ambulances and gun-toting pickups carried further members of the emergency services, who stood rigidly to attention, but were not so blind to the carnival atmosphere that they'd forgo the occasional wave to the crowd, which was going wild. A marching band came through, and then the army got involved: phalanx after phalanx of soldiers, striding as one. Their pickup trucks followed, each with a soldier attending the rollover bar-mounted grenade launcher. And then their armoured humvees rumbled past.

The navy wasn't about to be excluded by the parade's landlocked nature, towing a rigid inflatable attack boat down the thoroughfare, loaded with guns and hardened-looking marines. And then, not wanting to be left out, the air force joined in, with five helicopters flying very slowly along the parade route.

And it just kept on coming. Another marching band passed and then the teachers had their moment, followed by other government workers. Indigenous groups in their traditional dress rode past on horses. It went on for hours. We went off and grabbed a coffee and when we returned the mounted police were enjoying their moment in the spotlight. In fact, it seemed that the only people who didn't get an opportunity to march were the drug cartels whose activities have made the state of Michoacán – of which Morelia is the capital – one of the most violent in Mexico, or the vigilante groups that have risen up in response to them.

I'm sure the dauntingly high police presence that guarded the event had something to do with the cartel's decision not to gatecrash. Given that in 2017, 1277 murders were reported in Michoacán, we could understand the police presence.

After three hours, the parade seemed to peter out and we explored Morelia's UNESCO-protected centre, which is a monument to Spanish colonialism and the 19th century independence that followed it. Low-rise buildings lined the streets, while the various town squares were dominated by intricate cathedrals that date back to Spanish times. And then, as darkness fell, the floodlights were turned on and the stage in the main square came to life. A long speech was given by the town mayor before the moment everyone had been waiting for – the band began to play. And yes, it was a mariachi: my cue to go and find a beer well out of earshot.

The following morning, as we left the hotel into the bright sunlight, a pair of beautiful 1960s Ford Mustangs drove past, all gleaming paintwork and mirror chrome. They were heading for the main square where the parade had taken place the previous day and, like moths to a flame, we walked after them. As we did, a few more classic Fords rolled past and by the time we reached the square a car show was in full swing, organised by the local Ford club. About 30 Mustangs were lined up, along with a smattering of Focus STs. Parade fever was still running high and Sunday morning saw the turn of local charities and healthcare people to parade past, the effect being far more informal than the previous day's show of strength. Clearly, the party was an all weekend affair. But we needed to get a move on, and so after a breakfast surrounded by the cream of Mexico's classic Fords, we fired up our own classics and carried on, each of us with the same thought on our minds: sometimes, you end up in the right place at the right time.

26. CIVILISATIONS

02nd October 2017
19°41'N, 98°50'W. The Pyramid of the Sun,
Teotihuacán, Mexico.

FROM MY VANTAGE point 75 metres in the air, the plain of Teotihuacán stretched away beneath me. I was gazing out across what was once the largest city in the Americas. 17 centuries ago it was twice the size of London and over 100,000 people called it home. And what a sight it must have been.

Far below me, the ominously named Avenue of the Dead ran plumb-straight towards opposite horizons, a four-kilometre-long promenade lined with temples, murals and ruins. At its northern end, the wide avenue terminated at the Pyramid of the Moon, a solemn grey mountain of stone, built by hand over centuries. But despite its obvious bulk, it seemed strangely insignificant from where I was sitting. For I was atop the Pyramid of the Sun, which, being the third largest pyramid ever built, dominates the site. Its base covers 12^1/$_2$ acres, and its dense mass contains over a million cubic metres of rock. But there is a subtlety to the structure as well. Its position and orientation are dictated by astronomical cues, and its construction methods have survived innumerable earthquakes that have levelled many more modern structures. It shows that when they built the pyramid almost two millennia ago, the civilisations of Mesoamerica were as sophisticated as any in the world.

As we entered the region where some of the great societies of the Americas rose and fell, this was a lesson we'd be taught time and time again. Long before Columbus arrived on these shores, this part of America was a place of progress. A place where the empires of the Mayans, the Aztecs, the Teotilhauacáns, the Toltecs, and many more rose and fell with the ebb and flow of their civilisations.

A few days before we sat on the summit of the Pyramid of the Sun, we'd roamed a site where the pyramids of another ancient civilisation rose from the earth. The Guachimontones site near Tequila contains a series of stepped-rock pyramids up to 18 metres high and over 100 metres across, made by a civilisation called the Teuchitlán, which existed over 23 centuries ago. Now grassed over, these pyramids were once crowned by a wooden shaft which was used by priests in a ceremonial manner. Further, smaller pyramids dotted the site.

There's a statistic that goes along the lines of, in any major city, you're never more than 20 feet from a rat. We were beginning to think the same might be true of Mexico and pyramids. And we hadn't even reached the region where their most successful proponents had built their empire yet.

The Mayans.

These enigmatic people dominated a large area of Central America for millennia, and in that time they built one of the great civilisations. They developed the most advanced system of writing in the Americas and mastered mathematics. They made incredibly detailed observations of the sun, moon and stars, and created their own calendar. And they built great cities, where pyramids soared skywards, palaces sat inviolable and administrative offices stood aloof. They were a people who embraced both trade and conquest, and who understood the power of knowledge. Yet they never invented the wheel, and for centuries much of their world was in a state of slow collapse, even before Spanish germs and gunpowder finished it off late in the 17th century.

The famous city of Palenque, for example, was abandoned in the eighth century and was reclaimed by the jungle for almost a millennium before the allure of a lost city drew in archaeologists and adventure-seekers.

We fired up our engines, and left Teotihuacán to follow in their footsteps.

WITH SEVERAL THOUSAND miles already behind us, we were used to driving in Mexico now. The main roads weren't as bad as we'd expected, but progress tended to be slowed by the regular and expensive toll booths, and the occasional police checkpoints. We were also starting to encounter an obstacle which would plague us right the way through Latin America – the not-so-humble speed bump. Mexico took a 'bigger is better' approach to these intrusions and the ground clearance of our low-slung cars often wasn't up to the job, leaving us with two options: either approach the speed bumps at an angle or grit our teeth as scraping noises came from beneath the car. Neither was ideal.

Another adjustment you need to make to become a truly proficient Latin American motorist is interacting with those attempting to profit from your passing. At traffic lights, you're often besieged by people selling cold drinks or snacks. Others will wash your windscreen in return for a few coins, while yet more will attempt to sell you whatever they have to hand. On several occasions, I accelerated away from a toll booth only to see a figure on the verge, holding a stick out in front of us at windscreen height. And on the stick? A couple of parrots – for sale, obviously. The optimism of these guys, who clearly expected cars to screech to a halt due to being overcome by a sudden desire for a parrot, was mind-boggling. Optimism was clearly a thing in Latin America though. The person who tried to sell Kim five Labrador puppies through the window at a toll booth was clearly a glass-half-full kind of guy too.

"I just don't get it," was Brummy's take on it. "You're a Mexican and you don't have enough money. What makes you think the best way to make money is to sell puppies to passing cars? I mean, why not fruit or water? One grows on trees, the other literally falls from the sky. Why would you think puppies are a good idea?"

Several days of this curious new take on motoring took us to Palenque, and it didn't disappoint us. From the moment you enter the complex and find yourself beneath the stepped pyramid that forms the Temple of the Inscriptions, you're left in no doubt of the gravitas the place once had. As you explore beyond these big hitters, it's the scale of the site that leaves the deepest impression. We spent hours roaming the ruins, yet only around a tenth of the ancient city has been excavated. There are still secrets aplenty amid the jungles of the Americas.

FROM PALENQUE WE took rural roads to the border. The jungle thickened, the tarmac became more broken, and at every village the local people held a rope across the road, extolling a payment of a few coins for passage. Near the border, a military checkpoint with a dozen bored soldiers manning it gave our cars and documents the once over, before allowing us to continue. And then, after over 2000 miles of driving, Mexico was behind us. It was time to see what Guatemala had to offer.

27. GUATEMALA

06ᵗʰ October 2017
17°15'N, 90°59'W. El Ceibo, Guatemala.

THE FOREIGN OFFICE advice for Guatemala made for sobering reading. Recent, violent attacks on groups of British tourists. Frequent car-jacking and robberies on the route we'd be taking across the country. Express kidnappings, bogus police officers preying on travellers, and ambushers lying in wait on rural roads. And as if to emphasise that we weren't in Devon anymore, there was a warning not to travel on local buses due to frequent attacks on them, which are now apparently carried out using explosives. I guess that old-fashioned hold-ups simply weren't cutting it anymore, now the violent death count is running at over 5000 per year.

Not since my Africa trip had I been anywhere with quite the same unpredictable reputation.

The El Ceibo border crossing was completed in around three hours, the clean and professional Mexican operation contrasting with Guatemala, where a few rickety cabins sufficed for offices and a staff lunch break cost us an hour. And so we set about trying to reach the town of Flores before nightfall. Because our research had told us that if you're driving in Guatemala, bad things happen after dark.

Or do they? It's all too easy to be scared by the news and travel advice that you absorb when researching a trip. But should you let it dominate your planning? That's always a difficult decision. Take too bullish an attitude and you might increase your risk of becoming a victim. But if you're too timid, you'll never leave home. I always try to weigh the odds in my favour with sensible planning, defensive driving, and by trying to incorporate a degree of 'streetwiseness' into itinerary. And in this case, that meant reaching town before dark. Would we have been okay if we didn't? Probably, but the laws of probability say it would result in an ever-so-slightly higher likelihood of becoming another violent crime statistic. As it happens, there was only one time we felt even vaguely nervous on the run into Flores.

"Well that's a new one," Kim commented as it happened. "I've never been sat in a TVR listening to Mariah Carey while a bloke in a pickup truck points a machine gun at me before."

Fortunately, the guy lazily holding the gun as we rolled along in traffic didn't pull the trigger, and we safely arrived at Flores, site of one of the Maya's last stands against the Spanish, home of some fine colonial architecture, and a very pleasant lakeside spot in which to grab a beer and settle into country number 11.

And we weren't the only ones settling in, as Flores was clearly a popular spot on the backpacker circuit. The dreadlocked masses were seeing in the evening in the town's many bars while the street food vendors were geared up for the skinflint travellers, doing great business by serving dinners for a dollar or two. But why was Flores such a hit with the gap year crowd? It was a pleasant enough place alright, but I couldn't help thinking there had to be something more.

The answer lay hidden in the rolling hills about 40 miles to the north.

The legendary lost city of Tikal.

The ruins are located in thick jungle, and were once home to almost 100,000 people. They were abandoned 12 centuries ago, however, and today their only permanent residents are the animals which call the jungle home. A warning sign stood at the entrance to the complex, detailing some of the potential dangers we were about to face:

In Tikal Park you will see the howler monkey. They are slow and sedentary, they like to defecate on the heads of the people below to show their presence, and scream loudly.

Filled with fear of what lay in store for us, we headed into the jungle.

The ruins were in various stages of restoration. Some, such as the famous pyramids which punctuate the Great Plaza, have been completely rescued from the jungle and meticulously rebuilt. Others remain buried beneath centuries of advancing nature; ferns, creepers, and trees smothering what they've taken back.

The site is vast, and getting between the various structures involves braving the crap-hurling monkeys on long walks through the jungle. That alone was an experience. Lines of leafcutter ants wandered the undergrowth, stripping the green from the trees. Malevolent-looking spiders floated in space, their webs almost invisible around them. Birds darted through the canopy, flashes of bright colours racing past in an instant. The roar of howler monkeys echoed around us. And most appealingly, spider monkeys grazed slowly and deliberately in the trees, almost human in their expressions, yet superhuman in the way they leapt from branch to branch when they spotted the next meal.

And then there were the ruins themselves. Pyramids, temples and palaces rose above the treeline, providing liberating views across the canopy. Altars and lesser buildings blended in beneath, offering up a full-on Indiana Jones experience as we explored them. But some of the most impressive building works were also the most subtle. The reservoirs for instance, which watered the site, or the canals that fed them. We spent a full day walking in a mildly amazed state, never quite sure of what would appear out of the jungle next, and that evening we left with an acute case of Mayan overload.

And in case you're wondering, no, none of us were defecated on by a howler monkey, even though we tried our best to lure Brummy beneath them. Ah well, there's always next time.

FROM TIKAL, WE headed east to Belize. And doing so felt like something of a homecoming, for we were temporarily leaving the Spanish-speaking world for a nation where English is the official language and the banknotes still proudly bear a portrait of Her Royal Highness Queen Elizabeth II. Until 1981, Belize was a British colony and pro-British sentiment still runs high, due in part to the perceived fact that we've got their back when it comes to squabbles with their occasionally aggressive neighbour, Guatemala. Yes, this is a country that is proud to be Anglophile and different, standing apart from the crime rates and relative chaos of their Spanish-influenced neighbours.

This pro-British feeling is clear from the moment you cross the border from Guatemala and see the Union Jack is proudly displayed at the crossing, being given equal billing to the flag of Belize, as if to send a message to their neighbour. However, the real reason is somewhat less relevant to foreign affairs. Years ago during his take on a gap year, Prince Harry passed through the border crossing. Painted above the flags, a message reads 'Welcome Prince Harry.'

Kermit looked very much at home beneath the mural.

After the larger-than-life countries we'd visited so far on our trip across the Americas, Belize had a distinctly small-town feel. Literally, in the case of the capital, Belmopan, which has a whole 16,400 residents. We passed through the refreshingly untrafficked metropolis and onto the delightfully-named Hummingbird Highway, which would take us 50 miles through a glorious landscape of karst and woodland, to the Caribbean coast.

We stayed in the laid-back-to-horizontal beach town of Hopkins for a couple of days, in a hostel run by an elderly American called Joycelyn, who cooked a mean BBQ chicken – unfortunate for the chickens that roamed the beachfront site. It was nice to spend a few days off the road, as the pace we'd been maintaining since arriving in New York eight weeks earlier had been intense. This continuous activity, combined with the fact I was seldom alone and the predictable stresses that occur when a group of people are put together in such a situation, was making it rather difficult for me to manage my depression. It was still there, lingering, and while it was a frustrating thing to be burdened with on such a trip, my main concern was the fact I was only around halfway through the journey. What effect might future events have on me? The thought that I could drift back to the state I was in the year before departure worried me, as this would make the journey near impossible to complete and would turn it from the adventure of a lifetime, into the ordeal of a lifetime.

But as I enjoyed those few days off the road by the Caribbean coast, it gave me confidence. I could feel my mental state getting better, and this proved to me that I could control the black dog that was accompanying me on the trip.

Refreshed, we headed back into the relative chaos of Guatemala and continued our Central American odyssey.

IT WAS THE poorest place we'd been so far. Wooden shacks lined the road, their paint flaking and their corrugated metal roofs slowly rusting away. Vegetation crowded in closely around them, pinning them against the tarmac. Children played on the verges, and poultry often scattered before our front bumpers as we drove.

We were on the main road south across Guatemala, and it was one of the roads the Foreign Office had urged us not to take. But security wasn't the issue at the forefront of our minds. No, that other scourge of the sports car in Latin America had taken centre-stage: those damn speed bumps.

They came in waves, ten at a time, threatening to beach our cars. The Dodge had it worse than the TVR, its long chassis making it harder to negotiate them at a jaunty angle to prevent scraping. Our progress was slowed down to almost nothing as we bounced over them, and we continued nervously, because they wouldn't have to get a whole lot bigger to make the road impassable to us. The drive from the Belizean border to Guatemala City – the nation's capital – wasn't much more than three hundred miles but it ended up taking us a day and a half, broken up by a night in a rundown hotel in some nameless one-horse-town, and a traffic jam so long that Kim and I broke out the laptop and watched a film while we waited.

Guatemala City may have been home to over a million people but it needs to work on its PR, as it's not the sort of place that comes over very well in writing. Sentences like 'dirty, dangerous and downright forgettable,' as well as 'dangerous at night,' flowed from our guidebooks, and did little to pique our interest. So we rolled right on through the dusty carnage that passes for rush hour there and headed for an altogether more tranquil destination. Antigua.

THE LAID BACK colonial buildings had an easy-going splendour. They were the timeless survivors that had formed the backdrop for countless stories of ebb and flow. The town they were part of had been the capital of the Spanish colony of Guatemala for almost a quarter of a millennium. They'd survived earthquakes, volcanic eruptions, and the decline that followed the removal of the nation's capital status, when Guatemala City took over the role.

Antigua's loss actually turned out to be its gain, and the city is firmly on the up now, as tourists flood in to experience its laid-back charm. There's none of Guatemala City's dust and traffic here, and its cobbled streets are tranquil in comparison. With no crumbling concrete apartment blocks or overcrowding, Antigua offered a definite breath of fresh air in comparison to our earlier journey through the capital. The two cities do share one similarity though: it isn't advisable to wander the streets after dark. However, in Antigua, this is because your ears are likely to be assaulted by more mariachi and frankly, nothing is worth risking that for.

By day though, it's a lovely place to explore. There seems to be an interesting gem around every corner – a quirky café, spacious plaza, intricate church or earthquake-ravaged ruin. And beyond the streets lies a vista that elevates Antigua to another level of beauty. Surrounding the city, a trio of volcanoes punch up to the sky, all just under 4000m in height. They tower over the buildings completely, and rarely do you find yourself in a place where at least one of their summits isn't poking into view. And if it happens to be Volcán de Fuego's 3763m summit, you'll probably see a column of steam venting skywards too, as this is one volcano which is still very much active. It was almost as if Guatemala was reminding us that it still has an edgy side – a characteristic of this nation of extremes which would stay in our minds as our journey continued.

The road from Antigua to the border with El Salvador is infamous for its carjacking risk. From what we'd read, it was not a part of the journey to be taken lightly. Even in daylight it promised to be a dangerous drive, but one morning we put this to the back of our minds, got in the car and began this latest roll of the dice. After a few almost anticlimatic hours, we pulled into a petrol station for fuel and a cold drink, and happened to glance across the forecourt.

"Did you see that?" I asked Kim.

"Yeah, what on earth are they doing here?"

"I don't know, but there are more of them pulling in. Let's take Kermit over and say hello."

It turned out our eyes weren't deceiving us. A convoy of classic Ford Mustangs had indeed just driven past and pulled in next door. We burbled over to say hello. It was the Mustang club of Guatemala, of course – not a combination of words I ever thought I'd say.

I got chatting to a guy with a stunning light blue '66 coupé, and asked him about the road.

"Yeah, it's got a bit of a reputation," he said. "But it's generally fine. You'd have to be incredibly unlucky to have any issues along here. We come this way quite regularly with the club on our Sunday drives, heading to a restaurant for lunch, and it's always been fine."

"So, is there much of a car scene here in Guatemala?" I asked.

"There's a bit of a car culture, but it's not massive, because people don't have much money. Not like Mexico where there are more people with cash, and lots of car meets. But it's growing here, as more people can afford the hobby."

For the rest of the drive to the border, we rolled on feeling far more relaxed. No longer did the thick jungle lining the road seem to have the potential to be hiding danger. No, as the distance to the El Salvadorian border dropped to zero, we saw the countryside for what it truly was.

Simply breathtakingly beautiful.

28. BORDER WARS

16th October 2017
14°01'N, 89°54'W. CA-8 Highway,
Guatemala/El Salvador border.

THE BORDER CROSSING was tucked away in a steep-sided valley, the river running through it marking the arbitrary boundary where Guatemala ended and El Salvador began. We crossed the bridge and pulled up next to the glorified portacabin that had been pressed into service as the customs office. But the news wasn't good. The aloof officer in charge had only one word to say about Kermit's chances of being allowed into the country. A simple 'no.' As far as El Salvador is concerned, a right-hand drive car is simply too dangerous to be allowed to circulate on the nation's road network.

We fought our corner, but at this tiny border crossing, tucked away in the middle of nowhere, the customs officer was God, and he adopted a definite air of arrogance as he rejected our attempts to find a solution. No means no.

"That's it then," I said to Kim. "Let's head over to the bigger border crossing down by the coast and see if we have better luck there."

"Yeah, there's no point staying here anymore. Let's do it."

Luckily, my pre-trip research had flagged up a potential issue with El Salvador and right-hand drive vehicles, so in anticipation of the potential problem I'd not cancelled the TVR's Guatemalan Temporary Import Permit until we were 100 per cent sure we'd make it across the border. This mattered because once a permit is cancelled, the vehicle isn't allowed back into Guatemala for 90 days without a hefty payment, and the prospect of being stuck in no man's land with the mildly unpleasant customs officer for almost three months didn't really appeal.

The drive to the second border crossing took about an hour, through beautiful yet very poor rural communities, where people eked out a living in this mountainous corner of Central America. I don't think I've ever seen a place as green as those hills we rolled through after being denied entry to El Salvador. But soon enough, the verdant rural idyll phased into a dusty, run-down border town – the sort of place in which everything seems transitory, and where nobody ends up living out of choice. Yes, the small town of Hachadura exists as somewhere every visitor wants to spend the minimum possible time, and then get as far away as possible, pretty much from the moment they arrive.

It was a typical Latin American border. Big US-built trucks growled their way through customs, or waited on the concrete apron for their turn to pass. Small shanty cafés offered cold drinks, or a meal of rice and chicken, generally cooked over an open fire which was unbearably hot to be anywhere near, given that even the unheated air was well over 30°C. To assist with the inevitable border paperwork, some of the more enterprising shacks had a photocopier tucked away – something we'd be making heavy use of later in the day. The immigration buildings at least were reasonably clean and smart, and mercifully air conditioned, providing some relief for the endless stream of people who filed through, patiently waiting in line to hear the sound of their passport being stamped. But overall, the atmosphere was one of dust, heat and barely organised chaos.

We dived in, looking for a way to get Kermit across the border. If we failed, our only option would be to detour away from the relatively smooth tarmac of the Pan-American Highway by looping up across Honduras – not an option we were particularly psyched about.

On the El Salvadorian side of the border we were spotted by a fixer named Alexander. In his mid-twenties, speaking perfect English, and full of the confidence of someone on home turf, Alex was sure he could help.

How?

Simple. The one loophole in El Salvador's war on right-hand drive is the transit permit. Freight forwarding companies are allowed to apply for permission to transit right-hand drive vehicles across the country. These permits only last 24 hours and the penalty for over-running is substantial, but El Salvador is pretty small, being only 250 miles from border to border. And besides, we had a four-litre V8 to help us make it across in time.

Alex took us to the small office of one of the logistics businesses located at the border and we began to work through the paperwork. While on our own, Kim and I would have found the process almost impossible due to the language barrier and the fact we were outsiders, Alex knew the system and knew how to work it to achieve the result we wanted. Despite this, it still took several hours of forms, paperwork, and wandering between the customs offices, the freight company, and the ubiquitous shack with a photocopier but eventually, we had permission to complete a 24-hour transit of El Salvador.

We headed back to the Guatemalan side of the border, cancelled the TVR's Temporary Import Permit, had our passports stamped out, returned to El Salvador, completed immigration and started the clock ticking on our trip across a nation which ranks having the world's highest homicide rate amongst its claims to fame.

"So basically, we're now delivery drivers with the task of getting a TVR across the murder capital of the world in less than 24 hours?" said Kim.

"Oh yeah. I'm loving this."

"Me too," she replied with a grin as we rolled away from the border.

WE WERE ONLY a few miles into our mission when we arrived at the first police checkpoint, the staff of which got very excited when they noticed the steering wheel wasn't in the normal place. Fortunately, the documents we couldn't read, that we'd purchased off the freight company, seemed to do the trick, so the questioning moved on to other areas.

"Drugs?"

"No, no drugs."

"Money?"

"Oh no, we don't have any of that."

"Give us money."

"No."

I attempted to look serious and after a few moments, the policeman gestured that we could continue. We rolled on into the evening.

After a couple of hours, the road swung out of the interior and twisted its way through the steep cliffs that dropped down into the sea. It was glorious driving, a sinuous road passing through a landscape of rare drama, with the only fly in the ointment being the TVR's slipping clutch, which was now only able to transmit a fraction of the car's torque to its wheels.

Darkness came as we approached the surf-beaches of La Libertad, so we pulled over and camped outside a hostel, amid a sea of mango trees. The following morning, we took breakfast at a recently opened Subway, which felt just like a step back into the Western world. Or it would have, were it not for the grizzly-looking security guard clutching a double-barrelled shotgun, who was guarding the front door.

That afternoon, our first assignment as delivery drivers ended in success, with Kim and I making it to El Salvador's eastern border with 45 minutes to spare. As we crossed into Honduras, we became tourists once again. We also entered a rather safer country, as the yearly murder rate dropped from 83 per 100,000 people in El Salvador, to 57 in Honduras. For reference, back home in the UK it's 1.2.

HAVING CROSSED EL Salvador in under 24 hours, we repeated the feat in Honduras, nipping across the narrow Pacific south of the country rather quickly, with an overnight stop in Choluteca. No, we'd never heard of the place either.

And with the Dodge having already made it to Nicaragua, we didn't have time to hang around. We got moving from our overnight stop early, in an effort to catch them up, but progress turned out to be rather slow. Evidently, Honduras didn't consider a trip to the Nicaraguan border to be worthy of a smooth ride and we found ourselves on the worst road of the trip so far. Crater-like potholes kept our pace down, and in places the tarmac had disintegrated almost to nothing. Progress became a mixture of getting up speed when we could, before being forced to slow down to walking pace to tiptoe around the worst bits of road. Without much in the way of airflow, the heat in the car was stifling, and by the time we reached the border, Kim was feeling rather ill. With it being our fourth visit to a border crossing in 48 hours, I wasn't exactly psyched about getting stuck into the process either. But the motivation was there – Team Dodge were waiting for us at the colonial town of Granada, and the promise of pleasant bars and no more borders for a while was most appealing.

But first we had to get across this border. Kermit was sprayed with disinfectant and we unloaded all of our bags to be put through a scanner. Then the car was inspected by the police, the temporary import completed, the car insured, and once we'd paid a ten dollar entry tax, our passports were stamped and we were on our way. Another two hours of our lives lost to bureaucracy, as we cooked beneath the midday sun.

And Nicaragua didn't want to make progress too easy for us, either. Our first attempt at following a route to Granada gradually deteriorated into a 4x4 track, forcing us to backtrack. On our second attempt, we hit smoother tarmac and made reasonable progress, but even this wasn't without its issues. The police checkpoint, for instance, where the policeman asked me to reverse away from the barrier into a parking space, before attempting to fine me for reversing on the highway. Kim was still suffering and I was getting pretty tired so, forgetting my Spanish, I spoke rather aggressively at him in English, dropping in the occasional swear word, along with liberal use of the word 'embassy,' until he gave up and let us go.

We were still miles away from our destination when the sun set, an occurrence which coincided with rush hour in Nicaragua's capital, Managua. We crawled through the traffic for over an hour before we were released and sped through the final 30 miles to Granada, exhausted and relieved.

"What took you?" Brummy asked, appearing in front of the hotel.

"Bad roads, borders, dodgy police and shitty traffic. Is that enough for you?"

"It was fine for us," said Brummy. "Fancy a beer?"

"Damn right I do," I replied.

We headed out for dinner – in the local Chinese restaurant, naturally – then dropped into a nearby bar. As we were stood by the door, I made eye contact with a guy who was sat enjoying a beer. He looked quizzically at me, before asking: "are you Ben? Pub2Pub?"

"Erm, yeah, I am. How do you know that?"

"Your T-shirt – it says Pub2Pub. I'm Alan from Hotel Brio. It was pretty quiet so we've escaped here for a few days R&R."

"Ah yes, it makes sense now. That was kinda freaky, being recognised."

Though we'd never met, I knew of Alan from a website called PistonHeads. He'd been following our journey and had invited us to the hotel he'd recently bought with his girlfriend on Nicaragua's southern coast. To run into him 50 miles up the road was a rather unexpected, though pleasant, surprise.

The encounter did do something to illustrate the reach the trip was having. The longer we went on, the more the following we were gathering through our website and social media channels grew. Back home, the car itself had already become a minor celebrity in TVR circles, with anyone who has an interest in the marque seeming to know about Kermit's journey. Strangers had started sending us good luck messages or offers of assistance, and many folk were keen to be involved in the journey in some way, from Alan's invitation to come to his hotel, right up to the offer we received from a guy called Alvaro in Colombia, who was keen to join the expedition's entire South American leg. As people saw us progress, it was clear that our journey was striking a chord with them, and inspiring them to incorporate some adventure in their own lives, which was a nice feeling.

ALAN WAS SO persuasive about the glories of his hotel down by the coast that the following day we carried on to Playa Gigante, where Hotel Brio was. And a most pleasant and relaxed spot it proved to be. The beaches were clean and empty, their white sands running for miles along the edge of the Pacific. The few bars and restaurants were relaxed and easy-going places to while away the hours, and the hotel, overlooking the vista from its raised location above the town, had everything we could have needed. And to cap it all, the evenings bore witness to the most spectacular sunsets of the whole trip.

But Hotel Brio also marked the end of an era, because our right-hand drive issues in El Salvador had merely been the warm-up for the main event – Costa Rica, where right-hand drive cars are not only outlawed, but no handy transit rule exists either. The Dodge could continue, but the TVR couldn't. And as most of Team Dodge had their flights home booked from Panama a week after we arrived at Hotel Brio, we said our emotional goodbyes and they rolled on, leaving Kim and I alone with the TVR in Nicaragua.

29. NO MAN'S LAND

20th October 2017
11°23'N, 86°01'W. Hotel Brio, El Gigante, Nicaragua.

I'D KNOWN ABOUT the issues we'd be facing at the Costa Rican border since before we'd left the UK. Historically, there hadn't been any problems entering with right-hand drive cars, but a change in policy had seen a ban begin to be enforced in the months before Pub2Pub hit the road. As we'd progressed through the trip, it was always the big question mark in the route plan. There was no way to drive around Costa Rica, so just how were we going to be able to complete the journey?

We did have a few options, but none of them quite seemed to line up for us.

The first possibility was a shipping service between Nicaragua and Ecuador, which would bypass not only Costa Rica, but also Panama and Colombia. We missed a sailing of this service by a whisker when we arrived in Nicaragua, and the following voyage wasn't scheduled for another three weeks. I also found a potential container share from Honduras to Colombia, but the other overlanding vehicle in the share dropped out and I couldn't afford to go it alone. Then there was the option of having the TVR transported across Costa Rica to Panama as cargo on a lorry, but this seemed a pretty pricey option – especially as from Panama, I'd have to ship it again, around the impenetrable Darien Gap to Colombia.

So the options were to wait in Nicaragua for the shipment to Ecuador, or bite the bullet and attempt to truck the car across to Panama.

We went for the first option, and Kim and I started passing time in Nicaragua.

And we had at least a couple of weeks to kill. A return to Granada passed a few days, enjoying the fading colonial splendour, unique lakeside location, warm evenings and cheap beer. We headed back to Managua, the nondescript capital, to extend the TVR's Temporary Import Permit so it would be allowed in the country for longer. We popped over to Leon, where we watched the Day of the Dead celebrations in Nicaragua's other colonial jewel. Once Team Dodge had sold their steed in Costa Rica, Nick joined us again, and having left the TVR in Granada, we hired mopeds to explore the volcanic island of Omnotepe, before backpacking down to Panama, from where Nick and Kim continued on to Colombia, while I returned to Kermit.

All the time waiting and watching the days tick past, and the shipping date draw closer.

One positive of all the waiting was that it gave me time to see to Kermit's only really big issue – the slipping clutch. With help from the TVR Car Club back home, it was arranged that one of the UK's leading TVR garages – which goes by the rather apt name of 'Powers Performance' – would send one out to me. So, sending a clutch from the UK to Nicaragua, that's not going to go smoothly, is it? Wrong. In less than seven days door-to-door, the clutch kit had cleared customs and was ready to be fitted. I took the TVR to an independent Land Rover garage, who looked rather confused until I opened the bonnet and revealed the Rover V8. Once they understood, and after a few days of work, the clutch was swapped over. Kermit was also serviced, the new front shock absorbers were finally fitted and some welding was done on one of the suspension wishbones.

The TVR was all ready for South America. I just had to get it there.

And the news on that front wasn't good. While replacing the clutch, I heard from the shipping company that the November sailing had been cancelled. It would be over a month until the next voyage, if it even happened at all. After weeks of sitting around, that was the final straw.

I bit the bullet, booked a truck and headed for the Costa Rican border.

THE QUEUE OF lorries waiting to cross the border stretched back down the road for miles. The drivers were relaxing in the shade next to their machines, drinking coffee, playing cards or dozing on the tarmac. I overtook the line and swiftly exited Nicaragua. It felt good to finally be decisive after so many weeks biding time, waiting for non-existent ships. I felt energised with action, but driving through no man's land, I was stopped by the Costa Rican guards.

"No. You have to go back. This car is not allowed here."

I'd expected issues, but before I'd even made it to customs? The anti-right-hand drive sentiment was clearly pretty serious in Costa Rica.

"I know. I won't be driving on the road here. I'm meeting a truck at the border, to transport the car to Panama."

"Okay, you can go."

The flatbed car transporter – or 'grua,' as they're known in this part of the world – arrived as I was getting my passport stamped. The driver spoke almost no English, but some animated sign language was sufficient to get the car loaded and strapped down. I climbed into the cab, feeling strange to be transporting Kermit this way after so long behind the wheel, and we rolled over to the customs building.

It was already dark, and there was a definite slow-paced air prevailing. Eventually though, my truck driver made it to one of the windows, and entered into a discussion about the cargo. Now, my Spanish isn't great, but I could still tell that it wasn't going well. After a while, he headed outside and got on the phone to his boss, looking increasingly stressed. The head of the customs offices came out to talk to him.

This went on for about half an hour before someone who spoke English was summoned to talk to me, but I already knew what they were going to say.

The truck wouldn't be allowed to take the car across Costa Rica. It was only licensed for national transport, not international, and so the job was effectively beyond its pay grade. I attempted to contain my anger, as I knew I had to keep the customs officers on my side to have any chance of getting the car past them in the future but even so, I wasn't happy. I'd repeatedly pointed out to the truck company that it was an international transit and the car would need to be secured as cargo, and treated as such by customs. The bottom line was, they'd screwed up.

Following many apologies, the driver lowered Kermit back down onto the cracked tarmac and left. It was 10pm and my plan had unravelled already, before I'd even crossed the border. Hungry and tired but with no other option, I reclined Kermit's driver's seat and attempted to sleep. The customs area was bathed in sodium orange light, and trucks rolled past almost apologetically as I dozed off into a fragile slumber.

I JOLTED BACK into a confused consciousness. A rustling noise from the passenger side of the car had reached my sleepy mind. I glanced over to where the noise was coming from and saw its source. I'd left the window lowered slightly for ventilation and someone was now reaching through the gap, looking for the door handle, clearly oblivious to me, asleep on the other side of the car. As I came back into consciousness, it took me a few seconds to figure out what was going on. When I did, I shouted, "hey!" at the opportunistic robber.

Surprised, he glanced around quickly, then gestured at me to keep the noise down.

Being still mostly asleep – and unfailingly English – I apologised. But then my mind caught up, and I fired a torrent of abuse at the guy as he ran away across the border post.

I raised the windows a bit higher, and went back to sleep.

* * *

THE FOLLOWING MORNING I took stock of the situation and formulated a plan. Firstly, I decided I'd try everything I could to get special permission to enter Costa Rica with the car, and secondly, I'd get to the bottom of what went wrong with the truck, so the same mistakes wouldn't be made if I attempted that path again.

When it came to getting the car on the road in Costa Rica, I knew I'd have my work cut out. No-one had managed it yet, and if I was to be successful, I'd need help. So I racked my brain for any leads that might be of help. I posted messages asking for help on internet overlanding groups and on expat forums. I got in touch with the embassy and the local tourist boards. I spoke to some of the locals I'd met to see whether they might be able to assist in any way.

At this early stage, one person in particular was very pro-active in her attempts to help.

I'd met Melissa at a hostel in Managua, while I was having the clutch changed. We'd been out for dinner that evening and she'd flown home to Costa Rica the following morning. And when she heard of my predicament, she sprang into action.

And it turned out she was very well connected. For starters, she was friends with Costa Rica's Vice Minister for Transport, and also knew local lawyers, who were able to check on the laws that were preventing Kermit's entry. Armed with this potential assistance, we took several different approaches to try to get the car across the border.

I used my journalism connections to try to get special permission to bring in the car, banking on the good publicity I could bring Costa Rica. Melissa tried to get the Ministry of Transport to provide special permission. I discussed the situation with the lawyers in the Costa Rican capital, San José, and offered them a sum equal to the cost of the truck if they could find a way to get the car in.

That first morning at the border was a whirlwind of ideas, leads, and guarded optimism.

But I also began work on plan B – figuring out what had gone wrong with the truck the night before. In this respect, an El Salvadorian truck driver with some basic English was a great help to me. He explained why only certain trucks can make international transits, and took me to speak to some logistics companies based at the border. But their prices were eyewatering – measuring in the thousands of dollars. And if there's one thing I didn't have a surplus of it was dollars.

That first day flew past in a blur of action but by the end of it I was still at the border, I still didn't have a place to stay, and some of the leads had already begun to dry up.

Costa Rica's law was watertight. There were no loopholes through which I could gain entry, and the Ministry of Transport couldn't be seen to be bending the law to help.

For all the action, nothing had really changed as I settled down for another night sleeping in the TVR. Except for one thing – I now knew how important it was to keep the windows closed.

MY SECOND DAY in no man's land began with less of a spring in my step. The cramped cabin of a TVR, parked among the trucks in the edgy environment of a border post isn't conducive to sleep, but I worked on, trying to find a way out of the situation. I spoke to ex-pats in Costa Rica, and received offers of help from Panama. I continued to pursue the possibilities we'd dreamed up the previous day, both with Melissa and the lawyers. I heard back from the embassy, but there was nothing they could do. Gradually, I began to feel at home at this dusty outpost between two countries, where food came from a run-down trucker's restaurant, cold drinks from the shack just down the road from passport control and company from the Latin American truckers whose lives are lived on the Pan-American Highway.

I knew I couldn't stay there forever, of course. The nights sleeping in the car and the days trying to organise my escape would take their toll on me. And as our efforts to get the car permission to drive into Costa Rica were gradually extinguished, it became clear that my only options were to either attempt the truck across Costa Rica again or commit to a month-long wait for the ship from Nicaragua. Gradually, my presence at the border began to seem ever more futile.

"You need to return to Nicaragua," everyone told me. "You'll find a truck there far cheaper than you will here on the Costa Rican side."

And so after a few days of banging my head futilely against the Costa Rican brick wall, I decided to go back to Nicaragua, head to Hotel Brio and sort out a plan from there. After all, they had cold beer and beds, and that was all the incentive I needed.

I rolled back towards Nicaragua late on my third night at the border. It was spitting with rain, and far off lightning flashes lent a drama to my retreat.

I pulled up at the border and began the process of re-importing the car back into Nicaragua. It didn't go well.

"The car isn't allowed into Nicaragua," I was told almost immediately by the police chief. "Right-hand drive is not allowed here."

"But I've just spent over a month in Nicaragua with it, no problems."

"It's not coming in. It is illegal here."

"So why was I let in from Honduras a month ago?"

"It shouldn't have been allowed."

"Really? When I crossed the border from Honduras they said it was fine. When I went to the government offices in Managua to extend the Temporary Import Permit, they said it was fine. Now you're telling me it's not fine?"

"The law says it's not allowed in Nicaragua. It's not coming across the border."

"That's it. Take me to your commanding officer. I need to speak to him."

"You can't. He's gone home for the night."

"I don't care. You call him and get him back here."

It was 8pm when the guy in charge of the border post returned, and so far, my arguing had achieved nothing. Once the senior officer arrived, I continued pushing my case.

"So where are you going to go in Nicaragua?"

"I'll go to a hotel at Playa Gigante for a few days. I need to either organise a truck across Costa Rica, or head to Leon and deliver the car to the port, for shipping to Ecuador."

"You can't do that. Right-hand drive is not allowed in Nicaragua."

"Yes it is. This car has just spent five weeks on the road in Nicaragua. When I crossed the border from Honduras, it was no problem. When I extended the permit in Managua, there wasn't a problem. None of your country's police officers have a problem. It's only this border. You are in the wrong."

"I know my laws," the officer argued. "And I'm in charge here."

"I want you to call the customs office in Managua. They extended the permit. They're the ones who ultimately make the decisions."

"No. They're closed."

"So I'll stay here until they're open, and we'll call them in the morning."

The argument went on and on, back and forth, with me working the policeman's reluctance to go back up the chain to the country's head customs office for clarification. I kept working this angle; I could see he was scared of being embarrassed in front of his superiors.

After about 20 minutes, he disappeared for a conference with some of the other staff at the border post, and then returned to me.

"Okay, you can enter Nicaragua."

"Thank you. And the car?"

"Si."

I'd won. After several days living in no man's land, I was finally free again.

We completed the customs inspection of the car, my luggage was checked, my passport stamped, and I headed to the last desk before freedom, where the Temporary Import Permit is made out. They filled it in and handed it to me to sign. I read through it, but then I noticed that I was only being given a 48 hour Transit Permit to Honduras, rather than the usual 30 day Temporary Import Permit.

"Why only a Transit Permit? Why not 30 days?" I asked.

"That's what I was told to give you."

"Well I need a full permit. It's the weekend now, I can't arrange a truck across Costa Rica in only 48 hours. Where has the boss gone?"

"He's gone home again."

"Well I need a full 30 day permit. That's what we agreed."

"I don't have the authority to issue you one. You either have the transit permit now, or you'll have to wait until the morning and speak to the boss."

Feeling bullish and not about to give up without a fight, I opted to carry on the battle in the morning. The transit permit was torn up and I resigned myself to another night sleeping in the car.

There was a tap on the window. It was one of the border guards.

"You can't sleep here. It's not safe."

"Where should I sleep then?"

"Over there," he said, gesturing to a small compound about 100 metres away, glowing under the sodium lights. "My soldiers will keep you safe."

I thanked him, fired up the TVR and drove over.

The sliding entrance was guarded by a few teenage recruits whose uniforms hung of their slender frames like some tatty fancy dress outfit. Their guns looked real enough, though.

My intrusion into their dull routine was most welcome and I got chatting to one of the soldiers, who chain-smoked continuously as he told me about his life in simple Spanish, using my smartphone to translate.

"I have a girlfriend in Leon, and a daughter," he told me. "Where my family live, there's no work for me. But the army is good, so I live here. And I have another girlfriend in Rivas."

"How often do you go back to Leon?"

"Each month," he answered. "Where is your girl? Do you have women in England?"

"No," I replied. "It's a long story, but things don't seem to work out for me like that."

"You should get a Nicaraguan girlfriend. They're the best."

"Well if your boss would let me back into Nicaragua, I'd consider it."

As we chatted, I glanced around the compound they called home. Some tatty metal-framed bunk beds stood on an old concrete hardstanding. A weathered wall to one side and a rough corrugated roof offered their only protection from the elements. They had almost no personal possessions and didn't even have mosquito nets. One scruffy shack in the corner of the compound served as toilet and water supply, and they cooked outside this building, apparently using wood scavenged from the forest as fuel.

This was their world, for months at a time, and almost certainly for less than ten dollars a day. In comparison, the problem that was my temporary incarceration at the border seemed to pale into insignificance.

THE NEXT MORNING, I drove back over to the border post and had my meeting with the head of customs. Deeply rotund, profusely sweaty and with an air of arrogance, I disliked him immediately as he purposely kept me waiting as a demonstration of his authority. It was going to be a tough battle, but I enlisted a fixer to help with the language barrier, so at least I'd be able to argue my case. Which I did.

But initially I got nowhere. My fate was in the hands of someone who saw themselves as a little emperor of their domain, and who was annoyed that I hadn't been sent away from the border the previous night. Dealing with me was clearly beneath him.

But I didn't give up. I argued for 40 minutes, explaining that right-hand drive was a matter for the police rather than customs, so it was not his position to deny me entry. I laboured this point until he agreed that if the head of police said it was okay, he'd let the car back into Nicaragua.

My fixer and I headed over to see the head of police. Word had got around the border post by now, and his response was predictable.

"No."

"Show me the law which excludes right-hand drive vehicles," I demanded.

He took out a dusty copy of Nicaragua's rules of the road and presented it to me with the air of a victory. But I had a plan.

"I see. Thanks for showing me. I accept that this is your national law."

"So you must take your car back to Costa Rica," he replied.

"No. Are you aware that Nicaragua has agreed to abide by the 1977 Vienna Convention on Road Traffic?"

"Yes," he replied, clearly wondering where this was going.

"And as an international treaty, signed into law, this overrules your national road traffic laws?"

"Why are you telling me this?" he asked.

With help from my bi-lingual fixer, I explained.

"The 1977 Vienna Convention on Road Traffic states that if the vehicle meets all technical requirements in its country of registration, any conflicting requirements in the local country do not apply. This includes left and right-hand drive."

I showed him the wording of the convention, which I'd downloaded onto my phone in Spanish.

"As an international treaty, this overrides your national law, meaning you are breaking the law by not letting my car in."

"Nicaragua makes its own laws, and I am bound by them," he replied.

"You are a person of law, and I respect you for that," I replied, through my translator. "I know, as an educated person, you understand that this international convention overrides your national law. If you act against it, I will be forced to speak to my embassy and your superiors in Managua until we resolve this."

He sat silent for a few moments, looking at me and weighing up his options.

"Last night I was issued a transit permit," I told him. "This means the officers here last night understood my car was legally allowed into Nicaragua. I'm only asking for you to accept the same."

He stroked his moustache, pondering for a few more moments.

"Okay. You can enter," he eventually said. The words I was waiting for.

It was late morning, and I went back to find the head of customs and tell him. But he'd gone for a long lunch. I finally cornered him in his office when he returned a few hours later, and told him the good news.

"I must have it in writing that the head of police allows this," he said, not unreasonably.

But when I went back to the chief of police's office, he was gone. Asking around, we learned he'd gone home for the afternoon, and wouldn't be back until after the weekend. I went back to the customs office once again.

"Can't you phone him?" I asked.

"No," he replied. His patience with the situation was now zero. "We're finished here now. You will go back to the Costa Rican side of the border this afternoon."

"Oh really," I replied, full of anger. "We'll see about that."

Despite projecting a confident aura, I was now trapped. I couldn't enter Costa Rica with the car, and nor could I take it back into Nicaragua. Stuck in no man's land between the two borders, I either had to break the deadlock or find a lorry. Angered by the arrogance I'd experienced at the border that day, I decided to throw everything I could at the former option.

It was war.

And I decided to fight this war in a very British manner.

As noisily as possible, I parked Kermit right outside the main entrance into the immigration buildings. I hung the Union Jack in the rear window and mounted a portrait of the queen alongside it, which we'd brought along as a joke. I stuck a piece of A4 paper in each window, with a message in Spanish, reading:

Why is this car here?
On the 18th October, this car entered Nicaragua from Honduras and was declared legal. For five weeks, it was driven around Nicaragua and all the police I met said it was legal. On 10th November, I extended its permit at the DGA offices in Managua. They said it was legal. This week, after a few days in Costa Rica, I've tried to return to Nicaragua and the Peñas Blancas border crossing has declared it's illegal??!!
I am now speaking to the media and the embassy to resolve this.

And with the TVR now a very high-profile thorn in the side of the border post, I took to spending my days sitting next to it in my camping chair, drinking coffee and passing the time by laughing and joking with passers-by.

My goal with this rather ballsy approach was to get on the authorities' nerves. Not so much that they'd forcibly remove me and impound the car, but enough that they'll feel their authority was being undermined and their competence questioned, meaning they'd want me gone as soon as possible.

When several police crowded around me, demanding that I leave for the Costa Rican side of the border, I knew it was working.

"No. I'm staying here, and I'll be in Nicaragua tomorrow," I replied.

"No you aren't. You can't stay here. You must leave right away or we'll arrest you and take your car."

"On what charges? I've done nothing wrong," I asked, holding my nerve.

"You can't stay here. You have to go."

"I'm not going anywhere except back into Nicaragua."

And so ended every stand-off I had with the police, with me calling the bluff of their empty threats. As long as I did nothing wrong, there was nothing anyone could do to physically remove me from the border. The only option they had was to issue a permit saying Kermit was legal in Nicaragua. And as long as I was at the border, my security was their responsibility. If anything happened to the unwashed gringo in the vulnerable little car, it would be on their heads. Effectively, I was using my own security as leverage.

The deadlock lasted for the remainder of my time at the border and my life began to follow a very simple routine. I'd rise around 6am as the sun came up, and buy a succession of cheap coffees from the smiling old lady who sold them to people coming out of immigration. I'd then collar a customs officer who hadn't seen me before and try to get the paperwork rolling before their superiors arrived for work, but I never managed to pull off this ruse. My days were spent chatting amicably with people as they passed through the border – to the clear annoyance of the powers that be – while trying to find a way out of the situation. The car created a lot of interest and I was often asked to fire it up, a request I never turned down. And every time the border post shook to the shock and awe exhaust note of the big V8, I could see the authorities fill with a mixture of jealousy and annoyance. Food came from the open-fronted stall across the way, where rice and chicken was cooked over an open fire, and drinks were from the lady who spent her life sat by an ice bucket outside immigration, selling them to passers-by.

On most days, some other overlanders would pass through. Via the internet, my plight had become well known among others who were travelling along the Pan-American Highway, and other Europeans and Americans would offer messages of support, chat to me at the border, or see if I needed any supplies brought to me as I sat out my time there.

As the days drifted by, the officials' hatred of me grew, while the ordinary people at the border – the food and drink sellers, the truck drivers, the fixers – rallied around me. This strange, smiley gringo with the noisy little car, living among them while pissing off the authorities, really struck a chord with them, and despite the hostility, I felt surrounded by friends. And every time I saw my nemesis from the customs department in his sweaty blue polo shirt, I'd give him a smile and a wave, to his visible annoyance.

I wasn't going to be broken.

In total, I was living in no man's land and sleeping in the car for a week. On my last night there, I plucked up the courage to leave the car unguarded and go for a beer with one of the fixers. He'd told me he had some news about my situation.

"I've been speaking to the *aduana*," he said, already half-drunk. "And they tell me that they're going to give you a transit permit to take the car into Nicaragua tomorrow."

"How do you know?"

"I have a friend in the office," he told me. "Tomorrow, you'll be free."

"You're right, tomorrow I will be free. And thanks for letting me know," I told him. "But I'm not going to give them the satisfaction of deciding my fate. I've found a truck to Panama, and I'm leaving this evening."

THE TRUCK WAS a pokey little 7.5-tonner, but its load area was just large enough to accommodate the TVR. That night, we reversed it up to the raised concrete platform used by customs to gain access to the back of lorries and inspect their loads. I bounced the TVR up a rough grass verge onto the platform, and inched it into the back of the lorry. The paperwork was done, the car sealed in, and we passed through Costa Rican customs, and on into the night.

After a week living in no man's land, sleeping in the car, my ordeal was over.

Or was it?

30. VICTORY

29th November 2017
11°12'N, 85°36'W. Peñas Blancas,
Nicaragua/Costa Rica border.

IT WAS TEN in the evening when we finally cleared customs into Costa Rica and got under way. We drove for an hour into the night before Hrjairo, my driver, who was in his mid-twenties, decided to stop for a coffee. Me? I had a beer. I felt I'd earned it. Then we drove on for a bit before sleeping in the cab for a few hours, and then pushing on through the day, our worlds blurred by fatigue. It was late afternoon when we reached the border with Panama and rolled up to customs, intent on getting the car released and unloaded. How difficult could that be?

As it turned out, very difficult.

The people with the real power at the border had gone home for the day, and those who remained were unsure whether they should let the TVR in, because it was right-hand drive.

This was news to me. To my knowledge, no right-hand drive vehicle had ever been denied entry into Panama. In fact, I'd had an offer of help with this border from a guy who lived in Panama City and owned two Panamanian-registered, right-hand drive London black cabs. As I tried to negotiate the release of my cargo into Panama, only to find yet another brick wall going up, I could feel my willpower wilting. I'd done it; I'd gotten the car across Costa Rica. These further issues weren't supposed to be happening.

We were asked to come back the following day, so I checked us into a hotel at the border and bought Hrjairo and myself some much needed beers. But not before I'd showered: it had been over a week, and I smelt like a corpse.

CLEAN, RESTED AND refreshed, I returned to the border early the next morning, feeling far more confident.

"Right-hand drive cars *are* allowed into Panama," I kept telling myself. "I'm in the right here."

Unfortunately, the guy in charge of the border post disagreed. Once again overweight and with an air of arrogance about him – do these guys come off a production line or something? – I had a bad feeling about him right away. Through a translator, he told me what would be happening.

"You're going to have to take the car back to Nicaragua," he said. "It can't come into Panama."

"I can't take it back to Nicaragua," I explained. "They won't let it in."

"Okay, Honduras then."

"No," I pleaded. "I can't afford to have it trucked back to Honduras. It has to come into Panama."

"Where is it going after Panama?" he asked.

"To Colombia," I replied. "By ship to Cartagena."

"Right. The only way it can come into Panama is if the truck takes it directly to the port and unloads it there."

"That's another 500 kilometres on the truck, though. I can't afford that," I replied. "Look, no right-hand drive car has ever been denied entry into Panama. I've checked with lawyers in Panama City, and its legal here."

"You have your options," he replied. "This conversation is over."

And with that, he shut the door on me and walked away.

At that moment, I broke. I hit a wall.

For over a week, I'd hardly slept. I'd been doing everything I could to appear confident as I wrestled with a problem that felt far bigger than me. I'd been in a constant game of brinksmanship with the authorities and it had taken all my mental resources to keep going. It had been a battle, and when I loaded the car into that truck and left no man's land I thought I'd won. But that victory had just been smashed, and the struggle was suddenly back on, worse than ever. At that moment, I couldn't handle it, and I cracked.

I sat down on a concrete barrier under some stairs and for a moment, tears started rolling down my face. I was broken.

But I didn't have time for the luxury of self-pity. The truck had already been tied up on this job for longer than the company had planned, and Hrjairo's boss was putting pressure on him to unload my car and get the truck back to Nicaragua.

The problem was that the only place to unload it was at the bonded customs warehouse, about a kilometre up the road. We headed there with the lorry. As we drove, it seemed that Hrjairo had picked up some English in our time together.

"Fuck Panama,' he said enthusiastically. 'Fuck, fuck Panama."

I thought he made a very valid point.

At the warehouse, Hrjairo went into the offices to try to get permission to unload Kermit: effectively abandoning myself and the car at a government warehouse. While he was in the offices, I sent a rather desperate message to Helge, a Norwegian who was living in Panama, who'd got in touch when I was at the previous border to say that if I had any issues getting into Panama, let him know.

"I'll speak to a few people, and see what I can do," came his reply.

I didn't hold out much hope. The door had been slammed in my face very decisively, and I was pretty much out of options. I had the truck company demanding more money, Hrjairo eager to get away, and I honestly didn't know what to do.

And then I received another message from Helge, suggesting I go back to the customs offices, and ask if anything's changed.

And so, summoning my last dregs of willpower, I dragged myself back over to the border, and headed for the customs offices.

The door swung open as I approached. The customs officer who'd been so blunt with me was stood there, but his swagger had left him. He looked nervous, almost subservient, and was definitely paler than the last time I'd seen him. Amazingly, he could speak a little English now, which he had clearly refused to do before.

"Come in," he said, beckoning me into his office. "Can I get you a drink?

There's no problem, we'll have your car unloaded and on the road within half an hour."

"Okay," I said, "so there's no problem?"

"No problem," he replied. "Give me the papers and we'll get started. Is there anything else we can help you with?"

"No, just the car," I replied.

And he was true to his word. Within half an hour all the paperwork was complete, the truck's cargo was released, and the car was insured and temporarily imported onto Panama's road network. I headed back to the customs depot, and Hrjairo reversed the truck to the unloading platform. A burble of exhaust noise, and Kermit was free once again. We said our goodbyes, and I was free to go.

While I was doing this, I received a reply from Helge, who I'd messaged asking just how he'd managed to turn things around so suddenly.

It read: "Well, I'm friends with the father of the Vice-President. I had a word with him, he had a word with his daughter, and a call was made."

So, that explained it. The all-powerful border guard had received a phone call from the office of the Vice President, 'suggesting' they let the little green sports car in.

No wonder they all looked a bit shocked. They must have been wondering who the hell I was.

PEOPLE OFTEN ASK me how I coped during those ten days stuck between borders, with everything going against me – especially in light of the depression that had been defining my life before I hit the road. The answer is, except for that low point when I thought I'd snatched defeat from the jaws of victory, and everything seemed lost at the Panamanian border, it wasn't really an issue. In fact, the continuous stresses of the journey leading up to that point, trying to progress while best balancing the various aspirations of all the people on the trip and stay under budget were far tougher on my mental health. Once the border issues began, it was only me, the TVR and the task in hand. The simplicity of life made it easy to cope with, and I actually found myself sailing through the experience fairly serenely. I guess the moral is that with depression, lots of small niggles in life can be far more debilitating than one big issue. Or maybe I just take some perverse pleasure in getting into – and then out of – sticky situations. As Brummy is rather prone to saying: "if everyone else is standing in shit, Ben will be the only one laying in it."

* * *

HELGE TURNED OUT to be a bit of a legend. Not only did he get the country's second-in-command to help me out at the border, but he actually came up to the border himself to make sure I made it through okay. I met him there as I was finishing off the paperwork.

"Thanks so much for the help, Helge," I said. "I don't know what I'd have done without you."

"Oh, it's nothing," he replied. "It's how we do things here. If someone is in trouble, we help them. And I know that guy at the border, he's corrupt for sure. Some of them are great, but he's not one of the good ones."

We drove down to the town of David, where Helge introduced me to some of his other friends, who all knew of my predicament and had been poised to offer me any help they could. After a night in a hotel we carried on to Helge's house, about an hour from Panama City, where his wife was making a wonderful homecooked dinner for us.

Following my ten-day border ordeal, I'd definitely landed on my feet.

Helge had moved out from Norway many years before, and had created a good life for himself in Central America. He'd built his spacious bungalow from scratch, and it was filled with mementos and reminders from his life back in Norway.

It reminded us of Pub2Pub's earliest weeks, when fellow TVR owners in Norway had offered us their hospitality and made us feel at home as we were adjusting to life on the road. Now I was adjusting to life in Panama, and the welcome I received from those who'd sought to help me through my border issues made me feel like a minor celebrity.

But I still had a few more miles to go to complete the Central American leg of the journey. From Helge's house, I rolled across the Bridge of the Americas and in the midst of a torrential cloudburst, I found myself looking down upon the Panama Canal. Ships were making their way through this channel between the oceans while out to sea, many dozens more were sat awaiting their turn. It was one of the world's great construction projects, stretched out beneath me, and it marked a milestone in the trip. With 16,500 miles and 17 countries complete, only the South American continent now stood between the southernmost bar and myself.

To say I was happy would be an understatement.

I rode high through my time in Panama City. I went for coffee with the Vice President's father, and was interviewed on the only English language radio station. I met up with Barry, the ex-pat who owns several right-hand drive London cabs, and got my first go behind the wheel of one, out on

Panama Bay. I wandered the old town and the glorious modern waterfront. And with Helge, I visited a Christmas party for disadvantaged children laid on by Shriners International, a philanthropic group that he's a member of. When the moment came, I took the TVR to the Panama Canal's northern end, dropped it off at the Port of Manzanillo to be shipped past the Darien Gap, took the bus back to the city, and hopped on the next flight to Colombia.

SOUTH AMERICA

CUBA

GUATEMALA
HONDURAS

North
Atlantic
Ocean

Caribbean Sea

COSTA
RICA

Cartagena

VENEZUELA

Filandia

COLOMBIA

ECUADOR

Cuenca

Lima

PERU

BRAZIL

Cuzco

BOLIVIA

La Paz

Uyuni

URUGUAY

Buenos
Aires

Montevideo

South
Pacific
Ocean

ARGENTINA

South
Atlantic
Ocean

Santiago

CHILE

Falkland
Islands

Punta Arenas

Puerto Williams

Cape Horn

31. WAITING

10th December 2017
10°25'N, 75°32'W. Cartagena, Colombia.

THE OLD COLONIAL towns of Latin America all have an incontestable charm about them. The low rise charisma, spacious squares, laid back bars and towering churches create a welcoming atmosphere that immediately sets you at ease. However, after a while, their charms can merge into one and when you look back on your trip it can be difficult to tell them apart, so similar is the pattern to which they're built. As the months go by, you find your memories tangled into a state of slight confusion.

Was it Leon or Granada that had that great juice bar in the Plaza de Armas?

Where was it that we saw that awesome old Ford Cortina? Was it Antigua or Viejo Panama? Or maybe even El Fuerte, way back in Mexico?

After a while, it's the backdrop of these proud towns which anchors them in your mind, as this is the only characteristic which guarantees their uniqueness. It's the volcanoes towering above Antigua and the lakefront setting of Granada, which sets them apart, rather than the buildings themselves. This sameness is obviously selling short the unique charms of these places, which are all certainly worth a visit, but after so long in Central America, and especially after a month in Nicaragua, watching the clock tick down in such places, it felt like all these towns were built to the same rule book.

And when I alighted in Colombia, I found myself in the exception that proves the rule.

Yes, just like the continent to which it once served as a major gateway, the old town of Cartagena stands apart from the cities of Central America. It rises proudly next to the sea, unlike the towns earlier on our route, which seemed to hide inland. Rather than administration, its *raison d'être* was trade. And boy, they must have been good at it, because it's clear that in its day, this was one rich piece of real estate.

Compared to the other colonial towns we'd visited, the buildings stand taller, the balconies jut out with pride, and the swagger and confidence of the place is more convincing. The old port through which the money once flowed still stands preserved, and several replicas of famous sailing ships were moored at its quays during my visit.

The omnipresent wealth made this jewel in the crown of Spain's American Empire a place of potential rich pickings, coveted by everyone. Pirates were never far away, seeking to prey on either the galleons that carried plunder back to Spain, or the huge stockpiles of treasure held within the city. Even Francis Drake had a go, laying siege to Cartagena a few years before he sailed out of Plymouth to humiliate the Spanish Armada.

But this was no pacifist city resigned to its fate. The defensive walls and vast forts made it the best defended place in the Americas, and it weathered many sieges and assaults. Its history is one of blood and riches, of plunder and resilience. The endless silver of the Potosi mines flooded through on its journey to finance the Old World, and slaves from Africa flowed in the other direction, keeping Spain's imperial machine in motion.

What a stirring place from which to start my South American odyssey!

IT'S FORTUNATE THAT easy-going Cartagena is such a pleasant place to pass the time because, as it turned out, I was there for quite a while. What should have been a simple one or two day passage for the container ship to deliver the TVR to Cartagena's modern port, ended up taking nearer ten days, thanks to the vessel breaking down in Jamaica. A week after I arrived in Cartagena, Kermit was still sat in a metal box on the quay in Panama, as I wondered whether it would ever make it to South America, given all the obstacles that had been thrown up in its path recently. When it was finally loaded onto the ship, I half expected the vessel to sink in a final act of defiance.

Kermit was to be shipped around the roadless, impenetrable Darien Gap in a 40-foot container, which it was sharing with a BMW motorbike that was being ridden from Costa Rica to Ushuaia, and a Mexican couple's old Toyota hatchback, which was making a similar journey. One Friday, a week after arriving in Cartagena, we were all told the shipment had arrived and so set about getting it released. As the only non-Spanish speaker in the group, I very much took the back seat in this, as we rushed around with our shipping agent, jumping through all the countless bureaucratic hoops thrown up by the shipping company, customs, the port police and the port company itself.

We started the process bright and early on the Friday morning, with the goal of getting our vehicles released before the port shut on Saturday afternoon. Unfortunately, one and a half days of solid paperwork counts for little in this part of the world, and when Saturday lunchtime came, we were still a long way from even getting the container opened up. We resumed the battle early on Monday morning and were finally clear of the port and on the road in South America as the sun set that evening.

After all the issues I'd faced in the previous months – the cancelled ships, border issues, battles with authority, and this last delay getting Kermit out of Panama, it felt like an incredible victory. I was finally on the road in South America – the same continent as the southernmost bar.

All I had to do now was keep on driving south until I ran out of land. How hard could that be?

As it turns out, if you happen to find yourself driving south across Colombia, the answer is 'very,' because Colombia's topography doesn't exactly lend itself to rapid progress.

Colombia represents the northern extreme of The Andes mountain range, which would be dominating much of our progress in the coming months. And if Colombia was anything to go by, it wouldn't be easy. The main road south often climbed to almost 3000 metres, twisting left and right through the dense jungle. Out-of-breath trucks wheezed up the gradients at walking pace, while the twisty broken tarmac presented such poor sight lines that overtaking was often impossible, even with a four-litre V8 under your right foot.

Often, before the day's drive I'd look at the mapping on my phone, and it would suggest I'd be looking at an average speed of barely 20 miles per hour.

"I'll be the judge of that," I'd say to myself, striding confidently over to my thoroughbred sports car.

But the terrain always won, and I never did manage to beat the clock.

This wouldn't have been such a frustration if it wasn't for the fact that Colombia is a pretty damn big place. It's almost twice the size of Spain and if you tried to drive across Spain on twisting roads at 20 miles per hour, you'd probably get frustrated rather quickly, too. From Cartagena, the border with Ecuador was over 1000 miles away. That's a lot of hours behind the wheel. Alone in the TVR, which had now been my home for almost six months, I set about putting those miles behind me.

The roads weren't solely to blame for the initially frustrating lack of progress across Colombia, as navigation had become an issue too. I'd been finding my way around using Google Maps on my phone and this approach had worked reasonably well in Central America, where the Pan-American Highway offered the only real way across countries. However, in South America, where a web of roads of variable quality criss-cross the continent, it was often out of its depth. One way systems weren't recorded, leading to many frustrating detours in cities, and more annoyingly, it had no idea what the road conditions were like on the routes it planned. While this was often a minor frustration, with small detours from the main road on gravel or broken tarmac being suggested, on a few occasions it went wrong far more spectacularly. Such as the time in Medellín, when it tried to take me up the side of a mountain.

Now, Medellín doesn't have the best reputation. Back when Pablo Escobar's Medellín Cartel had made it the epicentre for the world's cocaine trade, it was the most murderous city in the world and every policeman had a $1000 price on their head. It's not like that now, but even so, driving through the run-down outskirts in a fancy green sports car still focuses the mind. So when Google began taking me through what felt like little more than a shanty-town during its quest to reach the main road to Bogatá, I may have wound the windows up a bit. The decaying buildings thinned out and the broken tarmac became rough cobblestones as the road climbed steeply, before changing to washed-out gravel and bedrock as it steepened yet again. I found myself crawling in first gear, slipping the clutch, with no chance to turn around and the underside of the car scraping almost continuously. But I could see the main road a few hundred metres above and so I pushed on as the conditions worsened. Large, sharp rocks began to appear on the road, and the burning smell from my clutch began to overpower that coming from the engine, which, thanks to the slow climb, was running hotter than it had in Death Valley.

And then I rounded a corner to find a bloke with a hoe, building the road.

I stopped about ten metres from him with smoke billowing from the clutch, and he stopped work and stared at this strange apparition from another world as it emerged from its own smoke screen.

In an exchange of broken Spanish, I established that there was no way to continue. The main road was close but in my low slung steed, it was about as attainable as the moon. There was only one thing for it. Several hundred metres of reversing through the jagged rocks to the first turning point, followed by an engine-cooling coast back down to the edge of town.

After all that, followed by another hour sat cooking under the sun in a superheated traffic jam, I was in such a bad mood with Google and the Colombian driving experience that I decided to sack off my original plan of going to Bogatá, via Pablo Escobar's enormous old mansion, where a herd of hippos roam and his original drug-smuggling aeroplane stands above the entrance gate, painted with zebra stripes.

He was clearly a guy with good taste.

As the clock ticked down towards Christmas, I decided a visit would have to wait for another time. I headed on south past the now-peaceful city centre and its enormous shopping centres, bound for Filandia.

32. A CHRISTMAS TALE

19th December 2017
6°57'N, 75°24'W. Yarumal, Colombia.

THERE'S ONE THING they don't tell you about Colombia: it's beautiful.

But then I guess talk of beauty doesn't sell newspapers. No, talk of drug wars, FARC kidnappings, and mass executions makes for far better copy if you're looking to draw people in. And while I'm not about to gloss over this aspect of Colombia's history, for it is definitely a part of life here, to become overly focussed on this one side of things would be to negate what it's really like to explore this unlucky country. And personally, I'd rather dwell on the mesmerising lushness of the scenery rather than the atrocities it may once have concealed. I'd rather focus on current Medellín's economic boom, rather than the research that once found that over 5000 of the city's residents were apparently paid to commit murder on at least one occasion during their youth.

Because as I travelled south, Colombia felt like a nation on the up, a place that would soon be seeing its time in the sun, that had been denied it for so long. A year before my visit, a peace deal had been signed between the FARC rebels and the government, bringing the decades-long insurgency to an end. The economy has performed well, with growth averaging over four per cent in the 21st century, and inflation has been kept reasonably in check. And if the crowds of free-spending tourists who packed out Cartagena are anything to go by, foreigners have decided that when it comes to finally checking out Colombia, the time is now. Yes, the Colombia I was driving across felt like a very different place to the one I'd read about in the news – except for a rather stressful few minutes to the south of Medellín, when thanks again to Google I found myself driving through a cocoa plantation, with every property in sight hidden behind tall, fortifying walls topped with barbed wire.

I treated Google maps with the utmost scepticism after that little detour.

* * *

HAVING PASSED THROUGH the tiny town of Filandia, I swung right onto a rough gravel track and started bouncing along at walking pace towards the evening's destination. Apparently it was a mile or two up the track, but that's pretty much all the help I had. I inched along the wet surface at a snail's pace, very aware that this wasn't exactly what Peter Wheeler had in mind when he'd designed the TVR Chimaera 25 years earlier.

A motorbike swung around the corner ahead, coming towards me. Its effortless progress showed just how out of place my TVR was here, though when the rider noticed the green sports car coming towards her, she did seem to wobble slightly with surprise. She pulled alongside my open window.

"Nice car," she said in greeting, her English accent rather unexpected in the circumstances.

"Thanks. The roads here don't seem to agree though," I replied.

"True, you soon get used to them though. Are you here for Steel Horse?"

"I am indeed. Am I in the right area?"

"Yeah, another mile up the track and it's on your right. I'm Yvette, I'm running the place over the winter. Are you here for Christmas?"

"Yeah, if that's okay?"

"I'm sure we'll fit you in. I'm just off into town for some supplies now, but if you head to the finca now, I'll be there in about half an hour."

"Sounds good, see you soon," I replied, continuing along the axle-twisting track.

YVETTE AND HER boyfriend had founded the Steel Horse Colombia hostel the previous year, when, having completed their motorcycle tour of South America, the prospect of returning to the grey UK in search of jobs didn't really appeal. So instead of joining the rat race, their solution was to ask themselves, where on their journey was the place they missed the most? The answer was the coffee-growing region around Filandia, and so they returned and bought an old farmhouse, with the goal of founding an overlander's retreat, which offers a taste of back home for those whose current home is the road.

They don't advertise, instead relying on the word of mouth which flows up and down the Pan-American Highway to draw people in. And that's how I'd found out about the place, with another overlander named Julie Tuck inviting me to come and join the Christmas party.

Set over two levels, the sprawling house was now everything a homesick overlander could ask for, and was a magnet for the motorcycles, 4x4s, trucks and converted vans that most people use for this type of extended journey. I pulled up and found that my TVR suddenly looked rather incongruous, as the only other two vehicles there were an enormous American pick-up with a camper conversion in its flatbed, and a huge blue Iveco 4x4 van named 'Cuthbert,' in which Julie and her husband, Marcus, were touring the world.

The van was their home for the five years or so they were planning to be on the road, and it certainly looked the part for the journey it was undertaking. Its tyres were designed for the worst mud the Amazon could throw at it, its bumper-mounted winch inspired confidence, and its snorkel gave it a wading depth deeper than Kermit is tall. The back of the van had been converted into a living quarters and had all the comforts you'd expect from such a thorough conversion, with the highlight for me being the seemingly unlimited supply of Yorkshire tea they offered. Every morning at Steel Horse, my day would begin with a successful attempt to scrounge a decent cuppa off these well-equipped roving Brits.

By Christmas Eve, the small courtyard had filled to capacity as other overlanders arrived. There was an old-fashioned Volkswagen campervan from Brazil, a Toyota Land Cruiser from Switzerland, a 4x4 Volkswagen van from Spain, and a British couple in a huge Chevrolet van in which they'd built a home, then named 'Elvis.' The assembled vehicles showed that when it comes to overlanding, there's more than one way to skin a cat – even if the TVR was still very much the outlier.

I was at Steel Horse for five days, and my time there turned out to be one of the highlights of the trip. Yvette was a great host, and each evening we'd all club in for a communal meal or BBQ. Christmas Eve saw us heading to one of the outbuildings after dark to throw heavy metal weights at targets made of gunpowder. If this sounds mildly ill-advised to you, you're probably right, but rest assured, it's the basic premise behind Colombia's national sport – Tejo, where teams aim to score points by exploding the gunpowder targets.

My top tip if you ever find yourself playing Tejo? Go easy on the beer. Once you can't remember how many bottles you've had, it becomes much more difficult.

Christmas Day was as close as you'll get to a British Christmas in rural Colombia. A roast dinner, an endless supply of beer, a game of Cards Against Humanity and a Hugh Grant movie to end the day. Meanwhile, the cows kept on grazing in the garden, the dogs argued among themselves and chased passing cars, and the cat kept sneaking into the bedrooms for some peace and quiet.

But when the clock ticks over to Boxing Day, how do you keep a traditional British Christmas rolling? With a day at the races, that's how. Yvette had a horse, I had a TVR, and rural Colombia had plenty of fields in which a duel could be held. We settled on a race from a standing start across a field which from the driver's seat, felt more like a ridge, with sharp drops on both sides of our path.

Having set one of the slowest times of the day last time I'd raced the TVR, back in Amarillo, Texas, I sure as hell wasn't going to let a horse beat me. And so, with our friends from Christmas Day watching, and Marcus and Julie's drone hovering overhead, we did battle. And what we found out was a statement of the bleeding obvious – a 240 horsepower TVR can beat a one horsepower horse in a straight line. But still, it was fun finding out.

We had three races, with the TVR experiencing varying degrees of lurid oversteer on the muddy surface, before the drone was crashed into a tree. After retrieving it, we called it a day and headed back to the finca, my head filled with glorious memories of speeding across a Colombian field with a horse to my right, dogs running all around and the V8 roaring away just in front of me.

Boxing Day was notable for one other thing. Kermit and I gained a travelling companion. Alvaro was a Colombian photojournalist who'd heard about the trip months earlier and got in touch to see whether it would be possible to tag along. I had a seat free for the South American leg and so I extended an invite. He arrived at Steel Horse on Boxing Day morning, keen to be part of the TVR's journey for as far as his funds would allow.

Fashionably dressed, with thin-rimmed spectacles and a rather studious style, Alvaro didn't exactly look like the adventurous sort, ready to take on the world as we battled our way across the Andes. But, glancing around the 20-odd people who'd assembled at Steel Horse for Christmas, neither did the rest of us. I've always found overlanding to be a very relaxed pursuit, open to anyone – not just grizzled bikers and mud-wrestling 4x4 types. As a Colombian local who'd spent the previous year using his incredible photography skills to record Latin America's esoteric car culture, I knew Alvaro would not only make for a great co-driver, but he'd also be able to document our South American adventure in a compelling manner too.

The following morning, after an extremely refreshing five days off the road, Alvaro and I checked Kermit over before waving our new-found friends goodbye as we bounced down the rough track back to Filandia, and then hit the road to Cali.

33. THE COLOMBIAN SOUTH

27th December 2017
3°26′N, 76°31′W. Cali, Colombia.

CALI IS MANY things to many people. To the locals, it's the beating heart of Colombia, where the religion is salsa and life is lived flat-out. To outsiders, it's a drugs cartel which once controlled 90 per cent of the world's cocaine market and was one of the most powerful crime syndicates the world has ever seen. And to me? It was the place where I finally got under the surface of car culture in Latin America.

How? Well, I have Alvaro to thank for that. There's very little homegrown automotive journalism in Colombia, meaning that those who do spread the word – such as Alvaro – are reasonably well known among the enthusiasts. So, the day before we headed to Cali, Alvaro got in touch with a few of the car clubs based there and suggested a meet up. When we arrived in the city, we were met by a 1950s American pickup truck which led us to our first port of call – a local businessman's collection of British classic cars. An anonymous door opened on a warehouse packed with classic Triumphs, MGs, Minis and Rovers, all in such good condition that they made Kermit look like something the cat had dragged in.

We spent an hour at the collection, but the fast-paced Spanish that characterised the conversations meant I left none the wiser as to its significance. The petrolhead pattern continued when we arrived at the hostel we'd be staying at. On seeing Kermit, the hostel owner showed us his fleet – a pristine 1970s convertible Mercedes SL living under a cover and in the garage, a far-from-pristine '60s Impala. This was clearly a city that loved cars.

As if to prove the point, later that evening, some friends of Alvaro, named Caesar and Juan, arrived outside the hostel in their early '80s BMW 5-series. We all piled in and were taken to the local garage where their car club loved to hang out into the early hours. Plenty of BMWs were in evidence, in varying states of restoration, along with some classic Americana, a few Japanese steeds from the 1980s, and even one and a half Model A Fords – just a chassis and engine counts as half a car, right? The walls were hung with motoring memorabilia, the workbenches scattered with parts under restoration. The place had an energy. It wasn't some showy garage, polished to perfection. It was somewhere real, where people worked hard for their dreams and cars were brought back to life, better than ever.

It's not remotely what I'd imagined a visit to Cali would entail.

After checking out the garage, we jumped into a pair of classic BMWs and a 1980s Honda and headed up into the hills for a late dinner. The road twisted skyward, and soon the city was a shining sweep of lights in the valley below. The perfect backdrop for a pizza and a beer at what was clearly one of Cali's best kept secrets. Once again, the Spanish flowed fast and free, but it didn't really matter to me. I'd come to one of the most infamous cities there is, and the local car enthusiasts had seen me as one of their own and taken it upon themselves to show me their world. As we rolled back down the hill into town I felt deeply content with life. The best travel experiences are those times when you unexpectedly find yourself getting beneath the surface of a place. To do that in the company of some great locals, from the back seat of a cherished early '80s BMW, well it doesn't get much better than that.

THE ROAD TO Pasto was a bit faster flowing than those further north – not that that's saying much. It still took us a full day to complete the 240 miles, partly thanks to a landslide which had severed the road at about half distance. However, luckily, more dangerous obstacles to our progress were kept at bay. Colombia's southern region near the border with Ecuador, still hasn't really calmed down after the recent ceasefire with FARC and as a result, the Pan-American Highway is heavily guarded, making it the only reasonably safe route down into the rest of South America. And when I say heavily guarded, I mean it. There were soldiers everywhere. You couldn't drive more than a kilometre without seeing a conscript by the side of the road. Now, you'd imagine this would create a rather tense atmosphere, but it actually had quite the opposite effect, as the soldiers all had orders to give a thumbs up to the passing motorists, so we sped along exchanging gestures of approval with what seemed like the entire Colombian Army. Whenever we drove past an army base, there were always at least 20 soldiers standing out front, flicking the thumb. To be honest, it was all rather surreal.

The reason for these thumbs up stems from the fact that during the rather dirty war with FARC, it wasn't only the rebels committing atrocities. In a world where it's impossible to tell civilian from guerrilla fighter, and where a Machiavellian approach had become an accepted tactic, some of the less moral corners of the army would occasionally be less than fussy when it came to filling their quotas of slain enemies. And over the years, trust between the armed forces and the public had slowly broken down.

This was the solution – eye contact and positive gestures. And while it sounds ridiculous, the two-way interaction seemed to work.

So for hundreds of miles we drove through a soldier-lined jungle, and it all felt very safe. The danger clearly wasn't over yet though. Sandbags and machine gun positions still lined the road, it's just that the soldiers now stood in front of them gesturing, rather than hiding behind them with their tin hats on. Colombia didn't have half its army deployed to the verge of the Pan-American Highway solely for PR purposes; they were there to maintain the new-found status-quo.

Pasto was a tight and gritty city of half a million people, 2500 metres up in the Andes. We arrived long after dark in the midst of a heavy downpour and set about finding a hostel for the night. It wasn't easy, as the biggest event of the year was about to kick off – the *Carnaval de Negros y Blancos*. I never did get to the bottom of what this mildly racist-sounding event was all about, but from the extensive setting-up that was going on when we arrived, it involves carnival floats, live music, lots of paint and foam being hurled around, and beer. Lots of beer.

It was a shame we couldn't hang around for another few days and be part of it, but we had to get going. It was late December, and I wanted to reach the southernmost pub by mid February, but we hadn't even made it out of the Northern Hemisphere yet. So the following morning we rolled onwards, through the mountains and past the gesturing soldiers, to the border with Ecuador.

34. THE VOLCANO

29th December 2017
0°48'N, 77°39'W. Ipiales, Colombia.

THE BORDER POST at Ipiales was tucked away in a charming river valley, but like most borders there was very little that was charming about the process of crossing it. In fact, it turned out to be one of the worst borders of the trip, albeit some way behind the Costa Rican and Panamanian crossings.

Leaving Colombia ended up taking a couple of hours, such was the queue for immigration, with the already high numbers of people travelling for Christmas or New Year being swollen by Venezuelan refugees, escaping their country's meltdown by entering Colombia before heading in a southerly direction.

But getting out of Colombia was nothing in comparison to getting into Ecuador. We queued for two and a half hours just to get our passports stamped. And then there was the car – again just getting to the window at customs to process the temporary import was almost an hour's work. The total time spent getting across, including buying insurance and grabbing a dinner of rice and fried chicken in a run-down restaurant on the Ecuadorian side was eight hours. Darkness was total by the time we actually rolled out into Pub2Pub's 20th country.

Ecuador handsomely rewarded our patience with unexpectedly perfect tarmac, well lit and impeccably marked roads and most excitingly, petrol at 24p per litre. Some TVR owners spend their whole lives dreaming of such good fortune. We headed to the old colonial town of San Gabriel, found a hotel with somewhere safe to park a TVR overnight, and then grabbed a full tank of gas, followed by a beer to celebrate making it across the border.

WE WERE RAPIDLY approaching one of the seminal moments of the entire expedition – the moment when we would cross the most famous datum of them all. The Equator. It would be a time to take stock of all we'd achieved. To look back with dignity and pride on battles won and obstacles overcome. And we were in the perfect place for it, for it was here, in 1739, that the members of the French Geodesic Mission first established the location of the Equator and hence were able to calculate the Earth's circumference. Their discovery eventually gave Ecuador its name. With these deep thoughts of great discovery and achievement in our minds, we pulled up to the modestly-named Mitad del Mundo – the middle of the world – ready to be humbled by the gravitas and dignity of this unique spot.

The tourist shops came quickly as we approached the monument. Dozens of them, all run by Ecuadorians in old-fashioned indigenous dress, each one selling exactly the same rubbish as the last. A fake llama farm sat next to the shops, looking strangely out of place. We approached the monument along a paved avenue, where kitschy fibreglass hummingbirds were spread among the busts of the expedition members – none of whom ever even visited this spot. Perhaps if they had, they could have pointed out that the monument hadn't actually been built on the Equator. The real line was apparently 240 metres away from the arbitrary line of yellow paint on which people queued to take their selfies, in front of the stone tower topped with a bronze globe, which apparently marked the centre of the world. We'd come looking for dignity, but instead we'd found cringe and profiteering.

"Okay, let's get out of here," said Alvaro, after about half an hour.

"I'm with you on that suggestion," I replied.

WHEN YOU PLAN a trip like this, you can never predict the moments that will disappoint, and those that will stay with you forever. Who could have predicted that the country named after the Equator would get a monument to it so wrong? Not me, that's for sure. But conversely, there are moments you never expect to blow you away, which end up touching your soul. One of those moments occurred the evening after our visit to the Mitad del Mundo.

The evening hadn't started well. We'd got hopelessly lost attempting to navigate through Ecuador's capital, Quito. Was it our fault, or Google's? I'm calling a draw, though I have to add that when Google tried to navigate our TVR down a flight of stairs for the second time in 20 minutes, Alvaro and I both saw the funny side. Obviously, our smartphones had decided to up the ante from sending us the wrong way along one-way streets, or up the side of mountains.

But eventually, we escaped the polluted melee of Quito and were heading south as the light began to fade. The hills to either side of the road towered high above us, restricting our view as we motored along. Then we swung around a corner and there it was, shimmering like perfection right in front of us.

The 5897-metre high cone of the Cotopaxi volcano cascaded down from the milky sky, its snow-clad slopes drifting to pink as the sun eased downwards. Wisps of smoke rose from the summit and lingered in the still evening air, gently hinting at the primeval power which lay hidden under the surface. Beneath the snowline, the mountain spread out into dark, rolling hills shaped by the ash showers and lava flows of millennia. To say it was an arresting view would be an understatement.

We pulled over and watched as the dusk light played upon the volcano. Channels and gullies formed by lava and rain stood out from the face as the sunlight caught them, while the clear air became infused with a wash of orange. We stood for a long time, watching the subtle interplay of light and shadow as it brought the captivating scene to life.

As we watched, a group of about a dozen local Ecuadorians wandered towards us. All were dressed in outlandishly garish jumpsuits and their faces were hidden behind masks shaped to look like monsters. Some members of the crowd carried the Ecuadorian flag, others fake rifles, while their most enterprising member had a collection bowl. As they approached they made muffled roars and growls through their masks, waved their arms in the air and pranced with a confident swagger, really getting into their monster role-play with conviction.

Despite appearances, the 12 monsters were friendly enough, especially once we'd made a donation. Their startling presence was part of the New Year's celebrations, which had clearly started a day early, and they were working their way through the various cars that had pulled over to admire the view, entertaining and collecting donations in equal measure. It was pretty clear they were having a great time.

After almost an hour parked by the road, being terrorised by monsters as the volcano loomed overhead, we climbed back into the TVR and carried on, driving into the landscape that had so enticed us from afar. That night, we stayed in a quiet guesthouse in the shadow of the mountain, and lingered on a chilly balcony late into the night, pointing our cameras at the snow-clad pyramid that towered above us into the starry sky.

Predictably, Alvaro's photos turned out to be way better than mine. No surprise there, then.

35. THE WASHOUT

31st December 2017
0°55'S, 78°36'W. Latacunga, Ecuador.

NEW YEAR'S EVE in this part of the world is definitely a big deal, and it had begun days earlier when we were driving down the boulevard of gesturing policemen back in Colombia. There, a carnival atmosphere had prevailed in many small villages, as locals in fancy dress stopped cars to demand a token donation. No donation meant you'd probably have a water balloon thrown at your car, and Kermit suffered a few direct hits that tested the watertightness of the hood to the limit. Beyond the limit, in fact. We'd known it wasn't watertight ever since Nicaragua when one particularly severe monsoon storm had resulted in me having to bail out the driver's footwell the following morning. But I digress.

These slightly comical attacks had given way to roaming packs of monsters once we'd crossed the border into Ecuador, and a sense of excitement about the upcoming, worldwide party was everywhere. And given all the hype we were rather excited too, as we rolled into the town of Latacunga, checked into a hostel, got Kermit parked somewhere secure, and went out to see what was in store for us that evening.

A large stage was being set up in the town's rain-soaked park, ready for an evening of live music, and as we'd finally left the world of mariachi behind, the thought of such a performance no longer filled me with terror. Many of the town's young men had taken the opportunity to dress in drag, complete with high heels and wigs, and were theatrically holding up traffic for donations. The shops were all full of face masks and figurines made of straw stuffed into old clothes and then made to look like either someone you dislike, or someone from popular culture. These 'old year effigy dolls' are burned at midnight, in a gesture designed to cleanse the negatives of the previous year from your life. Local politicians were a popular choice on whom to base them, as was Donald Trump. And it finally made sense that for the previous few days, we'd been seeing cars going past with near-life size Homer Simpsons or Shakiras strapped to the roof.

In Latacunga, some people clearly couldn't wait for the New Year and were already burning their dolls in the street during the afternoon. I guess 2018 couldn't come too soon for these folk.

The buzz seemed to have taken hold of everyone and the only things in town that mattered were the celebrations. Beer was already being drunk, the cafés were packed, and a truly memorable evening seemed in order.

At 5pm a chill breeze swept down from the mountains and the heavens opened. It wasn't the sort of rain you could ignore, not the sort of drizzle that you'd brave anyway. It completely dominated the experience of going outside, and it didn't let up. It rained right through the night.

Alvaro and I stayed in the hostel waiting for it to clear, but it didn't. And so cold and repelling was it that we never made it out to see what was happening at the now-almost-certainly-flooded park. We stayed in the hostel, talking cars, travel and music. We discovered a mutual appreciation for the humble Renault 4, I introduced him to the music of Muse and Feeder, and he got me up to speed on the Colombian music scene.

At midnight, the rain was heavier than ever. The distant detonations of a few fireworks echoed through the malevolent darkness and then our Ecuadorian New Year was over.

You win some, you lose some, I guess.

* * *

ECUADOR IS A wonderful place in which to have a TVR at your disposal. Up in the highlands, where the vegetation seems thinner than in Colombia, the traffic lighter and the roads better, it's a glorious place to drive. And that's before you pull into the petrol station and see fuel at $1.50 a gallon.

Whereas in Colombia, the Pan-American Highway had felt stunted by the landscape, and the progress across it had always felt hard-won, in Ecuador the subtly different topography meant the road seemed to flow with the terrain, rather than fight it. And with Kermit, driving along through the chill thin air, it was simply a great place to be. Timeless villages would come and go, always run down and with a gritty realism that made them seem charming, as if they saw the futility of trying too hard to impress. Clouds billowed around the ridges and summits above the road, sometimes sweeping down to encase us in a white tunnel. Animals grazed next to the tarmac on any patch of land flat enough to accommodate them, cows tethered to posts and flocks of sheep watched over by children. Occasionally we'd pass through a town, where a chaos of cobbled streets and ramshackle buildings would serve to thoroughly confuse Google Maps until we'd felt our way through to the other side. And just when we thought we knew the score, Ecuador would find some way to surprise us, be it with haunting volcanoes, monster-suited locals, or excessively kitsch tourist attractions.

In the city of Cuenca, the surprise took a different tangent, when we met up with a rather unlikely group of car enthusiasts – the Japanese Car Club of Ecuador. And in Ecuador, the Japanese car scene isn't all about the little Mazdas and Imprezas that we see back home. No, it focuses on a rather more utilitarian steed – the humble Datsun pickup truck.

But these guys really went to town with them. The engines had been souped up, the suspension lowered, the bodywork sharpened with a liberal application of the JDM style, and everything about them was as pristine as any cherished classic back home. We slotted Kermit into a convoy of six of these little beasts and went speeding around the town, taking in the sights two and a half kilometres above sea level. By the end of the visit, I was almost tempted to buy one until I heard the price they sell for. Fully restored? £8000 to £10,000. Even a standard one in reasonable condition would set you back £4000. And so the dream rapidly forming – of returning to Ecuador one day and buying one to explore the country more thoroughly – was put back on the shelf. After all, a Colombian Renault 4 could be had for less than half the price.

* * *

CUENCA WAS A very pretty town and it was a shame to pull ourselves away, but we'd set ourselves the goal of reaching Lima, in Peru, in time for the start of the Dakar Rally. This rather compelling mission gave us four days to complete about 1000 miles of driving on uncertain roads, and also negotiate the border crossing into Peru. Overly ambitious? We hit the road to find out, heading first through dizzying valleys to the southern Ecuadorian town of Machala – which made the rather heady claim of being the 'Banana Capital of the World' – before carrying on to the next international frontier, where Peru began.

36. THE DESERT

03rd January 2018
3°29'S, 80°13'W. Huaquillas, Ecuador.

THERE'S ONE THING you need to know if you're planning to drive across Peru. It's big. We're talking around 40 hours and over 1500 miles of driving to get from the border with Ecuador, down to Chile or Bolivia. While the sheer scale of the countries we were now crossing made me nostalgic for the more modestly proportioned nations of Central America, which could be driven across in a day, a masochistic part of me enjoys getting to grips with the big distances and watching them shrink as progress is made.

As I continued across South America, with milestones such as the Equator and various borders falling behind me, I began to take more interest in the big picture. Earlier in the trip, the enormity of what I was doing seemed so complete that I never really thought of where I was in the journey, or how far it was to the end. The figures were so large they became meaningless to me, except in a very arbitrary way. For instance, I remember, in Mexico, looking at the distance covered and working out that I'd completed one Mongol Rally and still had two more to go to reach the finish. The Mongol Rally is a yearly event that involves driving from England to Mongolia, and it was my first big trip. Now, I was effectively completing three of those drives back-to-back, which is a cool thing to ponder, but ultimately doesn't mean much.

Continued on page 193

An old taste of empire. A very British welcome for a very British car at the Belize border.

A Honduran pothole.

Volcán de Fuego smoking above the Colonial town of Antigua, Guatemala.

Living the Latin American trucker life while trapped
between the Nicaraguan and Costa Rican border.

Sunset over the Pacific, at San Juan del Sur, Nicaragua.

Changing the clutch in Managua, Nicaragua – the only major work the TVR required during its 27,000-mile trip.

Kermit at the Costa Rica/Panama border.

Life in no man's land. My home for a week.

Kermit looking right at home in a collection of classic British cars in Cali, Colombia.

The streets of Cartagena, Colombia.

Lost on the dirt tracks near Medellín, Colombia.

A day at the races:
I spent Boxing Day racing a horse
across a field in Filandia, rural Colombia.

Rounding a corner to come face to
face with the 5897m high Volcán
Cotopaxi, in Ecuador.

Ecuadorians all dressed up to celebrate New Year's Eve.

Meeting up with the Japanese car club of Cuenca, Ecuador, and their fine fleet of Datsun pickups.

A break in the monotony of crossing Peru's coastal desert.

Getting our UNESCO on with a visit to Peru's world famous Nazca lines.

Sports car heaven. A glimpse of the amazing driving roads that climb up onto the Altiplano between Nazca and Cuzco.

Looking across the historic streets of Cuzco, near Machu Picchu, Peru.

Exploring the highest capital city on Earth – La Paz, capital of Bolivia, 3650m above sea level.

Spending the afternoon with the Antique Car Club of Cuzco, and their varied selection of vehicles.

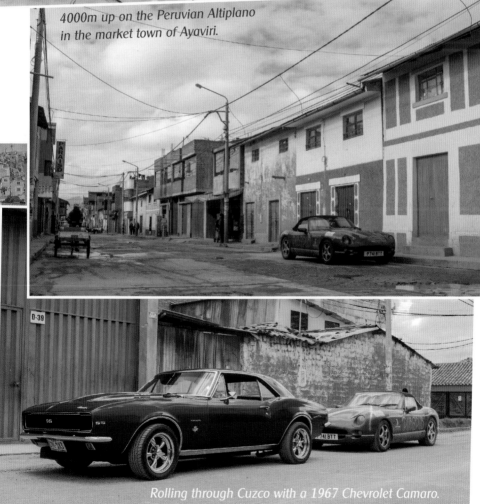

4000m up on the Peruvian Altiplano in the market town of Ayaviri.

Rolling through Cuzco with a 1967 Chevrolet Camaro.

Meeting the relics of another time. Steam trains rotting in the desert near Uyuni, southern Bolivia.

Caution – llamas. Crossing southern Bolivia, en-route to the Chilean border.

Driving the Salar de Uyuni, in southern Bolivia. The largest salt flat in the world, during rainy season it floods, turning its surface into a mirror.

Another shot from southern Bolivia.

El Mano del Deseirto – the hand of the desert – a sculpture located in the Atacama Desert, designed to emphasise human vulnerability in this unforgiving landscape.

Closing in on the disputed Falkland Islands as we cross Argentina.

Rolling over the plains of Argentinean Patagonia.

The advancing face of the Perito Moreno Glacier, Patagonia.

Moonrise over Bariloche, Patagonia.

Brooding skies over the Drake Passage, as we take a ship down through Tierra del Fuego, to the southernmost bar.

Bar Analij – the southernmost bar.

Big sky country on Argentina's answer to Route 66. Ruta 40, seen here in Southern Patagonia.

Grabbing a beer in the world's southernmost bar.

On the campsite in Santa Cruz, Patagonia, during the long drive back up to Uruguay.

Kermit's first evening back in the UK – at the Maypole Inn in Yapton, Sussex.

Kermit taking pride of place at the TVR Car Club 'season opener' at Burghley.

TVRs lined up at the finish line at the Two Bridges Hotel, Dartmoor, eight and a half months and 27,000 miles since starting the journey there.

However, now I was in South America, and on the same continent as the southernmost bar, the distances had became a lot more real and I started to obsess over them. Every morning during breakfast, checking our progress became part of my routine. Using Google, I could see how far it was to the southernmost bar, how many hours of driving I could expect, and how it compared to what I'd covered since I'd arrived in Cartagena a few weeks before. My mind would play the figures over, working out percentages and daily averages. Having been on the road for six months already, for the first time the final destination felt within reach, and I was beginning to obsess about getting there.

But it was still most of a continent away. That 1500 mile drive across Peru was just the beginning. Beyond that there was Bolivia, Chile and Argentina to cross. To reach the southernmost bar, I was looking at a total of around 6000 miles, but with six months and over 17,000 miles already behind me, that still counted as 'near.'

I still had to take the drive stage by stage, though. Leg by leg, mile by mile. On the worst roads, I wouldn't be thinking beyond the next pothole or speedbump.

"Just get past there," I'd tell myself, "and then worry about what's next. If you keep doing that, eventually you'll reach better tarmac."

This mental focus was good for my mind, which I was aware had not found the continuous, cumulative pressures of the trip easy. My sanctuary became these calculations and the close attention that the driving demanded. Because when your whole world is focussing on negotiating a rough track or a confusing city, you don't have the extra capacity to be depressed. I think focussing on distances and progress was a kind of therapy, which kept my mental issues in check. As we drove, I'd count down the distance to the day's destination, juggling the numbers in my mind.

"85 kilometres to Chimbote. That's 62 minus nine miles, so 53 miles. We're averaging about 50 miles an hour, so add in a little bit for getting into town, and we'll be at the hostel in about an hour and 20. So, just after 7pm."

I'd play the numbers through my mind in this manner dozens of times each day, delighting in our progress as I felt the final bar draw closer. Every distance sign at the side of the road would trigger an avalanche of mental arithmetic. However, don't take this obsessing with the destination to imply I wasn't enjoying the journey – I was. I guess it was just a bit of a coping mechanism to relax my mind and keep it occupied so it wouldn't drift onto other less appealing subjects and begin to ruminate, as my idle mind was wont to do.

* * *

THE ROAD TO Lima is long and dusty; 1000 miles of reasonably smooth tarmac crossing Peru's coastal desert. It's a surreal place. Sand eddies across the road, sometimes blowing in through Kermit's open windows from the dry land all around. Dunes bulk upwards, sculpted by the wind into unique, bulbous shapes. The air acquires a chill, unexpected when the Equator is still only a few hundred miles to the north. And as you drive, the Pacific Ocean often flits into view to your right, the breakers rolling in to stain the parched sands.

With the world's largest ocean to your side and the rainforests barely having left your rear view mirror, it's an utterly surreal place. A blank, empty strip of land, sandwiched between two worlds that seethe with life.

But there's one part of this landscape in which life is abundant. It is home to almost ten million people and covers over 1000 square miles. It's one of Latin America's great cities, and it's called Lima.

If you put ten million people together in one place, you're guaranteed one thing. Traffic. Even 20 miles out, the roads were filled to capacity. Everyone hustled to get ahead as they sped along through the fumes and dust, flowing around the buses that would suddenly stop in the road, and seemingly oblivious to people crossing as the melee surged around them. It was dark as we entered the city, Alvaro wrestling with the navigation as I played chicken with the late rush hour traffic. The frantic intensity, the bright lights, and the sensation of urgency were invigorating after so long out in the coastal desert, counting down the miles at a steady 55 miles per hour. We swung around taxi-choked roundabouts, growled along the boulevards, and watched the engine temperature gauge with interest when progress was halted by the weight of traffic. After a full day on the road, it got incredibly hot beneath the insulating fibreglass bonnet, and so it always felt like there was little margin for error when rolling into a big city after a ten-hour day but despite this, we never overheated.

Back in 20th-century Blackpool, they were building much tougher cars than most people realise.

But our visit to Lima wouldn't be altogether devoid of car-related shenanigans, and there were a few things we'd need to see to in the coming days. But first, we had to navigate our way to the hostel in Miraflores and relax. After all, we'd just driven to the capital of Peru in a 20-year-old TVR. That's got to be worth a beer, right?

HELICOPTERS HUNG MOTIONLESS overhead as the crowd drifted towards the brightly-coloured flags and banners which packed out the area. We followed them, heading to the start line of one of the more esoteric yet awesome sporting events out there – the Dakar Rally.

The idea behind the rally is simple. You can enter on a motorbike or quad bike, in a 4x4 or even in a truck, but whatever machinery you bring along, you're going to have to complete over 5000 miles in 14 days, much of it off-road, and much of it against the clock. Fatalities aren't unheard of and in many years, only half of the entrants make it to the finish line.

And there I was, thinking Pub2Pub was a hardcore undertaking.

The start of the event is as much a parade as anything else, with each of the 335 entrants rolling past the crowds before taking their position at the official start line, then being waved off into the adventure. It was great to see the machinery up close, each vehicle having been pushed to the limits of what's possible when it comes to fit-for-purpose engineering designed to take on a desert at speed. Kermit felt incredibly compromised in comparison, especially when I visualised it next to one of the Russian Kamaz trucks, which sported a crew of three, packed almost 1000 horsepower, and tipped the scales at around 18 tonnes. Serious stuff.

Our original plan was to travel up to Bolivia with the rally, spectating on some of the off-road legs, and generally soaking up the atmosphere of this most rarefied of motorsports. However, the more we thought about the option of racing off in pursuit of Carlos Sainz and co, the more we realised that discretion is the better part of valour, and we really should give the car some TLC before unleashing it against the Peruvian Altiplano; we'd be in Lima for another few days.

The main reason for this was that Kermit had developed its first major issue since the slipping clutch. When pulling away from a speed bump or traffic light, a distinct judder could now be felt through the drivetrain. Was it a broken engine mount, or maybe a warped clutch plate? Or perhaps we were down a cylinder or two and hadn't noticed? Whatever it was, it made sense to get it looked into before we left the largest city for some time, a reasoning which only got stronger when we found out there was an independent Land Rover garage on the other side of town. One Monday morning, we ended our routine of taking lazy walks around the waterfront area of Miraflores and took the car to have it checked over.

The garage may not have been pretty, having a distinctly back-street, oil-and-rag vibe about it, but it didn't take them long to find the issue. One of the ballasting resistors on the distributor had failed and a couple of the plug extenders were shorting out, meaning that, at times – generally under load –

we were dropping down to five or six cylinders. This unbalanced the engine enough to cause the judder. The garage couldn't source spare parts so we simply took out the resistor and removed the plug extenders, insulating the leads by wrapping them in gaffa tape. While this isn't generally the way TVR owners tend to approach repairs, I was feeling rather bullish. After all, it only had to cover another 6000 miles and it would be back in Europe. Could it cover 6000 miles like that? Sure it could. Onwards we went, with my faith that Kermit was going to go the distance remaining unshaken.

37. THE ALTIPLANO

10th January 2018
14°49'S, 74°56'W. Nazca, Peru.

WE'D DRIVEN ON for six hours since leaving Lima and found ourselves in a rocky plain that stretched for miles beneath the mottled grey sky. The colour seemed bleached from the landscape, which was rendered only in graduations of an unattractive sandy brown. Anonymous hills rose in the distance, visible in outline only, their detail hidden by the dust in the air.

We had somehow stumbled into a landscape even more coarse and unwelcoming than the coastal desert through which we'd driven for days to get to Lima. At least there the sand brought a softness to the landscape, and wherever you are in the world, there's a romance to driving among sand dunes, an air of the exotic. Here though, there was only a rocky plain across which the chill wind howled, as bleak and unforgiving as the moon.

But we were so glad our journey had led us here.

We climbed the staircase which led to the observation tower's small viewing platform. The metal structure shook with hollow vibrations as we did so, focussing on the steps beneath our feet as we spiralled up. When there was no more height to be gained, we looked out across the empty wasteland, and the glorious treasures that were etched into its surface.

Directly beneath us, the stylised outline of a tree stretched out across the bone-dry ground. Almost 100 metres across, the shape had been cut into the earth millennia ago by digging away the mottled-brown topsoil to reveal the lighter earth below. Next to the tree, a pair of hands had been dug into the desert's surface. There was also a lizard, its body severed by the Pan-

American Highway that passed through the site. Signs of more geoglyphs hewn from the gravelly earth stretched into the distance.

We were looking out across the famous Nazca Lines, and if we're honest, we didn't quite know what to make of them.

We weren't the only ones, as these enigmatic relics have baffled many archaeologists over the years. There are hundreds of designs and the trenches that form them have a combined length of over 800 miles; but what was the purpose of this massive undertaking? No-one knows for sure. Some say they are aligned to perform celestial observations; others believe they are designed to be seen by deities high above. But ultimately, no-one really knows.

Just like the TVR's ongoing reliability, the lines remain an enigma to be debated by future scholars ad infinitum.

THERE AREN'T MANY places in South America whose names carry more historical gravitas than Nazca, but the morning after viewing the lines, we hit the road to one of them – Cuzco. Former capital of the ancient Inca Empire, and gateway to the famous lost city of Machu Picchu, this exotic city sits over three kilometres above sea level and was once the centre of an empire that stretched all the way from Colombia to Chile's Atacama Desert. It sits in my mind as one of those places whose exotic allure is infinite, and is every bit the equal to the mysteries of Llasa or Timbuktu, Samarkand or Bagan. What a destination to be travelling to!

But road trips aren't about the destination, they're about the journey. And somehow, the drive to Cuzco turned out to be even more memorable than the place itself.

Shortly after we'd left Nazca, the road hit the sheer wall of Peru's Altiplano. The sand and gravel landscape thrust up into the sky and the colour green made a welcome return as we began our climb up onto one of the world's largest plateaus, an otherworldly place that stretches for thousands of miles through the thin air, between 3000 and 4000 metres above sea level.

The road took this challenge head-on, twisting and turning as it rose, sometimes flowing through fast open corners that teetered above the abyss, at other times contorting into stacked hairpins that could be attacked at ten tenths. The TVR felt good after its fettling in Lima a few days earlier so I drove enthusiastically. There was almost no traffic and the front tyres squealed with understeer as we entered the tightest hairpins, while, with all the weight in the boot, the car's rear end felt planted as we accelerated out of them.

As we climbed higher, the temperature dropped and the view opened out, the parched yellow hills spilling back down to the coastal desert far beneath us. But I was aware of this only in passing, as my concentration was on the road, pushing hard as this perfect ribbon of tarmac cycled beneath my perfect car and the mysterious city of Cuzco drew closer.

A few hours after leaving Nazca, we found ourselves four kilometres above sea level, in a completely different world. We'd reached the Altiplano. Shallow lakes dotted the rolling grassy plain, while snowcapped mountains reached higher around us. Llamas and vicuñas grazed by the roadside, their herders never far away. The sky felt close now, the low cloud sweeping down to meet us and occasionally strafing Kermit with barrages of rain. We roared through this magnificent landscape for hour after hour, the TVR feeling completely at home as its sporting and grand touring credentials merged into one. And how was I feeling? All was good in my world, as I was having the best driving day of my life.

Ten hours of this motoring perfection saw us in the tatty town of Cachora, where ramshackle buildings lean against each other on the edge of an Andean ridge. We found a hotel and went for food, and as the adrenaline wore off for the first time that day I realised just how tired I was. But sat in the mouldering front room of a run-down house in this shambolic corner of Peru, drinking Inca Cola as chicken cooked on an open fire, I realised something else: there was nowhere else I'd rather be. I was in the middle of the adventure, living life by the moment, a perfect car at my disposal, and the perfect landscape in which to enjoy it.

The following day, another four hours of hairpins and vistas would take us to the legendary capital of the Incas. I smiled at the thought. Aren't moments like that what life is all about?

EVERYONE TAKES THEIR own unique memories away from a visit to Cuzco. For some, the highlight is exploring the richly storied streets and plazas, which bask in over a thousand years of history. For others, it will be the hallowed side trip to the most famous lost city of them all – Machu Picchu. And for me? Easy. What on earth could possibly be more memorable than cruising around the former capital of the Inca Empire in convoy with a raucously loud '67 Chevrolet Camaro?

Once again, Alvaro's contact list had come through for us, and we met up with the Club Automovil Antiguo Del Cuzco on our second day there. And a very wide-ranging bunch they were too, bringing everything from the Camaro to a Lotus Seven, from a '20s Ford pickup to an MGB sports car. And obviously, with this being Peru, they brought a bottle of Pisco too, and the enduring friendship between the car enthusiasts of Peru, Colombia and the UK was toasted very thoroughly.

Thanks to a landslide taking out the railway, we never did make it to the lost city of Machu Picchu, but that didn't really seem to matter. For the 1.4 million people who visit every year, it's surely the highlight of their time in this part of the world, but somehow I doubt I would have found it any more memorable than roaring around town with that midnight blue '67 Chevy, before making new friends over shots of Pisco while admiring the assembled classic metal in this far flung corner of Peru.

Cuzco, you did yourself proud.

IT HAD BEEN raining for hours: heavy, mountain rain that seemed to sheet across the landscape, chilling the air as it soaked everything. The headlights of the oncoming traffic dazzled as the wipers struggled to clear the windscreen, which misted up continuously as our TVR's watertightness was overcome by the onslaught. The downpour went on for hours as we rolled east through the thin air, eventually clearing as we approached the day's highpoint – the 4338m high Abra la Raya pass.

But the weather wasn't about to let us complete the day without another challenge. It built up ominously on the horizon over the empty plain as the sun set. A bulging black cloud spread itself across our path, blocky downpours connecting it to the ground, and lightning lashing out to the empty plain below. We had to brave it as there was only one road. We rolled on towards our fate.

Beneath the cloud, the darkness was almost total. Only a smudge of light spanning the horizon reached us from the world beyond. The rain came thicker and the lightning became more frequent. And there was nothing else there to attract it: just us, the soaking tarmac and the vast emptiness of the plain around us.

We drove on nervously, hoping our luck would hold. It seemed to take forever to make it through the maelstrom as the lightning slowly closed in on our metal-framed machine, but eventually we emerged unscathed into a world where the sanctuary of a small Quechua town glowed on the horizon. We headed there, and rolled through muddy, flooded streets past dimly lit buildings tinged with sadness, until we found a hotel.

They say the highs of life are better appreciated when you have the contrasting lows, and looking back, as I drifted off to sleep in that neglected town four kilometres up on the Altiplano, that day's hard won miles contrasted with the drive to Cuzco so completely that they made it seem all the sweeter.

38. BOLIVIA

16th January 2018
16°14'S, 69°17'W. Lake Titicaca, Peru.

THE SPARKLING, CRYSTAL blueness stretched away into the distance, shimmering in the rain-washed air. A few small boats towed their wakes through the vastness, but there was nothing else between us and the horizon. The appearance of purity, brought on by the altitude, was hypnotising. We were driving along the shores of Lake Titicaca, and thanks to the air being one third thinner than it is at sea level, I'd never seen anywhere like it before. The highest navigable body of water in the world, Lake Titicaca exists 3800 metres up in the Andean sky. We rolled on in silence towards the Bolivian border, soaking up the strange beauty all around us.

But we never reached the border. About ten miles from the frontier, the villagers were hard at work, building a road block. Just before we'd arrived, in a frenzy of activity they'd dragged boulders, rocks and turf across the tarmac, sealing off the main road between Peru and Bolivia. And with their work complete, they stood back and admired it, chatting and joking to each other as the lightly trafficked road came to a halt.

They looked an unlikely group to be taking such action. The women were dressed in traditional Quechua clothes, all bright pastel colours, wide-brimmed hats and woollens, while the men wore cheap Chinese copies of western clothes. But however they looked, they'd done it. They'd stopped the traffic. Alvaro went and had a chat with them to see what the score was.

"They're angry because one of their political leaders – their favourite political leader – has been arrested and thrown in jail for corruption," he said. "This guy fights for them in Lima, they say, so they're protesting against the arrest."

"Will they let us through?" I asked.

"No," was the predictable answer.

We waited for about an hour. The police popped down, took a look at what was happening and went away again. Alvaro chatted to some of the truck drivers, and was told that last time, this merry band managed to close the road for three days. I looked at the map. There was another road into

Bolivia, which took a less frequented border crossing up by the lake. We did a U-turn, headed along the shores of Lake Titicaca for one last time, and then crossed the border.

IF YOU'VE BEEN in South America for a while and you feel like you're getting to know the place, head to Bolivia. Then prepare to have everything you thought you knew turned on its head. This is the one nation on our route across South America which stands apart, an unpredictable place that walks to its own beat, always with pride but sometimes with a hint of sadness as well.

It's one of those places where you're never quite sure what's going to happen next, and after a while nothing that happens will surprise you anymore. If you thought an Ecuadorian New Year was a trifle strange, you haven't seen anything yet.

A market run by witches, where you can buy a dried llama foetus to bury in the foundations of your newly-built house for luck? Yes, that's perfectly normal here. Police cars that were originally stolen in Chile, then smuggled across the border to start a new life with the Bolivian coppers? Well, why not? Middle-aged, professional female wrestlers in bowler hats, battering each other in the ring? It's big business in La Paz. And for the pièce de résistance, how about a president who was once a coca grower, and who, on gaining the presidency, promptly threw out the US National Drugs Administration and declared it every Bolivian's right to grow coca? It happened, and there's even a Coca museum in La Paz, complete with a mock-up of a cocaine lab and a mannequin masquerading as a TV-stealing addict. Yes, this is Latin America wrought weird and raw. And that's what makes it so exciting.

We rolled into La Paz late in the evening and promptly spent several hours stuck in chaotic traffic jams that were going nowhere, trying to negotiate the unfathomable neighbourhoods that clung to the city's precipitous slopes. La Paz lies over three kilometres up, in a steep-sided bowl, which traps the pollution and makes driving a nightmare. It's under control though. The Bolivian government has deployed a small army of people dressed in zebra costumes to stand at intersections, calming the traffic and apparently helping it flow. And no, I'm not making this up. Meanwhile, the sensible people had shunned the zebras' good intentions and were travelling high above us, in the cable cars which climb to the bowl's rim.

By the time we'd fought our way through to the place where we were staying, we were exhausted, but we were also curious about this crazy place around us. So, when someone suggested heading out for a beer, who were we to argue?

IF YOU'RE ON a road trip and you find yourself in La Paz, there's only really one road in town – the much hyped 'most dangerous road in the world.' Its official title is the North Yungas Road, but the world knows it by an altogether more sobering moniker: Death Road.

The highway packs a lot into its 40-odd miles. Starting 4700 metres above sea level, the mostly gravel surface plummets from the mountains into the steaming jungle, as it weaves down to its finish at an altitude of 1300 metres. But what makes it famous, and what's really given it its reputation, is the drop which lies just to your left as you make your descent.

Yes, for much of its distance, the road, which is generally between three and four metres wide, terminates in a sheer unguarded drop into the tree canopy, up to 600 metres below. The other side of this vertiginous track is generally a sheer rock face, meaning there's no escape. If you make a mistake, you're either in the rock face or plummeting into the abyss.

No wonder that at the height of its notoriety, the road was claiming up to 300 lives a year.

Back in those bad old days, the North Yungas Road was the main route out of La Paz to the north east. Today, however, a bypass is in operation, meaning the risk of taking to the air while avoiding a head-on collision with a badly-driven bus is much reduced. Despite this, it still focuses the mind, and Alvaro in particular was concerned, particularly when the morning dawned with forecasts of rain.

"I'm not comfortable driving it in the rain. We need to be careful," he told me over breakfast.

"I agree, this isn't the place to try something stupid. We'll go up there, and if the rain is too bad, we won't drive it."

"Okay. I'm nervous of the risk," he said, agitated.

We finished our coffees and headed up the hill out of La Paz, to our date with Death Road.

AT 4700 METRES the rain fell ominously, soaking both the tarmac and the police checkpoints where we were half-heartedly checked for drugs as we passed. We rolled through the spray as torrents of water gushed down from the rock faces above. We weren't on Death Road yet, but even so, the omens weren't good.

When we arrived at the turn-off that led onto the famous road, we stopped for a chat. The rain had eased back to drizzle but the surface was still wet. Looking ahead as the track ran innocuously away from us, I felt perfectly comfortable. I'd driven plenty of bad roads in my time. I'd teetered above abysses at the handlebars of an auto-rickshaw in the Himalayas, battled across mud and gravel in Africa, and surfed along sandy tracks in Kazakhstan. It was situations like this that I lived for and my confidence in such situations is complete.

"Come on, Alvaro, let's do it."

"Okay, I guess so," he replied, unconvinced.

"It'll be fine, trust me. I'm sure I've driven worse before, and we can always come back if it gets too bad."

With that, I checked the engine's fluids, gave the tyres the once over, and set off down Death Road in my TVR.

It started innocently enough, a gravel track lined with tall grasses and broken cliffs. But very soon, such pleasantries were left behind, and the road opened up into the spectacular drive-in-the-sky experience that has made it so famous. Vertical cliffs hundreds of metres high soared above us to our right, sometimes unleashing waterfalls that fell directly onto the road, making it very much a roof-on undertaking. To our left, there was air. Clouds swirled ominously below us in the abyss, sometimes ballooning up in greeting, sometimes clearing to reveal the jungle canopy far below. Between the sheer cliff and the plunging drop was our world, about three and a half metres wide, hewn from rough gravel, and sweeping left and right as the landscape dictated.

My approach to safely negotiating the road was simple. I ignored the drop. It's a similar mental tactic to that used in rock climbing, where if you focus on the fact you're in a difficult situation, you're far more likely to fall than you are if you blank it out and focus solely on the climbing. So, I did exactly that. I treated Death Road as just another 40-mile gravel track and drove it sensibly in that manner. Admittedly, this approach terrified Alvaro on a few occasions, when I put the wheels of his side of the car within inches of the drop while negotiating particularly rough sections of the road, but still. Over 20,000 miles into the trip, I was so familiar with the car that knowing exactly where the wheels were wasn't a problem. Despite the hype this road receives, our descent turned out to be most smooth and uneventful in the end. The few oncoming vehicles were easily passed, and we had plenty of opportunities to enjoy the view – even if I generally refused to get out of the car, given how bad the handbrake is, and how the engine was sometimes reluctant to restart at altitude, because let's face it, it would have been a shame to lose Kermit over the edge after all we'd been through. But the scenery was immense. The eagle's eye view afforded to us by the road gave us a magnificent perspective out across the near-impenetrable mountains and jungle, which raced away to the horizon. For most of the road, we descended in a relaxed manner, enjoying the scenery, stopping for photos, and slowly picking out the best line across the rough surface. Even the two small rivers that required fording near the bottom didn't present the TVR with any issues and we put Death Road behind us with minimal stress, and not even a single death.

BACK IN LA Paz that evening, we headed out to celebrate, and characteristically, Bolivia threw us another one of its curveballs. Alvaro and I were sat having a few beers with some other European travellers who were in a similarly positive mood, having descended Death Road on mountain bikes that day, when they suggested heading to another bar, with a glint in their eyes.

"Come on, it'll be fun," our new-found friends told us. "You haven't seen La Paz until you've seen this place."

"I'm not sure," said Alvaro. "What sort of bar is it?"

"You'll see when you get there. Trust us."

"Sod it," I said. "Sounds interesting, let's check it out."

We left the hostel and jumped in a taxi that was waiting outside. Our friends told the taxi driver to take us to 'Route 36,' and away we went, speeding through the seedy, unloved streets of the world's highest – and weirdest – capital.

The taxi driver dropped us in an anonymous street, with little illumination for the mouldering buildings. Rain was falling very lightly and an unsmiling guy was stood next to an unmarked door, oblivious to the dampness.

The taxi driver said something to him and he nodded, beckoning us inside. We went up the stairs of a scruffy hallway, our friends confident and Alvaro and I somewhat more cautious, and were met by two more serious-looking locals, to whom we each paid 20 Bolivianos to enter.

Inside the room it was almost dark. A few customers were sitting at tables, talking excitedly. A makeshift bar stood in the corner, looking like it had been thrown down a few days ago. In fact, as I glanced around, I could see that everything looked similarly makeshift. The whole bar, the furniture, the wall coverings, it was all transitory.

And then I noticed that nobody was drinking. Each dimly-lit table had a couple of plastic plates on it. And on each plate, there were a few lines of white powder. Suddenly, the shifty-looking, fast-talking clientele made sense.

We were in that jewel in Bolivia's touristic crown – La Paz's illegal cocaine bar.

Anywhere else in the world, this experience would seem somewhat odd, but in Bolivia, where strange is the new normal, it made perfect sense. Route 36 has been running under the radar for years, moving location every few weeks and not allowing locals in, to avoid blowing its cover. However, as the taxi drivers seemed to know where it is from week to week, the chances are the authorities do too, which suggests that it only remains open due to the influence of someone with a fair bit of power, or the bribery of someone with a fair bit of money.

We were shown to a table and a waitress (is it still a waitress in a cocaine bar? Who knows?) came over to take our order. All the people we were with went for the standard order off the house menu – a gram of cocaine, artistically presented in four lines on a blue plastic plate. However, Alvaro and I have never had any interest in such illegal highs, so we each ordered a beer instead.

Whereas I was rather tickled by the whole experience, Alvaro was feeling somewhat uncomfortable – coming from a country that has been torn apart by the cocaine trade, that's understandable. We stayed for an hour or so, watching as our friends upped the conversational tempo and started talking through – rather than to – each other, and then we went to leave. The guy on the door kept us inside until the coast was clear and a taxi was sat outside then we were free to go into the rain-strafed night.

39. THE SALT SEA

19th January 2018
20°32'S, 66°50'W. Near Uyuni, Bolivia.

THERE WERE MOMENTS when I could have sworn we were back in New Mexico: the rolling green lands, dotted with hills and devoid of development; the long straight roads, alternating between two lanes and dual carriageway; and the big sky, dominating everything as it domed overhead with its scattering of thunderstorms. But there were signs we were in Bolivia, too.

Llamas, for instance, which aren't exactly ten a penny in the Midwest. Or the fact that every time we went into a petrol station, we had to bribe the attendant to sell us petrol at the local price, rather than the foreigner's rate – which was about three times higher. Or the times we were stopped by police and a pantomime of document checking and bribe-seeking ensued. And then there was that time when we were nearing Uyuni and a sudden snowstorm exploded overhead, leaving us driving in a whiteout for about 15 miles before we emerged into a soul-stirring sunset. Yeah, despite the Altiplano's similarity to some other landscapes, Bolivia still did things its own way. And there's nothing that defines Bolivia more in the eyes of the world than the landscape we were heading towards.

THE SALAR DE Uyuni is a place that had sat in my mind for years, intriguing me and beckoning me to visit. It's the world's largest salt flat, covering an area not far off the size of Northern Ireland. So what does that mean in terms of numbers? Ten billion tonnes of salt, in an area that measures 80 miles across and is so flat that NASA use it for calibrating their satellites. Compelling.

We simply had to drive it.

There was only one problem. Our visit coincided with the rainy season, and the salt flats were flooded.

Ever the optimist, I decided we should take a look anyway. We drove up to the access point which is the usual way onto the salt flats if you're visiting from Uyuni, but the signs weren't good. Almost every other vehicle was a Toyota Land Cruiser 4x4, ferrying tourists out onto this natural wonder of the world. The few folk not in Land Cruisers had gone one better, showing up in full-blown trucks. We were in our dainty little TVR and frankly, watching the big boys fording the runnels which had formed where the water was running off the salt flat, I didn't fancy our chances.

I parked by the first runnel and jumped out to take a closer look.

The view to the horizon was incredible. Nothing but an endless sheet of salt, covered by about an inch of water. I knew the TVR could handle that – its ground clearance wasn't that low. The problem was getting to it. As the water ran off the salt flat, it had cut several grooves in which it flowed freely, between 20 and 30 centimetres deep. The bottom of these grooves was soft salt, and the descent into and out of them wasn't exactly gradual.

I took my shoes off and paced them, feeling for a way across, but it all seemed too deep for the TVR, with the engine's air intake mounted vulnerably in the low-slung nose. If we got it wrong and drew water into

Kermit's big V8, we'd destroy the engine, and for what? The opportunity to drive a few miles on the flooded salt flat? When I first looked at what we'd have to drive through, it seemed an unjustifiable risk. However, unwilling to just leave, I wandered the problem area for about 15 minutes, imagining different routes through the waters, and as I did so, I could feel a cavalier confidence rising in me.

"Screw it, let's do it," I shouted over to Alvaro, who was clearly having similar thoughts.

"Yeah, let's," he replied.

So it was unanimous then. I put my shoes back on and ducked into the car.

The TVR may have lacked the ground clearance, wading depth, and four-wheel drive of our Land Cruiser-wielding friends, but it did have one big thing going for it – it trod lightly. Kermit's low weight and sports car wide tyres meant it put much less pressure on the salt than a Land Cruiser, and so could skim over soft areas where a big 4x4 might sink in and get stuck. I used this fact to my advantage to get past the first area of deep water, skimming over a waterlogged area of salt while everyone else was wading through a foot of water just upstream. Salt flew everywhere as I took this obstacle at speed, relying on momentum and lightness to carry me across the problem area successfully. With this first obstacle crossed, there were now two more runnels standing between Kermit and its release onto the endless expanse of salt. And there was no way around these two; the car would have to wade. So, I jammed the plastic lid off my food box in front of the engine's air intake so the water churned up by our bow wave wouldn't hit it directly, and then followed the line I'd mapped out on foot half an hour earlier. The car bounced around violently, salty water was hurled everywhere, and balancing the traction to climb out of the runnels was a very delicate act but somehow, it did it. Against the odds, and the advice of the Land Cruiser-driving masses, we'd made it onto the salt flat. I breathed a massive sigh of relief. The most stressful 40 minutes of the trip were behind me.

And after the tension of the briny water-crossings, what an incredible place to find ourselves! The thin layer of water had turned the salt flat into the world's largest mirror. The sky was reflected in the ground beneath us and the surface across which we were driving became an expanse of blue, dotted with dappled clouds. The horizon disappeared, the heavens and earth merged into one, and the sensation was very much one of driving in the sky. Those 40 minutes of stress and the high-stakes roll of the dice we'd played in getting the car out there had been very much worth it. We rolled around for an hour or so, soaking up the unique landscape, doing doughnuts, taking photos and savouring one of the most surreal and beautiful moments of the trip. Sometimes, we'd just stop, get out of the car and stare, saying nothing. The impact of the landscape was such that no words were necessary. And then, with our souls lifted higher than at any other stage of the trip, we attempted to drive back to the world beyond the surrealism. The engine began to splutter, running roughly before we ground to a halt. Dead on the salt.

Damn.

"What do you think it is?" asked Alvaro.

"It's probably just some water getting into the electrics. Hopefully once we've dried it out it'll fire right back up," I replied, crossing my fingers.

I opened the bonnet, and the first thing which struck me was that everything – literally everything – was covered in salt. It caked the exhausts, where it had been baked on, and had plastered the engine in a thick, briny layer. I set about cleaning all the electrical contacts, opening every connection and spraying excessive amounts of WD40. After ten minutes of this and a considerable amount of cranking, the engine burst into life once again and we retraced our route back to terra-firma.

Looking back, I'd never put Kermit through that sort of treatment again. It was a pretty terrible way to treat a classic car and it was as much by luck as judgement that we came out of the experience with no lasting damage. But do I regret it? Not one bit. Life is for the living and if you're almost four kilometres above sea level, roaring across the world's largest mirror in your pride-and-joy sports car, you're probably living pretty well. Even if the result had been a hefty garage bill it would've been worth it, just for those memories that will stay with me forever.

If you're a TVR owner, reading the last few pages has probably resulted in you breaking out in a cold sweat, as you imagine all the damage that salty water could do to the chassis. Well, rest assured the first thing we did once we got back into town was to spend an hour going over every inch of it with a pressure washer, hosing off all the corrosive salt. And as I write this a year and an MOT test after that incredible day when we drove in the sky, it seems like we got away with it.

SAFELY BACK IN Uyuni, with the car cleaner than ever and the memories of finally achieving my dream of driving Bolivia's salt flats still racing through my mind, I wandered among the wind-worn buildings of the melancholy town. The wide streets always felt strangely underpopulated, while the salt and sand of its surroundings tinted everything. It was the definition of a transit town; who'd want to live here, braving the cutting wind, thin air and omnipresent cold for years on end?

I surely wasn't the first of my people to have these thoughts, either. In the late 19th century, dozens of British engineers came to this bleak and remote corner of Bolivia, carrying with them the knowledge and expertise of the Industrial Revolution. They were here to drag the Altiplano into the steam age.

The mines around this part of Bolivia were rich, but transporting their spoils to the sea for shipment to world markets was a challenge. The coast was hundreds of miles away and almost four kilometres lower than the Altiplano. But the British were experts in railway construction and solved these issues, linking Uyuni to the sea ports of the Atacama's Pacific coast.

As well as the expertise, Britain also supplied the technology. Locomotives, built in Victorian steelworks half a world away, were shipped out to ply the tracks. They worked for their keep for half a century, climbing up and down from the coast until the mines were depleted and their *raison d'être* was gone.

They make for a forlorn sight today, sitting on the edge of town. Once proud and dynamic locomotives now sit abandoned in the desert, their patina of rust complete as they slowly dissolve in the salty air. We drove among them in the TVR, their weathered hulks towering over us as they sat in their final resting places, while rubbish from the town's nearby dump blew amongst them. Some had been stripped and were missing boilers or other parts, but most sat complete, proud reminders of a world which no longer existed.

It was time to go. We loaded up Kermit and drove on, past the graveyard of locomotives and out into the desert.

40. THE WILDERNESS

22nd January 2018
21°20'S, 67°28'W. Southern Bolivia.

AS WE SET off down the gravel track out of Uyuni, almost 300 miles and a border crossing lay between us and the next town, so we'd loaded the back of the TVR with supplies – food, water and five gallons of extra fuel. The route would take us across the northern edge of the other-worldly Salvador Dalí Desert, past steaming volcanoes, exposed salt flats, and sandstone rock formations which had been sculpted by millennia of wind and sand.

We were nervous as we set off. Did we have enough fuel and water? Was Kermit up to such a long stint off-tarmac? What would the conditions under our wheels be like? And what if we broke down? Memories of being stranded in African deserts flooded back to me as Uyuni disappeared in the rear view mirror.

It was a strange sensation given there were still thousands of miles to go, but this stretch of gravel through the uninhabited desert felt like the final hurdle. If Kermit was going to fail to go the distance, I was convinced this is where it would happen. I tried to flush the negative thoughts of my previous desert-crossing issues from my mind and focus on the driving, but they kept creeping back, niggling me.

The flatness relented as we drove, Uyuni's dustbowl giving way to mighty volcanoes shimmering on the horizon. The landscape was so vast and unfeatured, and the distances so great, that they'd stay with us for hours on end, as if we were on a ship, slowly steaming past some far-off mountain.

We drove for hours, the gravel smooth, the landscape gradually changing. Grey hills rose from the horizon, the haze washing out any colour from them until we drew closer and it relented, allowing their mottled rusty colours to show through. Some of them were volcanic and steam vented from fissures high in their sides. And then we noticed something.

We were making much better time than we'd anticipated. The Chilean border, which represented the halfway point of our drive from Uyuni to Calama, hoved into view. It was only just after lunchtime, yet we'd not expected to reach the border before nightfall. Trains clunked past on the nearby railway line as we wandered inside and began the paperwork.

It took a few hours to get into Chile. First, there was the predictable drugs inspection, with a very excitable dog clambering over every inch of Kermit. Given that the last three countries we'd passed through – Bolivia, Peru and Colombia – account for almost all the world's cocaine production, you can understand why the Chileans take this pretty seriously. The second delay was equally predictable: right-hand drive.

We were taken to the police station in the border village while the police checked their laws to see whether we were legal in their country. They spent 15 minutes pouring over the small print of their road traffic act, as I prepared for the battle which seemed to be coming. I'd had plenty of practice in

Central America, after all. This shouldn't be too hard.

But then with a smile and a signature on some paperwork, we were free to go.

"If he decides to overtake anything, make sure you're awake. You're the eyes," the policeman said to Alvaro as we wandered back to the car.

We'd not been able to find any information on the road conditions on the Chilean side of the border and so we were pleasantly surprised to find smooth tarmac speeding our progress. We didn't make it to Calama that night though, instead camping out in the Atacama Desert, beneath a sky filled with stars.

AFTER THE OFFBEAT weirdness of Bolivia, Chile felt like a return to Europe. In Calama, we found smooth, well-marked roads, courteous drivers, unblemished buildings, and an aura of prosperity we hadn't felt in weeks. Most exciting for me, however, was that we also found Shell V-Power fuel. Kermit would no longer be forced to exist on a diet of cheap Bolivian gas, its price bartered down by Alvaro and its usefulness driven up with octane booster. I filled the tank and paid for it on my credit card, which was another novelty.

We may have been picking up some European vibes, but our road trip was still very much a South American affair. We were in the driest desert on the planet – the Atacama. Nothing grew here. It was a huge swathe of emptiness, with only the occasional mine or astronomical observatory breaking the trend. Santiago, Chile's capital, was 1000 miles away, and for all its mod-cons and pleasantries, Calama was, well, kind of dull. It was time to hit the road again.

FOR DAYS, WE drove across the nothingness. Our companions on the tarmac were mining lorries and pick-up trucks, fuelling the wealth-extraction to our north. The landscape was gravel and sand. No life broke its absolute bleakness and it made for monotonous driving, where the biggest challenge was simply staying awake. Sometimes we'd pass a mangled vehicle that had speared off into the desert after its driver had failed the challenge. The authorities left these battered carcasses of vehicles where they came to rest as warnings to others.

After leaving Calama, we came upon a huge sculpture of a hand protruding from the desert. Standing 11 metres tall and finished in concrete, the sculpture symbolises the helplessness and vulnerability of man. I can't imagine a better setting in which to make such a statement as this, in the most inhospitable landscape I'd ever been through. We stopped and took some photos before continuing south, through a world where water doesn't exist, and 50 miles without so much as a signpost is the norm.

I normally love deserts, citing them as my favourite landscape, but this was just too much. To be visually appealing, a desert needs its monotony broken by a trace of life, a hint that the landscape is capable of being welcoming. The Atacama goes beyond this. While I'm sure other parts of it live up to their beautiful reputation, the bit we spent days driving through didn't bring to mind any romantic desert ideals. In my eyes it was simply a wasteland, where a dull hazy sky and washed out gravel plains combined to bleach any beauty from the vistas.

But nothing lasts forever. Following day after day of counting down the miles to Santiago, green began to creep back into our world. Not quite the rampant green that had accompanied much of the journey, but it didn't matter. It was a sign of progress. And the towns began to change, becoming less utilitarian and mining-focussed and more like the sort of place you'd actually want to explore. Trees began to appear and the mining machines that had dominated the roads to the north were replaced by normal folk going about their days, in their newish Korean or Japanese hatchbacks. Vibrancy was coming back into the world after the blandness of the north. Then we swept into Santiago, Chile's cosmopolitan capital city, and it all made sense.

41. ON CAR CULTURE

26th January 2018
33°22'S, 70°31'W. Santiago, Chile.

IT WAS ALMOST midnight and we were at a service station on the edge of Santiago. White light flooded the parking lot and as a few policemen looked on the cars rolled in. Every niche of car culture was represented. A gleaming white Nissan Skyline from the late '90s growled its way across the forecourt, followed by a classic Volkswagen Squareback. There were lowered Fiat Uno pick-ups, brand new Ford Focus STs, and perfect early Renault 5s which really caught my eye. This was the car scene in Chile stripped bare, a late night meet bringing the community together as one.

"It's pretty quiet tonight," explained Nick, our host – who randomly happened to own one of Chile's only Rover 75s. "Normally on a Thursday night you'll get some Porsches and more of the *Fast and Furious* stuff, but it's the holiday season at the moment, so lots of people aren't around."

His explanation tailed off as a particularly vocal Ford Mustang burbled past.

"The car scene in Chile is still pretty small," he continued. "It's growing, but interesting cars are so expensive here. There's a free trade area at Arica where they bring lots of stuff in from Japan, but by the time it's converted to left-hand drive and the import paperwork is done, the prices go crazy. You're looking at $10,000 for an old Miata, for instance. Still, everyone loves the Japanese stuff. And the scene is a bit different to what you have in the UK. Over there, there are so many enthusiasts that each group kinda does their own thing. The Porsche guys do their thing, the Japanese guys do theirs, and they don't really meet. Here, because it's a much smaller scene, everyone just gets together whatever. It doesn't matter what you drive. As long as you love cars, that's all that matters."

As he talked, and my jealousy for the lack of snobbery in the Chilean scene grew, the cars kept coming and going. At one end of the meet, the service station's car wash was doing a great trade getting the enthusiasts' cars looking their best. At the other end, a pitched battle seemed to be going on at the petrol pumps, where a few unlucky ordinary motorists had stopped for fuel, and were now trying to find a way past all the cherished metal and get back on the highway though it was impossible. Even on this 'quiet' night, so many cars had turned out for the meet that the parking lot was jammed and nobody was going anywhere fast. Except that is, the enthusiasts who were heading home, roaring back onto the road with maximum noise as the police looked on.

"It's fine," Nick told us. "If you do anything stupid the police will radio ahead and you'll be caught. But as long as you're sensible, there aren't any problems. We have a good relationship with the police."

At half past midnight the meet was still in full swing, with everyone enjoying the cool night air. But we had plans for the following day, and so we piled into Nick's car and eased our way back through the assorted precious metal and roaring exhausts, onto the road to our hostel.

IT WAS A petrolhead's dream. The garage workshop wasn't short of space, and they'd filled it well. A blood-red Ferrari 348 sat under a dust cover, next to a perfectly restored Chevrolet pick-up from the '50s, and a classic

Maserati. Opposite was parked a Rolls-Royce Silver Ghost, while down on the garage floor, work was in full swing. A Porsche 993 was up on the ramps for its annual service, and an AC Cobra replica had dropped by for a tune-up. A Mustang was in for a replacement engine, and as for the Morgan, well, the Morgan just sat there looking more than a little confused at being so far from home.

And who could blame it? Because really, who expects to find such a broad, impassioned petrolhead culture somewhere like Santiago? Not me, that's for sure, but the trip just kept on showing that car culture transcends country and race. It brings people together around a common interest, and that alone is something to be celebrated.

We left the workshop and walked across the street to a showroom. But this was a showroom with a difference, because none of the cars were for sale. They were being stored for wealthy collectors. Pride of place in the middle of the gleaming room was an Aston Martin One-77, a 740hp, $3,000,000 monster which certainly stole the show with its presence. And that was quite an achievement, as it sat in the middle of a masterclass of exotica: a Lamborghini Gallardo was to its left, a Ferrari Testarossa to its right, and other spots in the room were taken by everything from a Mercedes AMG race car to one of the Delorians used to film the *Back to the Future* movies. Chile could surely impress with some interesting motors, provided you knew where to look.

One of the obvious places to look is in the museums. We visited two during our time in Santiago. The Salon Antique Car Museum was first, and we were shown around the 400-strong collection by the museum's founder and owner, a flamboyant chap named Gabriel. And who would have thought this corner of Latin America would harbour such an extensive cross-section of historic vehicles? The collection had everything from Armstrong Siddeleys and Tatras to a T34 tank and a Volvo 240.

Next on the list was the Jedimar Museum. This houses a personal collection which has been amassed by the family who own one of Chile's most successful bus companies, and it doesn't disappoint. You want to be made homesick by an encounter with a Lotus Esprit or a Jaguar E-Type? This is the place. Or maybe you want to wish you worked harder at school, by tripping over a Ford GT40 or targa rally-prepared Ferrari 250 GTE? This collection will do that, too, before leaving you in awe of the Jedimar jewel in the crown − a glorious Bugatti Type 35.

On an adventure like this, it's the unexpected highs that leave the deepest impression. And who could have predicted when I hit the road six months,

23 countries, and 20,000 miles earlier that Santiago's highlight would be the city's unexpected car culture? Thanks to Nick and the other motoring enthusiasts who'd provided us with such a warm welcome, we left Santiago with heads full of memories I could never have foreseen, and a deep appreciation for how cars can bring people together.

42. THE LONGEST ROAD

28th January 2018
40°34'S, 73°07'W. Osorno, Chile.

THE BULK OF South America was behind us now, but there was still 2000 miles of road remaining between us and the southernmost bar. Fortunately for us, Chile was allowing us to make progress pretty easily, and we covered a quarter of the remaining distance in one long, hot day behind the wheel, the landscape phasing to verdant as we drove on for hour after hour, until we found ourselves in the rolling greenery of Chile's Lake District.

So how did we celebrate our arrival in this wonderful playground of nature? A day or two making the most of the hiking trails, or maybe an afternoon in rented kayaks enjoying the crystal-clear waters? Not even close. Given our Chilean experience so far, you won't be surprised to learn that the main tourist activity we undertook in Chile's Lake District was a visit to the Studebaker Museum.

What on earth is a museum dedicated to one of the United States' more obscure motoring marques doing in this remote corner of rural Chile? It's a perfectly rational question, and one which we never quite found the answer to, but even so, it was fairly fitting that our last memories before crossing the border into Argentina would involve another unexpected dose of car culture, given our experiences in Santiago a few days before. It also mirrored my time behind the wheel of a Studebaker in Cuba quite nicely too, which now felt like it was so long ago that it may as well have been a completely different trip.

The road rose as we headed up to the Cardenal Antonio Samoré Pass which marked the border between Chile and Argentina. As seems fairly traditional in South America, these two nations have had their differences in the past, and given their occasional disputes, it wasn't surprising that the two border posts were separated by 40 kilometres and a 1314m high mountain pass. It was holiday season, and the crossing was busy with tourists, but after an hour spent waiting in various lines we'd checked out of Chile and were rolling through a landscape which was once a forest, but had recently been decimated by fire. Insects swirled around us when we stopped the car, the only sign of life in this scorched dead world.

When we'd completed the drive through this surreal landscape to the Argentinean border, we were immediately reminded of another territorial dispute that Argentina has. Only this time, it was with my country.

'*Las Malvinas Son Argentina's Para Siempre,*' read the sign on the TV screen above passport control, overlaid on a map of the Falkland Islands. 'The Malvinas are Argentina's forever' is apparently the most important message that can be conveyed to those waiting to have their passports stamped at this remote border crossing in the Andes. Given that I was an English person, in a fancy English car, sporting (most definitely non-provocative) English number plates, I hoped the sentiment would be left at the border. If it wasn't, there was the potential for the trip to have a nasty sting in its tail, and hence I didn't know what sort of world I would find as I rolled into Argentina.

But what I did find was paradise.

The glistening lakes went on for miles, flooding the valleys that twisted through the sea of mountains. On the lakeshores the shrubs and grasses were dotted with thistles, while higher up rock and woodland predominated. The air was sweet and fragrant, the chill breeze so fresh it almost jarred. And the road flowed through this landscape, sweeping us gloriously on across the Argentine Lake District – which you really should visit if you get the chance – to the enigmatic town of Bariloche.

Tumbling down a steep hillside to a perfect lakeshore on what feels like the outer edge of the world, Bariloche is a place where myth and rumour blur into one. Some of the myths are famous. For instance in 1945, when escaping Nazis wanted somewhere far off the radar in which to live out their days, this was the place they chose. And if you know where to look, Hitler's birthday is apparently still celebrated every year in a behind-closed-doors party. Bariloche isn't only a gateway to an immense landscape of rare beauty, it's also a gateway to strangeness.

We checked into a hostel and spent a few days taking in Bariloche's charms. Whatever lies beneath the surface of this place, on a superficial level, it's pleasant enough, if slightly odd. For reasons known only to the city planners who developed the place in the 1930s, the centre has been built to look like a Swiss ski resort and has a definite alpine feel to it, majoring on exposed stonework and heavy timber framing and making it unlike anywhere else I'd seen in South America. However, as the city acts as a gateway to Patagonia, this outdoorsy vibe doesn't seem too out of place. The floods of tourists that pass through the town en route to the famous landscapes further south give credibility to the unusual appearance. After a few days taking in this surreal place, I followed the crowds too, rolling onto Ruta 40, heading south to the end of the world.

I say 'I' because Bariloche marked the end of Alvaro's Pub2Pub adventure. With his finances low, Alvaro took the 20-hour bus to Buenos Aires, to continue his adventures in the world of car culture in a slightly more cost-effective manner. Kermit and I continued alone, to complete the final stages of the dream I'd had in that Dartmoor pub four years earlier.

If the opportunity to experience South America was a big part of what drew me to make that plan all those years before, it was Patagonia which held the greatest allure. Because just like the town which marks its gateway, Patagonia is a place of legend, rendered larger than life. To me, it has always seemed to hang out over the edge of the known world, surrounded by unknown oceans and steeped in the romance of adventure. It's a land where giant sloths once roamed, and sabre-toothed tigers hunted in their tracks. A place where the wind is so strong it is sometimes impossible to stand, and where the rains can sweep in for months on end. A place of endless plains, incomparable mountains, smothering ice caps and churning seas. And to me, as someone who'd spent the previous decade driving across the remote landscapes of the world, in an abstract sense, it was the place that represented the end of the road. If you fire up your engine in England and start to drive, there is nowhere in the world that is further away. In that decade of adventure I'd ticked off the more accessible overlanding destinations first – Asia, Scandinavia, Africa – and now I was finally here. The endless enchantment that is Patagonia lay just beyond Bariloche's limits, and I had a TVR at my disposal. Situations don't get much better.

RUTA 40 WAS my companion on the journey south. Argentina's answer to Route 66, it's one of only two roads which cross the vastness of Patagonia. With the long-cherished draw of the southernmost bar fuelling my progress, I followed it keenly, my mile-counting and mental arithmetic in overdrive.

"Okay, so it's 1200 miles to Punta Arenas, and 800 miles to El Chaltén," I said to myself, as Pink Floyd's music complemented the landscape. "So at this speed, that's about 16 hours driving. I can smash ten out today, which leaves six for the morning, including the dodgy gravel section. So El Chaltén tomorrow, then a day hike to Cerro Torre, then on to El Calafate for a bit, and I should be in Punta Arenas in a week."

These thoughts played like a loop in my mind as I drove, interspersed with moments when my subconscious would dwell on how the car was doing, as I had become determined to complete the trip without a major breakdown. This stemmed from a feeling that I was on the verge of doing something great for the TVR brand. Always mocked for their unreliability, if Kermit completed this trip without any more problems it would give the brand a boost just as it was being relaunched, and also give fellow TVR owners some ammunition to fire back when the pub bore makes their predictable jokes on the subject. I was willing Kermit to do it, and reliability became another obsession with which my mind whiled away the long hours on the road.

Despite this focus on reliability, that strange confidence I'd had in the car since early on in the trip had never changed. It sounds ridiculous, but after so long on the road, I was so connected to the car that I could almost feel it talking to me. And the dialogue said it wasn't going to fail. My conviction that Kermit was going to complete the trip without any issues was complete and had never been shaken. It was going to do this. I just knew it.

I ROLLED ON through the world I'd been dreaming of for years. The dusty grasslands were my constant companion, endlessly similar yet somehow endlessly compelling at the same time. It was an empty, prehistoric world, where dinosaurs wouldn't look at all out of place. Only the road broke the timelessness of my surroundings, and the fact that every 60 or 80 miles a YPF petrol station or weather-worn village would rise from the horizon, serving to emphasise the remoteness. But there was more than just the grandeur of nothingness, as for most of my drive across Patagonia I was shadowed by beauty. Far to the west and flickering in and out of view, the southern reaches of the Andes tracked my journey. Proud faces of stone and snow, they scrolled slowly past me as the grasslands flickered along in parallax.

The Andes are the longest mountain range in the world, stretching for over 4000 miles along the length of South America. I'd first encountered them in Colombia as they rose virtually from the Caribbean, and now at the range's southernmost extent, I was seeing them drop back into the sea. And it was probably my imagination, but as the mountains finally descended from the sky, I swear that I could feel the continent narrowing around me, thinning out before breaking up into the desolate islands of Tierra del Fuego, where the southernmost bar awaited.

But it was very possible that I was imagining things, having been on the road for what was starting to feel like far too long. I rolled on in my own little bubble, lost in my thoughts as I soaked up the landscape I'd long dreamed about, and counted down the miles. Always counting down the miles. On my first day of driving in Patagonia, I was so swept up by the road trip equivalent of 'summit fever' that I drove until it was pitch black before pulling over for the night, to sleep in the car and be on my way at first light. I switched off the engine, and silence droned in my ears after 12 hours of near non-stop TVR noise. When I walked around the car to stretch my legs before sleeping, I could see the exhaust manifolds glowing red hot through the bonnet vents, while the most beautiful sky I'd ever seen hung above me. To many, grabbing a few hours' sleep in the driver's seat of an old car, parked in the middle of nowhere, before rising at dawn for another long day on the road wouldn't be a particularly appealing prospect. But to me, on that night beneath that unfamiliar, beautiful sky, it was perfect. Just me, the car and the adventure.

The next day, I faced what I considered to be the drive's final crux – the 50 miles of gravel, which, for some reason, is the only part of Ruta 40 in Patagonia that isn't paved. Impassable in rain, I was fortunate with the weather conditions, but Kermit still ground out on the thick gravel repeatedly as I drove. I counted down the miles, patting the dashboard and encouraging Kermit as I drove, saying things like, "come on, Kermit, you've got this."

The fact I was now talking to Kermit was further proof, if any were required, that I'd been on the road for too long.

PATAGONIA MAY HAVE been calling me for years, but there was one part of the landscape which I'd been drawn to for decades. Ever since seeing a photo of the improbable spire of Cerro Torre in a climbing magazine many years before, I'd wanted to see the mountain for myself. I knew my climbing skills would never be sufficient for me to ascend it, but just to see it would be a dream. As I rolled in to El Chaltén – the village at the mountain's base – at dusk, it shimmered distantly on the horizon next to its larger and more famous neighbour, Mount Fitz Roy. I was on a massive high. I'd just driven to Cerro Torre in my TVR! I grinned as I drove, and punched the air so hard that I almost crashed.

The following day I made the long, steep hike to the glacial lake at the base of the mountain, to get a proper view of this incredible peak. Icebergs floated in the lake, having been melted into improbable shapes by the surprisingly warm sun. A glacier fell from the mountain's base, from where the incredible spike of ice-streaked granite rose to the sky. I'd done it. Almost 20 years after seeing that grainy photo in a climbing magazine, I'd made it to the exact place where that photo of the mountain had been taken.

And the one cloud in the sky hid it from view.

It was certainly an anticlimax, but then you win some, you lose some, I guess. I sat on the glacial moraines for an hour or so, drinking the beer I'd carried up especially for the moment, and had chilled amid the icebergs of the lake, then walked back down to the town. And as I drove away from El Chaltén and the still-cloudy Fitz Roy Massif, I knew I'd be back some day. Cerro Torre wouldn't be unfinished business forever.

THE ICE HAD travelled 19 miles from the glacier's origin high on the mountain to the lagoon at its base, but now it was time. In blocks the size of apartment buildings, the frozen water calved from the glacier's advancing, 150-metre tall face, sending waves rippling out across the lake. It was spellbinding and addictive, waiting for the next chunk to detach and enjoying the surroundings as I did so. And what a spectacle! The Perito Moreno Glacier measures over three miles across by the time it noses into the waters where it terminates, and all around the Patagonian scenery provided a setting which befits such a wonder of nature. A spellbinding sweep of mountain, forest and ice.

My long-cherished dreams of Patagonia were being answered, and then some.

I WAS AT the very bottom of the continent now and South America was beginning to fracture around me. The seas and straits were becoming closer together on the map and the signs which, ever since I'd passed into Argentina, had been counting down the distance to Las Malvinas were telling me that the islands were now less than 400 miles away. I crossed back into Chile, rolled past the Torres Del Paine massif and found myself in a broken world where neither land nor sea dominates. It was a place of scudding clouds, salty air and tiny settlements clinging onto the edge of the world. A sculpture of a giant ground sloth towered above a roundabout as I rolled into Puerto Natales, a fitting symbol of this place where I could easily believe that monsters roamed. And then, after a day wandering the bleak outpost streets, layered up against the biting southerly wind, I drove the last few hours to Punta Arenas, and almost wept as I rolled into town, because after more than 23,000 miles of driving, this was as far south as Kermit and

I would go together. I parked the indefatigable piece of Blackpool fibreglass and boarded a boat to the last bar on earth.

43. THE VOYAGE

08ᵗʰ February 2018
53°07′S, 70°51′W. Punta Arenas, Chile.

I WALKED UP a ramp onto the ship that was to take me to the southernmost bar. It was a small vessel, painted orange and named the MV Yaghan, after the indigenous people who first eked out an existence down here among the islands and bays of Tierra del Fuego. A few vehicles were being carried and there were around 50 passengers, most of whom were Chilean. Rhythmic vibrations rose through the metal structure as the diesel engines were started and our 36-hour voyage began, as we slipped our moorings into the Strait of Magellan.

This strait would carry us almost to the Drake Passage, before we took the Beagle Channel to Puerto Williams. Could there be a more evocative selection of names with which to end this odyssey? Magellan was one of the shining lights of the golden age of exploration. The Beagle was the vessel that carried Darwin through these waters on his voyage of discovery to the Galapagos, and Sir Francis Drake had circumnavigated the world via these waters. Drake's voyage began and ended in Devon, too. Maybe there's something in the water there?

As we slowly sailed away from Punta Arenas, I gazed out across the strait, dwelling on the names and the history of these legendary feats of seafaring. Magellan, Drake, Darwin: they were larger than life: great men, real explorers whose deeds made my little car-based journeys look like the follies they are. I'd known their names, obviously, but they'd always seemed so far-off to me, both in terms of geography and time. I could never gain a true appreciation of what they went through – I mean, how could I relate to the loss of five of the six ships under Drake's command, as he'd endured on his lap of the world? However, sailing these waters after overcoming my own personal challenges gave me the smallest glimpse of what they'd dealt with. As the sun went down over the mile-wide Strait of Magellan and I watched the shores disappear, I felt nothing but respect for these hard men of the ocean.

* * *

IT WAS LATE in the evening and all the other passengers were sleeping, but sleep was the last thing on my mind. I went outside, quietly closing the heavy wooden doors. The vessel rocked very gently beneath me and the engines continued their monotone grumble. A few lights glowed dimly, illuminating the deck, while the vessel's navigation lights floated in space, red and green. But there was nothing else. The darkness was complete, and a cold breeze came out of the night, flecking me with a salty spray.

As my eyes adjusted to the lack of light, I began to discern a few stars, shining through gaps in the clouds. My only reference to the world beyond the ship. I smiled to myself.

"I'm actually going to do this," I thought. Then the biting cold drove me back inside.

I AWOKE TO a lazy grey dawn. The sea was still calm and mountains crowded all around. Their low summits were crowned with a dusting of snow, while their slopes were near-black and steep. It reminded me of Scotland.

But there were differences. As I stood near the bow, I watched penguins dive nonchalantly beneath the vessel as we approached. Whales appeared in the channel too, blowing jets of water in the air and splashing their tails down onto the water's surface. And then there were the seals, playing amongst the waves or basking on rocky islands.

It was seven months since I'd stood on the deck of that boat 800 miles from the North Pole, as we sailed into Pyramiden for the northernmost beer. That was 20,000 miles of driving and 24 countries ago, and here I was again, sailing to a bar. It lent a pleasing symmetry to the trip.

"I'm going to do this," I told myself again, smiling.

The Beagle Channel narrowed and the mountains pressed in around us, their steep slopes rising sheer from the sea to their summits, over 1000 metres up. Glaciers began to spill down between them, sometimes releasing icebergs into the ominous waters. The white snow caps of the highest mountains merged with the clouds above and the dark slopes were matched by the blue-grey sea. There was a foreboding drama to the landscape, unmatched by anything else the trip had thrown up. Man had no place here, in these unpredictable waters, among the unyielding mountains.

But I didn't care.

"I can't believe I'm going to do this," I said to myself.

I thought back to everything I'd overcome to be here. The smothering depression that had crushed me before the trip, and the time, just over a year earlier, when I'd felt so powerless and unequal to the challenge that I'd cancelled the whole thing. I thought about what a struggle it had been to raise the money for the journey, and wondered how on earth I'd managed to get across Costa Rica. And as I'd been away for so long, I thought about family and friends back home, on the far side of the world, and I missed them.

I drifted through the whole day like this, a happy yet thoughtful passenger, enjoying the novelty of having nothing to do but watch the world go by. My fate was in the hands of the ship's crew and that suited me just fine. As the light faded for the second time on the voyage, I felt we must be close. I could see the lights of Ushuaia – Argentina's southernmost city – glowing against the cloud base in the distance. Puerto Williams was just a few miles further on.

IT WAS ONE in the morning, but something was different. As I drifted into consciousness, I noticed the engine's rhythm had changed. It was no longer running at full speed, and a few lights were floating in the darkness, outside the window. We'd arrived at the end of the world.

A gentle drizzle was falling, but there was no wind. I disembarked with some Chilean trekkers who'd come to take a five-day hike to the south of the island and we wandered off to find the campsite. The little circles of light from our head torches lit up the puddles in the dirt track as we walked.

On the campsite, there was a wooden hut from which light flooded out. Still half asleep, I pitched my tent then went inside. A wood-burning stove sat in the corner, pumping out heat, while about a dozen new arrivals huddled around it, chatting excitedly about the weather and their plans. Others had clearly been too tired to pitch their tents and had simply rolled out their sleeping bags on the floor and passed out. It was the bustle of a bunkhouse back home in the mountains, but I was too tired for it.

I went to my tent and drifted off to sleep, with 'I can't believe I'm actually here' still drifting through my mind.

THE CITY I'D spent the previous seven months reaching turned out to be a slapdash kind of place. Tatty wooden houses sprawled among the grass, with neglected wooden picket fences marking their boundaries. Many were surrounded by the detritus of frontier life. Broken cars, tools and building materials. Damp, neglected roads stretched between them, roamed by weather-beaten people and dogs. Down by the tiny naval base, a scruffy wooden pole was stacked with distance markers, and one of them declared

London to be 15,223km away. But any big city may as well have been another world away; the whole place felt at the mercy of the elements, trapped between mountain and sea, while the clouds pressed down above. Nature felt close, as if this was the outermost marker of civilisation.

And I still couldn't believe that after all the effort and tribulations I'd made it there.

I checked into a hostel and wandered the town as the afternoon passed. The irony of having spent seven months getting to Puerto Williams, only to end up waiting for the bar to open was not lost on me. I must have strolled every street in the place as the rain fell and the wind bustled down the muddy streets. Then, at just after seven in the evening, I popped out for a beer.

From the outside, it was just another single storey shack, but inside the wooden walls, the bar was a pleasant enough place to be. The bar itself had been crudely painted to resemble cemented stones and behind it, the shelves were cluttered with unfamiliar spirits and the fridge was stocked with beer. A short, rather rotund lady stood there awaiting my order.

"Hola, un cerveza Tierra de Humos, pour favoir."

I sat down and she brought the bottle over with a glass.

And as I started to pour the drink, a smile began to spread across my face. It grew and grew, until I started laughing under my breath. Then I composed myself, and took a sip of beer.

I'd done it.

And at that moment, a feeling of lightness washed over me as a huge weight was suddenly lifted from my shoulders. For the first time in years, I was free. I fought to hold back the tears.

Ever since I'd had the idea for Pub2Pub four years before, it had been a huge, inescapable part of my life. Whatever I was doing, it was always there at the back of my mind and until that moment I didn't realise just what a huge, crushing pressure it had been for me to battle through depression and all the other obstacles and make it happen. But as I took that sip of beer, it all fell into place. I suddenly felt a foot taller and a stone lighter. I'd done it. I was free. The tears started to roll down my cheeks.

I glanced around the bar. Other than the lady who'd served my drink, the only other person there was a Brazilian backpacker. She was writing in her journal while she waited for food and I didn't feel like speaking to her anyway. There was no way I could explain this to a stranger at that moment.

It had been the biggest challenge of my life, and had dominated my world for years but with that sip of beer, it was complete. And at that moment I knew it had totally been worth it. The sweetest victories are those earned through adversity and it was those four years of toil that meant this was more than just a beer. It was one of the defining moments of my life.

But was it over? As I'd been wandering around town earlier, I noticed that a building on the southern side of town had 'Bar Analij' painted on the door. But it didn't look like a bar. It was a green-painted timber house with lace curtains hanging in the windows. In the cold light of day, I was convinced it was a red herring. But when I strolled past on the way back to my hostel, a flashing sign sat on the window sill, which read 'abierto': open.

So this was the real southernmost bar. Bar Analij. The bar's name gave me a sudden feeling of unease.

Had I just driven 20,000 miles to go for a beer in a rural Chilean gay bar?

I grasped the door handle, unsure of what to expect. I still half believed I was walking into someone's living room. But the door did indeed open into a bar. Just, maybe not the kind of bar you'd usually gravitate to. Plastic patio furniture was laid out in what was formerly a front room. Chilean rodeo posters brightened up the scruffy walls, while a TV in the corner was showing Chilean line dancing, with the volume cranked up to 11. A makeshift wood burner sat near the door pumping out heat and in the far corner, there was the bar. Two local middle-aged men sat on the bar stools, and a young guy stood behind the counter, serving them. They all turned to stare at me as I entered. Momentarily, I felt uneasy, as if I was trespassing and I shouldn't be there, but then I remembered I'd just driven 20,000 miles for a drink in this place; and I was damn well going to have one.

The bar's total stock consisted of a bottle of Grant's Whisky and a domestic fridge full of Cervaza Austral. I ordered one of the beers, which came in a litre bottle, and sat down at the bar.

The locals tried to strike up a conversation, but my Spanish wasn't up to it and I found them difficult to understand. I'm sure they would have found me pretty difficult to understand too, if I tried to explain to them what the hell I was doing there. So slightly awkwardly, I sat with my beer as the line dancing music blasted out across the bar, drinking rather faster than I usually would.

So this was it? This was the place I'd just spent all that time driving to? The sheer ridiculousness of the whole thing began to sink in, and I smiled at the thought.

Within half an hour of my arrival, I finished the beer, paid and walked back past the patio furniture and rodeo posters, out of the Bar Analij and through the cold, wet night to my hostel, grinning like a Cheshire cat all the way.

It hadn't been remotely close to what I'd expected, but I didn't care. It had been totally worth it.

44. THE CONFLICT

15th February 2018
51°37'S, 69°34'W. Rio Gallegos, Argentina.

I WAS ABOUT six hours into the 2000 mile drive back up to Uruguay, from where the TVR was to be shipped back to Europe, and I had just crossed back into Argentina. I rolled up to the police checkpoint and was directed to pull over.

It was the standard routine. A bored policeman trying to make sense of my foreign passport, driving licence and car documents, followed by a cursory walk around the car. But this time, it was different. The policeman really didn't seem to approve of this foreign TVR, and disappeared into the tiny office, to speak to his boss, before returning, looking stern.

"*Esta bien?*" I asked. "*Puedo ir?*"

"No," he replied.

Using my phone to translate, he explained that I couldn't pass because one of my headlights was broken. I had to go back to the town of Rio Gallegos, a few miles back down the road, and get it fixed.

"But I have a hotel booked in Santa Cruz," I argued. "Can't I get it fixed there?"

"No, you'll go back," he replied. "You can't continue."

I insisted on speaking to the commanding officer, but it seemed that the orders had come from the head of the checkpoint. The fancy little English car couldn't continue. And as I could understand their point I would have accepted their decision if it weren't for one thing.

It was a busy checkpoint, and a steady stream of Argentinean cars were passing through, many of which also sported non-functional headlights, or were breaking the law by running with no lights on at all. Hell, a few even had flat tyres, or bumpers hanging off. But the police weren't stopping any of them, only me.

I wasn't having that.

I carried on arguing with the boss of the checkpoint but got nowhere. After telling me my car would be impounded if I didn't go back, he refused to speak to me. So, I did what any sensible person would do. I went back out to the checkpoint and pointed out every car with a visible defect to the policeman waving the traffic through.

"That car has a light out too. You must impound him too," I'd shout across the tarmac. "You're not doing your job."

I was clearly a nuisance. After a while, the checkpoint commander was called back out. I stared him down.

"Es porque soy Ingles, si?" I said. "It's because I'm English, yes?"

I continued in my broken Spanish. "Carro Argentinain, no es problemo, bero carro Inglais, es un problem. Es porque soy Inglais. Ablar es porque soy Inglais." I challenged him to admit the reason he'd detained me, but none of the locals, was because I was English.

He didn't have an answer.

I kept going, pointing out other cars with defects and repeating "es porque soy Ingles, si?"

He wouldn't admit it and I was creating quite a scene at the checkpoint now. The traffic was queuing back towards Rio Gallegos, which, coincidentally, is an important military base and the location of the airfield from which Mirage and Skyhawk fighter planes flew their missions during the Falklands Conflict. But obviously these policemen were professional, and the fact I was English couldn't possibly affect their professional judgement, right?

"Admit that you're only holding me because I'm English and I'll go back. Otherwise, I'm carrying on to Santa Cruz, and I'll fix the headlight there," I said.

20 minutes and one very heated argument after I arrived at the checkpoint, I was waved on. I continued the long drive north, past a sign that read 'Las Malvinas, 530km,' and on to Santa Cruz. I guess it could have been worse though. At least no-one threw stones at my British-registered sports car.

THAT EVENING, I pulled into the municipal campsite and hid my car at the far end of the area of scorched grass, attempting to obscure its identity with my tent as best I could, for I was in Puerto Santa Cruz; and Puerto Santa Cruz was a navy town.

It was also a dusty, unappealing grid of timber houses, unsmiling people, and unrestrained dogs, which seemed to like nothing better than to take out their aggression on any passers-by. I walked the wide streets into town, taking in the dusty settlement's vibe.

Murals on walls and buildings declared the Malvinas to belong to Argentina, while at a road junction, a sculpture depicting the islands towered over my head. Other junctions were marked by artillery pieces, and a preserved gun from the front of a warship stood proudly by a roundabout. Some of the street names caught my attention too: Avenue Belgrano, Avenue Heroes de Malvinas.

I was glad I'd hidden the car.

I tried to withdraw money at both of the banks in town, but neither were connected to the international banking system and I only had about 80 dollars cash. I changed the notes into the local currency – giving me the opportunity to admire the map of Las Malvinas on the 50 peso note – and put most of the cash straight into Kermit's petrol tank. I had just enough left for some bread and a couple of beers. I wasn't planning on hanging around for long.

But in the end, I was detained for longer than I'd expected, and the reason was one I couldn't have foreseen. A few days earlier, when I was back in Punta Arenas collecting Kermit, I'd sent out a couple of press releases to the local news outlets who'd covered Pub2Pub's launch. These had resulted in BBC Devon running a short online story, which went live while I was sleeping in my tent in Puerto Santa Cruz. The feature had done pretty well at a local level so was promoted to the national BBC news site, and, thanks to the time difference, by the time I awoke, the Pub2Pub story was the second most-read article across the whole BBC news network. When I surfaced and wandered down to the petrol station to grab a coffee while making use of their wifi, Kermit was a bigger news story than Trump. One and a half million people had read the story in its first eight hours online, and coverage had snowballed from there.

As I got within range of the petrol station's wifi connection, my phone seemed to explode. I had emails from magazine editors asking for articles, and from radio shows requesting interviews. Strangers were finding the expedition on Facebook and wishing me well, while friends were sending me links from the coverage as it spread around the world. Back home, the *Daily Mail, Mirror,* and *Star* had picked up the story, while around the world it had already been covered by media outlets in Japan, and the *Hindustan Times* in India.

A friend messaged me to tell me that he'd been queuing to buy bread at a bakery in southern France and overheard the people next to him talking about a crazy English guy who was driving around the world in a TVR. Even Jennifer messaged from my past, having just spat coffee across her sofa when she heard my journey being run as a news story on BBC Radio 2.

The result of all this coverage was that the Pub2Pub story was read by over ten million people around the world that weekend, and many of them probably thought driving a sports car across the globe would be an impossibly glamorous experience. But as I spent my day sat in the petrol station, rationing my consumption of their cheap coffee because of my money shortage while trying to keep up with all the emails and hoping no war veterans spotted the TVR, it really didn't feel so.

Before returning to my tent, I read some of the comments on the original BBC story. Most were positive and clearly appreciated my daft achievement. However, some were the opposite, and accused me of being some rich, showoff toff with an endless supply of money, who clearly hasn't done a day's work in my life.

Back on the $2-a-night campsite, I couldn't stop chuckling to myself. Online, people were arguing about whether I was some kind of hero or a rich spoilt cad with an attention addiction. But in reality, I was neither. I had less than five dollars cash left and I was sitting in the dirt, fixing a headlight on my old car while drinking a couple of bottles of the only beer I could afford. Whatever peoples' perceptions, I was no different to anyone else. I was just a normal guy who'd battled his way through depression and thrown everything he could at achieving a dream.

By half past nine, the beer was gone and I didn't have enough money to buy any more. I went to sleep with my head still spinning from the most surreal day of the trip so far.

I CONTINUED THE long haul through Argentina, covering around 400 miles a day while attempting to keep up with the constant news coverage and content requests. Within a few days of the BBC feature, over a hundred articles describing my trip had appeared, but my existence hadn't really changed. My life still revolved around getting the TVR to the end of its journey as cheaply as possible, and this close to the end of the trip, after so long on the road, homesickness was building. The night after leaving Puerto Santa Cruz, I slept in the car on a petrol station forecourt to save money. The following night, I pulled into the town of Gaiman.

Welsh settlers had founded the town in the 1870s, having moved to Patagonia to escape the irritations of their overbearing English neighbours and live their lives by their own rules. They'd built a Patagonian approximation of a Welsh town, maintained their language and traditions, and sustained themselves the only way they knew how – through sheep farming. But they never saw the homeland they loved again, and the streets felt tinged with an all-encompassing yet non-specific sadness. The original Welsh-speaking settlers would have called this feeling *hiraeth*, a word for which there is no direct English translation. But as I walked the melancholy riverbank and touched the weeping willow trees planted by those first homesick Welshmen all those years before, I felt it too and was overcome with a longing for home.

The next morning, in this sad village in rural Argentina, Kermit was recognised from the news coverage for the first time, and I wondered what home I would be coming back to.

I rolled on towards the finish. The night after leaving Gaiman, I once again slept in the car to save money, then the following night I found the cheapest hotel I could. It looked welcoming enough from outside, but an Argentinean flag hung in reception with a map of Las Malvinas drawn on, surrounded by signatures of war veterans. However, the staff were great and I was treated with nothing less than respect. Argentina continued to feel like a conundrum I felt I'd never understand.

I spent a few days in Buenos Aires, but didn't really do much with my time there. I was exhausted and simply wanted to go home. I'd been living too close to my limits for too long, and the continuous pressures of driving, dealing with the media coverage, and the homesickness had worn me down, and depression was beginning to swirl thicker around me. I skipped the sightseeing opportunities of this great city and instead attempted to have some downtime to relax. I'd wander aimlessly around the streets, or sit in the hostel browsing the internet, giving my mind some breathing space after the long haul back up through Argentina.

Then I finally boarded the ferry to Uruguay and drove for the last few hours up the coast to Montevideo. There, I dropped Kermit off at the docks to be loaded on the ship that would return it to the comforting familiarity of Europe.

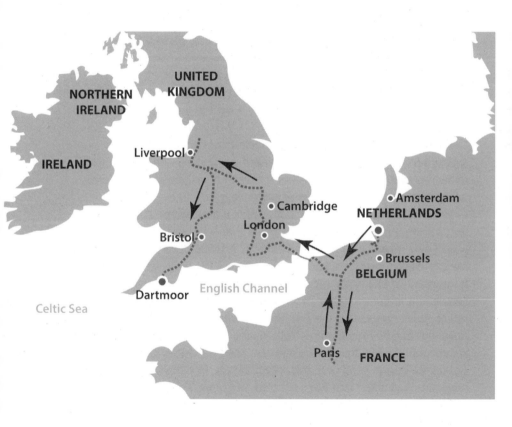

45. THE FINISH LINE

02nd March 2018
51°09'N, 0°10'W. Gatwick Airport, Great Britain.

THE AIRBUS DROPPED out of the clouds, revealing a landscape of bitter white. Snow lay thick on the ground with only the roads offering respite, their black tarmac jarring against the smothered countryside. It was my first sight of Britain for half a year, but this wasn't a typical winter's day at Gatwick. I'd flown back straight into the jaws of the so-called 'Beast from the East,' a particularly hyped snowstorm that had hit a few days previously.

My sister collected me from Gatwick in the little red Micra we'd taken to Norway the previous summer, and I did what every self respecting Brit would do when returning after six months away. I went to the fish and chip shop and then the pub.

But it was strange being back and I felt lost. I couldn't readjust to saying hello in English, the people around me seemed different to how I'd remembered them, and the weather – which I obviously have to discuss, being English and all – was the ultimate curveball.

However, as I sat there in the once-familiar atmosphere of an English pub, having a beer with my sister, in many ways I wasn't back yet. The trip wasn't over. Kermit was somewhere on the Atlantic Ocean, making its way back to Europe, and I still had to drive it across the finish line on Dartmoor, from where I'd begun the trip the previous summer. So, a few weeks after setting foot in the UK again, I was back on the move, taking an overnight bus to Antwerp to collect the TVR. The bus was the cheapest I could find and arrived at three in the morning. With nowhere to stay, I wandered the cold streets until the first train to the port ran, and then dozed off in the freezing station, waiting to head over and collect the car. In Colombia, the collection procedure had taken four days, but back in Europe I was firing up Kermit within 20 minutes and rolling onto the roads of northern Belgium.

The 1500 miles I covered making my way back to the start point turned into something of a victory lap. I headed back to The Netherlands to revisit the guys at the Glym9 garage, who had hosted me on the second day of the trip, and then went down to Paris to catch up with Philippe and his Porsche. On my return to England, I went to the TVR Car Club's first event of the year and Kermit was given a hero's welcome. It was a washout, but even so, several hundred TVRs attended the event at Burghley House. Kermit was given pride of place outside the front door of the manor house and a steady flow of people came to see the car they'd been following for the past eight months as it made its way across the globe. Many of them wanted to speak to me, too. Uneasy with being the centre of attention, I felt like a bit of a fraud as people congratulated me on my achievement – my comfort zone was the wilds of Patagonia, not this.

I continued the tour, still counting down the miles to the finish line. But now, there were only a few hundred left. I gave a talk to another group of TVR owners in Cheshire, and then rolled down to my parent's house near Bristol. From there, with 27,000 miles behind me, there were only 140 to go.

My mum joined me in Kermit's passenger seat for the final run across Dartmoor to the finish line at the Two Bridges Hotel, and it meant the world to her. In Kermit's rear view mirror, my sister drove the red Micra we'd bought at the start of the trip, followed by a line of TVRs that stretched into the distance: a rolling guard of honour for a very special car. The wintry undulations of my home turf scrolled past as I drove and I was no longer counting down the miles, for I was home already. With a dab of the brakes and a blink of the indicator, I swung into the grounds of the Two Bridges Hotel, from where I'd left over eight months earlier. Friends and a few members of the press had already gathered there, waiting for my return. I parked and turned off the engine, and to the very British sound of a round of applause, it was done.

46. CLOSURE

13th October 2018
50°44'N, 3°23'W. Rockbeare, Great Britain.

THEY SAY THAT every big trip you make changes you as a person. When you come back, you aren't the same person who set off all those months before. You can't be, having experienced so much. And Pub2Pub certainly changed me. It brought me to a new place in my life. Over a decade after I set off on my first road trip into the unknown, I was able to commit myself to a life of driving adventure. Effectively, Pub2Pub was my big break.

The writing commissions started flooding in and the recognition the Pub2Pub brand now carried enabled me to launch Pub2Pub Adventures, a business dedicated to bringing adventurous road tripping to the masses. The autumn after I'd returned to the UK, the new business ran its first organised road trip, with Kermit leading a convoy of sports cars down to a bar called the Eagle's Nest, in Bavaria. The new business presented me with an exciting future and I looked forward to seeing where it would take me. But I wasn't where I wanted to be yet, because there was one aspect of my life that took rather longer to change.

YEARS EARLIER, WHEN I was suffocated by depression, I'd cancelled Pub2Pub because I couldn't see how I'd be able to dig deep enough to make it happen under the circumstances. But in the end making Pub2Pub happen was the easy bit. Beating depression itself took rather longer.

Before departure, by taking the pressure off myself and making changes to my life, I'd managed to get my mental health into a state that allowed me to make the trip happen. But I wasn't free from the problem. It stayed with me right through the trip, always buried somewhere in my mind. It was something I tried to manage by trying not to do too much and making sure I got as much downtime as possible. But managing is very different to curing, and in effect, while on the trip, my strategy was one of putting off confronting the issue until I was back.

And when I got home I didn't have to go looking for it. The depression that I'd been ignoring for the previous eight months found me again.

For months, as spring turned into summer, I was at its mercy. Knowing the futility of trying to do too much, I'd often only manage an hour or two of work each day. But the only way to beat it was to listen to myself, and not try to push too hard. It was frustrating. I had so many dreams for the future with my new business, and so many ideas for where to take the Pub2Pub project next. But they had to wait until I was ready. I had to be patient. I'd know when I was finally there.

IT WAS ALMOST two years since that day at Laura's wedding. Two years since I'd sat there on the end of the bed, staring at the carpet, unable to face the world. Two years since I'd felt more hopeless and defeated than ever before and, looking into my future and seeing only darkness, I'd cancelled the trip.

The sun was blazing through Laura's kitchen window and inside there was a hive of activity. Laughter and chatter filled the air as party food was made on an industrial scale. A month earlier, Laura had asked me to be godfather to her son, Austin, and having accepted, I was helping with preparations for his first birthday party. All around me, the room bustled with strangers from Laura's and her husband Chris' family, but I was fine. I was enjoying it. I worked away, making sandwiches, preparing drinks, chatting, and loading the cars.

In another hour, we'd be heading over to the village hall for the party. Lots of my friends would be there, strangers, too. It promised to be a fun afternoon of small-talk and child care, of pleasant introductions to strangers and catching up with those I'd not seen in a while. It was the sort of occasion that, in the months before Pub2Pub, I would have dreaded. But not now.

And then it hit me.

I was looking forward to it. I felt fine.

As I loaded the sandwiches and the birthday cake into my car, I couldn't help but smile to myself. Not a passing, throwaway smile. No, my face was infected by a ridiculous, over-the-top smile that wouldn't go away. Because it was at that moment I noticed the clouds had finally lifted. I was no longer that battered shell of a person who'd been so crushed by depression that he'd cancelled the trip less than two years before. The moment I'd been coveting more than any other for the past few years had finally arrived. I'd left the black dog of depression behind, and I was free.

The journey was over. And what an incredible journey it had been.

In any given year in the UK, mental health problems such as depression affect one in four adults. People from all walks of life experience problems, and some of society's highest fliers have battled with mental health issues. Isaac Newton, Ernest Hemingway, Steven Fry, and Winston Churchill have all suffered from depression. It's nothing to be ashamed of.

If you or someone you know is suffering from depressive illness, the charity Mind can help you understand the illness, and is able to offer various forms of emergency support if required. You can find out more by visiting www. mind.org.uk.

If depression is affecting your day-to-day life, don't hesitate to see your GP about it. It's every bit as real an illness as the flu.

And, just like the flu, it can be beaten.

Ben Coombs

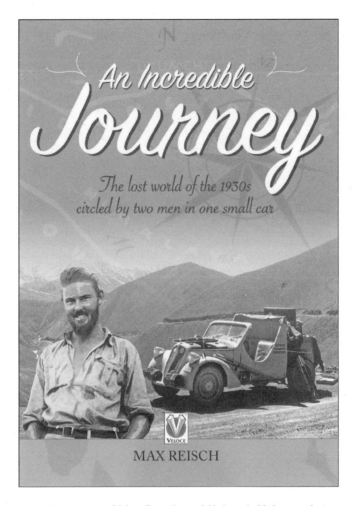

The compelling story of Max Reisch and Helmuth Hahmann's journey across Asia in 1935 in a Steyr 100. It is a story of adventure and discovery, revealing the countries, people and problems that they encountered along the way. With stunning period photographs, this book provides a historic and fascinating insight into a pre-WW2 world.

ISBN: 978-1-787111-65-3
Paperback · 21x14.8cm · 288 pages · 231 pictures

For more information and price details, visit our website at www.veloce.co.uk
email: info@veloce.co.uk · Tel: +44(0)1305 260068

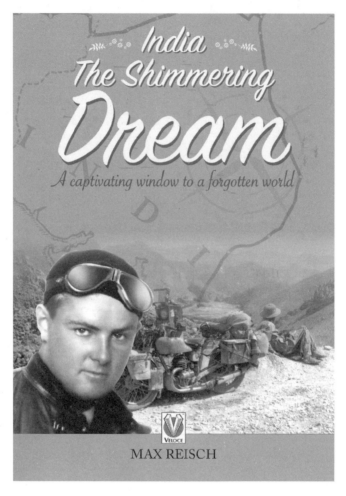

An extraordinary account of a remarkable motorcycle journey made in 1933, through Iraq, Iran and Baluchistan (now part of Pakistan) to India. Wonderful descriptions of the people and cultures, now nearly forgotten, yet still hugely relevant today, are brought evocatively to life by the stunning period photos.

ISBN: 978-1-787112-94-0
Paperback · 21x14.8cm · 192 pages · 96 pictures

For more information and price details, visit our website at www.veloce.co.uk
email: info@veloce.co.uk · Tel: +44(0)1305 260068

Following his dismissal from a job he never should have had, the author packs a tent, some snacks, and a suit, and sets out on a two-wheeled adventure across Europe. With no idea where he's going, and only two very large and confusing maps to rely on, he heads out to prove that planning and forethought are the very antithesis of a motorcycle adventure.

ISBN: 978-1-845843-99-1
Paperback · 21x14.8cm · 144 pages
129 colour and b&w pictures

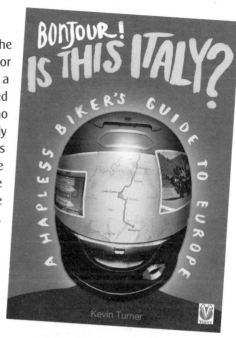

Kevin Turner heads off on another ill-thought out adventure, this time aiming for the towering waterfalls of Norway, before heading east to Moscow. This fascinating adventure – part sprint, part marathon – charts the perils, pitfalls and thrills of a 6000-mile solo motorcycle journey across Europe, Scandinavia and into Asia. The author's observations and anecdotes transform this motorcycle guidebook into a laugh-a-minute page turner, which inspires and entertains in equal measure.

ISBN: 978-1-845846-22-0
Paperback · 21x14.8cm · 160 pages
134 colour pictures

For more information and price details, visit our website at www.veloce.co.uk
email: info@veloce.co.uk · Tel: +44(0)1305 260068